Patience and Fortitude

PATIENCE AND
FORTITUDE

FIORELLO LA GUARDIA

A Biography by
WILLIAM MANNERS

New York and London
HARCOURT BRACE JOVANOVICH

Printed in the United States of America

The quotation from Ernest Hemingway's *A Farewell to Arms* is used by permission of Charles Scribner's Sons.

Library of Congress Cataloging in Publication Data

Manners, William, 1907–
Patience and fortitude.

Bibliography: p.
1. La Guardia, Fiorello Henry, 1882–1947. I. Title.
E748.L23M33   974.7′1′040924   [B]   76–895
ISBN 0–15–171290–5

First edition

B C D E

For Ande . . . .

ACKNOWLEDGMENTS

This alphabetical listing of those who helped me, in all manner of ways, scarcely conveys the extent of my thanks and appreciation: Dr. George Baehr, Adolf A. Berle, Beatrice Bishop Berle, Walter D. Binger, William C. Chanler, Willam R. Emerson, Lloyd K. Garrison, William B. Goodman, Anna Rosenberg Hoffman, Warren King, Dr. Emanuel S. Knishkowy, Marie La Guardia, Wayne Lawson, Felix Leon, Alice Roosevelt Longworth, Jane Harris Manners, Julie Elizabeth Manners, Tracy Barbara Manners, Joseph W. Marshall, Pearl Bernstein Max, David R. McIlwaine, Paul McLaughlin, Robert Moses, Scott Nearing, Pauline M. Newman, Morris S. Novik, Cara Sheridan O'Donnell, Justine Wise Polier, Roberta Pryor, A. Philip Randolph, Seymour N. Siegal, Bliss K. Thorne, Helen G. Tierney, William J. Walsh and those who asked to remain anonymous.

Patience and
Fortitude

CHAPTER ONE

WITH TWO LINES, PETER PINDAR PINNED DOWN
man's insatiable thirst for recognition. "What rage for fame attends
both great and small!/Better be damned than mentioned not at all."
Thus the politician, eager for even the ephemeral assurance of applause, may strive to do good or achieve notoriety. But ovations van-
ish with the speed of sound, and posthumous glory—one's name en-
graved in weather-obliterated cornerstones—is no more satisfactory.

In his lifetime, Fiorello La Guardia's accomplishments as a congressman and as mayor of New York—an office synonymous with the
end of a career—were known to every man in the street. The Little
Flower had compassion for the underprivileged and an ever-driving
determination during his twelve-year rule in New York City to produce an efficient administration of honest city government. (The volt-
age of this determination was temper, "mostly synthetic—to gain a
point, to effect a subjection, to exhibit himself in a righteous role." One
of his municipal officials said admiringly, "Jesus Christ, he's a son of a
bitch, but you believe—he's able to engender this feeling of loyalty—
that what he's doing is right.")

La Guardia's works and blazing personality made him a figure of
international renown. At the end of World War II, a Sergeant Stanley
Rosenthal of Brooklyn sent La Guardia a snapshot he had taken of a
wall in Pozzuoli, Italy. On the wall in huge white letters was LA
GUARDIA; on two adjoining walls in equally large white letters FDR,
CHURCHILL.

Today, a generation later—such is the evanescence of fame—the
young know La Guardia only as an airport. And should La Guardia's
name be mentioned to their parents, an unvarying response occurs.

3

They identify La Guardia by one specific act, because that act epitomized his humanity; they exclaim, "Remember when La Guardia read comics on the radio to the kids!"

Every Sunday, from Mayor La Guardia's spacious office in the southwest corner of the ground floor of City Hall, "Talk to the People" went forth from WNYC, 830 on your radio dial. The Mayor conducted his colloquial, salty, fatherly, admonitory, conspiratorial, bombastic monologues with close to two million listeners.

Almost all tuned in primarily to be entertained; La Guardia's commissioners, of course, switched on their sets because they never knew when he might give them a direct order in the course of a broadcast and expect immediate action. Even Robert Moses listened. The Little Flower always put on a good show; he was compelling, unpredictable, amusing, and as endearing as a panda. His showmanship was both innate and premeditated. ("He was always acting," Deputy Commissioner Walter D. Binger stated. Once at a municipal function, in pointing out the importance of dramatization in getting something across to the public, La Guardia leaned over from his position on the dais and said as he looked down at a table of twelve lovely actresses who had been placed there just for show, "Now, young ladies, just how would you dramatize sewage treatment?")

La Guardia's relationship with radio had not always been thus. At the beginning of his mayoralty he had neither an understanding nor an appreciation of radio's valuable potential. In fact, on the third day of January, 1934, three days after Fiorello La Guardia became mayor, he swore in Seymour Siegel, a young stock exchange statistician and son of a former Congressional colleague, as assistant program manager and then said to him, "Now, go across the street and shut that joint down." "That joint" was WNYC, New York City's ten-year-old municipal radio station. Indeed, it had been one of La Guardia's campaign promises to eliminate the station because it was an unnecessary expense.

WNYC was built in 1924 by Grover Whalen, commissioner of plant and structures. (The Plant and Structures Department had charge of the B's in city government: Ferry Boats, Bridges, Buses and Broadcasting.) Whalen, "with a silk hat on his head and a gardenia in his lapel," official greeter of distinguished guests of the City of New York, became so enamored of the concept of mass communication that he persuaded the Board of Estimate to appropriate $50,000 to establish a city station. Unable to buy a transmitter in the United States because of the General Electric, AT&T and Westinghouse monopoly, Whalen journeyed to Brazil, bought a transmitter there, brought it back and set it up in the Municipal Building. He persuaded a former employer, John Wanamaker, to supply furnishings and WNYC went into operation in July 1924.

During its first ten years, the station provided a somewhat casual kind of broadcasting. It would go on the air at 10:00 in the morning, or possibly 10:20 or 10:27. At noon it would shut down, and everyone would go out to lunch. And at 5:30 P.M., it would go off the air.

In those days, WNYC did not own a single phonograph record. Therefore, every morning at nine, a city limousine would drive up to a gramophone shop at Fifth Avenue and 59th Street and the chauffeur would borrow one or two albums. He would return to the station with them, where they would be played from ten to eleven—the "Masterwork Hour." The chauffeur would then drive to 59th Street and return the albums to the shelf. A major crisis occurred the day one of the records was broken, and no one on the staff knew "where in the hell [they were] going to get the buck and a quarter to pay for this."

The mayors during that first decade of broadcasting—Hylan, Walker and O'Brien—had no interest in the city station, although ponderous, red-headed and red-mustached Mayor John Francis Hylan, at one point, was struck with the idea of sitting down in front of a microphone and reading *The Autobiography of John F. Hylan* from cover to cover. The American Civil Liberties Union, however, instituted a taxpayers' suit, charging that Hylan was using the public airwaves for private political purposes. (The ACLU overlooked the more serious charge of Hylan's being a "cheerless bore.") Eventually, Hylan, as mayor, couldn't use the municipal station. When, for example, he appeared at a luncheon at the Commodore Hotel, everything was broadcast until Mayor Hylan rose to speak and then the microphone was turned off. Thus the station appeared to have no value whatsoever for politicians.

Ten days after Seymour Siegel was sent across the street to "shut that joint down" he handed a one-page report to La Guardia which stated that there was nothing wrong with the station that a little management couldn't fix. Furthermore, if the Mayor were to give up the station, he would be relinquishing a very valuable franchise for all time. La Guardia gave this statement some thought and then named a three-man commission (which included William Paley of CBS) to make a further study. Several months later, the commission presented its conclusions, which were the same as Siegel's.

It was at this time that La Guardia and the New York press had ended their honeymoon. Certain reporters, he was sure, were out to get him. He frequently wrote letters to Arthur Hays Sulzberger, publisher of the *Times*, strongly suggesting that he fire Paul Crowell, one of his reporters. (Crowell's wit was epitomized by his sardonic statement: "An empty limousine drew up in front of City Hall and Commissioner X got out.") Each time Sulzberger sent La Guardia's demand to Crowell with the question "What can I answer to this?" Crowell would write a reply to La Guardia which said, in substance, that Crowell was a first-rate, indispensable reporter, the publisher would sign it and off it would go to the Mayor. Obviously, such maneuvers did not brighten La Guardia's rapport with the pressroom (Room 9) at City Hall. But they did guide him to the realization that radio was an instrument of power, of communication, by which he could go directly to the people in the handling of their problems and thus circumvent the distortions that resulted from being misquoted.

From then on, through the years, La Guardia went on the air to denounce "tinhorns" and "chiselers" and, in the case of one fraudulent operation, in which relatives of men killed in World War II were victimized, to shout, "Cut that out! If you don't, I'll announce your name next Sunday. Get me?"; to rally New Yorkers after a snowstorm; to shape up commissioners; and even, from time to time, to address a personal message to his wife, ignoring the FCC's view of such direct, point-to-point communications as violations. He was equal to "Now look, honey, I want that spaghetti done . . ."

In the interval between his broadcasts, the WNYC staff was made aware that he listened to the station constantly. "You know," recalled Siegel, "he'd phone you at two o'clock in the morning. He'd want to know why there had been a delay of thirty seconds—sometime during the previous day. You figured, what the hell, the guy must be listening to the station all the time. Or how else would he know that?"

And although La Guardia made no attempt to censor a pioneering series on venereal disease (at a time when NBC wouldn't permit the surgeon general of the United States to utter "syphilis" on the air) he became infuriated when he heard avant-garde composers like Schön-berg or Stravinsky on the "Masterwork Hour." On one such occasion, the phone at WNYC rang and the Mayor's falsetto demanded, "Cut that trash off the air! Play Tchaikovsky!"

Conservative though his musical taste may have been, La Guardia made radical innovations after he decided to keep WNYC in operation. In his efforts to do something for the consumer, to help the housewife spend her money wisely, he appointed Frances Foley Gannon, widow of a Supreme Court justice, as deputy commissioner of markets. Every morning at 8:25, for the next twenty-five years, Mrs. Gannon went on the air with the best food buys.

La Guardia's regularly scheduled "Talk to the People" began at the end of 1941. Immediately following Pearl Harbor, he had gone on the air with an emergency address and then rushed off to the West Coast to assess the danger of attack there. The Sunday after his return, he made the first of a regular series of braodcasts from City Hall, already directly wired with WNYC to handle possible emergencies. The Mayor's "Talk to the People" presented an auditory pastiche which not only revealed what was going on in the world, but also gave advice on what to buy and what not to buy and on how to get rid of cockroaches in the kitchen, as well as notes on blackouts, dollops of morale for those doing volunteer work, and comments on food in connection with rationing.

"Oh, fish! Oh, fish," he exclaimed one Sunday. "Well, I had my usual call today from Mr. Triggs, head of the OPA Fish Division. Triggs says the filet situation will clear up, and of course if Triggs says so I believe him, so we'll wait and see." He shoved his heavy horn-rimmed glasses onto his forehead, out of the way. "Apples! Another beautiful black market's in the making, and as for snap beans, I've asked the OPA to be ready with information for wholesalers and retailers—no reason why they can't have the information." He pushed his glasses to his nose. "But go slow in buying those snap beans until next week, when the full crop comes in. . . . Oranges! Yes, I'm going to talk about oranges again. They spoof me. Especially a bunch of cheap dirty low-down politicians. Well, I won't go into it." The glasses had slipped far down on his nose, giving him a confiding, paternal quality. "But there's no reason why you can't buy oranges by the pound rather than by the dozen. I told my wife about this, and she said she'd never done it before and I said well, you used to buy bananas by the dozen, and now you buy them by the pound. She said she never thought of that. Again I warn you chicken dealers!" He placed his face right up to the microphone, a belligerent, nose-to-nose confrontation with those chicken dealers. "I'm not fooling. No more monkey business!"

On July 1, 1945, a Sunday that would prove memorable, the Mayor, as always, arrived at City Hall an hour before he was to go on the air. During the week, as was his custom, he had tossed bits of paper with one or two words scrawled on them into the bottom drawer of his desk—reminders of subjects he might refer to in the broadcast on the forthcoming Sunday. Throughout this particular week, he had also badgered Morris Novik, the station director, for special ideas because of an impending strike of the Newspaper and Mail Deliverers Union. The strike of 1,500 members, employed on eleven metropolitan newspapers, was expected to break on Saturday night, so that there would be no Sunday paper in New York City; that was the best way to do it, the workers felt. The strike had come exactly as expected.

Now La Guardia pulled out the desk drawer and turned it upside down; the notes fluttered to the desk top. He looked the notes over, mentally reviewed their possibilities, discarded a few. (Slips quite frequently had the word *fish* on them. After meat rationing began, he recommended the eating of fish so often that New Yorkers began calling him "the Little Flounder" instead of the Little Flower.)

At 12:55, five minutes before the broadcast, La Guardia went into the men's room just off his office. This interval served an additional purpose; during it, the people who had come to witness the broadcast and had lined up in the City Hall rotunda—tourists in New York, commissioners, officials from other cities—were herded into La Guardia's office to the hundred chairs that had been set up. It was so large an office that during the time a supplicant walked across it to the desk, he might feel himself getting smaller and smaller and smaller, like Lewis Carroll's Alice. The mammoth walnut desk fit the office's scale; the Mayor, of course, didn't. A pasta- or *knaydl*-like, bulkiness made him appear shorter than his five feet two inches. (When a photograph was taken of His Honor and Bess Myerson, the willowy, newly crowned Miss America, the photographer called out, "Mr. Mayor, why don't you stand up?" "God damn it," bellowed the Mayor, "I *am* standing up!")

Seated now, he was tieless, coatless; his white shirt was opened wide at the throat, with coiled black hair released like sofa stuffing. Perspiration trickled down his cheeks and his stocky body fidgeted. It appeared that the heat, part of a three-day heat wave, had conspired with the low black swivel chair in which he sat to make him uncomfortable. Portraits of La Guardia's predecessors gazed down at him: Gaynor, whose pince-nez and goatee—suggesting distinction—contradicted a wild eccentricity; Democratic Mayor George Brinton McClellan, Jr., an aristocratic son of the Civil War general and one who had really bucked Tammany leaders; John Purroy Mitchel, elected at thirty-four, negated as a reformer by Hearst simply because the Vanderbilts called him Jack.

As broadcast time became imminent, visitors and reporters sat in a silent, reverential semicircle before the Mayor. The City Hall chimes tolled, and this was a sign-on; the announcer in his introduction referred to the historic bells of City Hall striking the hour "in the city of opportunity where seven and a half million people live in peace and harmony and enjoy the benefits of Democracy." (This was also WNYC's standard sign-off and had been written by La Guardia.) Then the martial beat of the program's recorded theme, "The Marine Hymn," began. ". . . First to fight for right and freedom and to keep our honor clean. /We are proud to bear the ti-tle of the United States Marines." La Guardia, bouncing a bit in his chair, appeared to be absorbed by the music.

He now flung his hand up, indicating to Joe Fischler that he introduce him. "And speaking from his desk at City Hall," Fischler announced, "His Honor the Mayor."

The Mayor continued to bounce in his chair, as the flow of his ad-libbing carried him along. This made it necessary for Hon Hong Wei, the station's brilliant engineer and an infinitely patient man, to use all his skill in maintaining a steady level.

La Guardia talked on a variety of subjects. He included a didactic lecture concerning cabbage, *Brassica oleracea capitata:* cabbage was plentiful, cabbage could be made into a tasty dish, the water in which cabbage was boiled should not be thrown away. He then said, "If you have any children, bring them around the radio in thirty seconds. I have a message for them." Without a pause, he pointed out that he knew the children were disappointed because they "did not get the funnies." Then he turned to the director of the station with a semi-belligerent "listen, Morris," and went on to tell Morris he wanted some time set aside every day—during the strike—for the reading of the funnies to the kids. And he didn't want any excuses. "You know your programs are not so hot, so you can always find some space. You find someone who can read the funnies and who can describe them. And if you cannot find anyone, I will do it. I do not have time to do it, but I will do it. I want something like this . . ."

With the colored comic section of the *Sunday News* spread out on his desk and turned to Dick Tracy, La Guardia then presented a performance to be emulated in all future readings of funnies to the children of New York City. *Ahhhhh,* what do we have here? The gardener. Stabbed! Bleeding—all over the floor. Blood. . . . All this, he explained, smiling benignly at the microphone, was just "a reminder of what has happened to date." Then he talked to his audience—in the hushed voice of strictest confidence—about Dick Tracy, the detective on the trail "of a maid named Breathless," a detective tireless in pursuit, slender of form, not like Police Commissioner Lou Valentine's detectives, who, inexplicably, got fat. Now, get this picture. Breathless has hidden herself . . . in a laundry truck . . . along with a pot of money. Money! Taut suspense was in the Little Flower's falsetto. Fifty . . . thousand . . . dollars. In a pot. Now, the truck stops for a traffic light. You should always stop, children, when the light's red. Oh, the money—all that money—is spilling out of the pot . . . And now we see "Dick Tracy with his fine chiseled profile, talking to dignified Mrs. Van Hoosen." What's this? That laundry truck driver. Yes, he's found Breathless! And what does he say? He says, "Well, mangle my shorts and call me rough-dry! I've never picked up a bag like this before." The Mayor folded the comics, still flat on his desk. "We will find out what happens tomorrow, and we will let you know in case you cannot get the papers at home."

The audience reacted with a spontaneous round of applause.

After the remainder of the broadcast, La Guardia repaired once again to the men's room, then emerged to meet with his staff for a review of the broadcast before the press came in.

"What did you think of it?" he asked Morris Novik.

Novik, who recalled that La Guardia's performance "didn't mean a damn thing to me because I wasn't brought up with the funnies—reading the comics," replied, "Mayor, I don't know, but the people who were here certainly liked it."

The other staff members were very enthusiastic. It was great, they said.

"Well, Novik, the big shot," La Guardia complained, "he doesn't think it was so great."

Novik shook his head. "I didn't say it wasn't any good. I just couldn't understand it. But I could tell you how to improve on it. You said to the parents, 'Bring your kids to the radio in thirty seconds.' Most kids are down on the street playing and thirty seconds isn't enough time. If I knew what you were going to do, I would have made the suggestion right at the beginning of the program to bring the kids up because I have something to tell them in fifteen minutes."

La Guardia threw up his hands in disgust. "God damn it," he shouted, "there isn't anything I can do right!"

Although the reading of the comics proved to be the high point of the broadcast, the program had been concluded by Ed Durlacher's Top Hands, a fiddle-playing, cowboy-attired group, performing to publicize a weekly, municipally sponsored square dance at Riverside Drive and 105th Street.

"It brings me back to my younger days in Arizona," La Guardia told Ed Durlacher. (Nostalgia for a time fifty years in the past when he had followed the adventures of the Yellow Kid in the *World* and lived among cowboys in Prescott, Arizona, was natural, understandable. Now his days in Congress—1917-1933—were long over and his tenure as Mayor of New York—1933-1945—neared its end. These were the major undertakings of his life, of which only two years, two months and twenty days remained.) "How about a sample of that square dance they call the lancers? You start and I'll pick it up."

The Mayor did indeed pick it up:

> Chase that rabbit, chase that squirrel,
> Chase that pretty girl around the world.
> Hurry, boy, don't be slow.
> Chase that girl and around you go.

La Guardia pounded the desk to the tempo of the melody, too caught up in the rhythm and the song's admonitions to take time to wipe the perspiration streaming down his face. The Top Hands sawed away with comparable intensity and industry.

> Chase that 'possom, chase that coon,
> Chase that great big old baboon.
> Couple up two, buckle up four,
> Circle left in the middle of the floor.

The music came to an abrupt end and, after pausing briefly to catch his breath and return from a childhood in Arizona, Mayor Fiorello La Guardia concluded that Sunday's performance with his radio signature.

"Patience and Fortitude," he told his audience—and, as always, it was a command.

CHAPTER TWO

TO THE NINE-YEAR-OLD BOY, TRAVELING WITH HIS parents, sister and brother from a barracks in New York State to Fort Huachuca in the Arizona Territory, the journey was endless. Anticipation—as well as the rigors of 1891 travel—made the miles long, the hours interminable. Being a child, he had a joyous, innocent view of army post life that could not include the reality of a trooper's nine-dollar monthly paycheck—or the hardships of isolation and monotony. One soldier expressed a universal anguish of the military when he looked at the majestic magenta beauty of the mountains hemming in the fort at which he was stationed and cried out, "God damn you! You're always there!" The wife of another, with comparable bitterness, accused the War Department of having a special hellish talent for locating posts in areas distinguished by desolation, heat and insects.

But Achille Luigi Carlo La Guardia—the boy's father and an army bandmaster—accepted the stark facts of military life. When he had enlisted, he had consented not to claim "special privilege by reason of being married." Thus orders—ignoring the burdensome expense of travel and the trials of getting settled—moved him and his family every few years—or oftener: Fort Sully, South Dakota; Sacket's Harbor, New York; and now Fort Huachuca, Arizona—approximately a dozen miles from the Mexican border.

Seven months later, another order sent the La Guardias several hundred miles northwest to Fort Whipple. As they approached the fort from the desert, with its atmosphere a blend of May heat and dust, the fragrance of pine seemed to promise a less Spartan life. But the fort, snuggled down comfortably in its own ring of mountains, appeared a replica of all forts.

Here Fiorello La Guardia was to spend six years; as an adult, he would term them "a happy wholesome boyhood." The fort had been established to protect those involved in the newly discovered gold mines, for this had been the hunting grounds of the Apache, "notorious for extreme cruelty," the white man insisted, "as well as for cunning and endurance." But in 1886 the treacherous Geronimo's mother, wife and three children had been killed and Geronimo had been exiled to and imprisoned in Fort Marion, Florida; and twelve years earlier the last big Indian battle had been fought at Wounded Knee Creek. Still, the days at Fort Whipple continued to be delineated by reveille and taps, and now there was only beauty—no strain of alarm or urgency— as the longing sound of the bugle merged with the sun-bright Arizona air.

Although Fiorello did not remember the Lower East Side of New York—he had left it at the age of three—he did not need comparison to enhance the immensities of his desert playground. And he could never forget the kind of events that lodge in a boy's memory: riding burros, shooting a gun—with a man helping him hold it. And Prescott, a mere mile and a half down a winding dirt road, had infinite appeal. It was the archetype of all frontier towns: false front, covered walk, flat and unpaved street. Its boisterous cosmopolitan population must also have appealed to Fiorello's penchant for life at a crescendoed pitch; it required three breweries, twenty saloons and more than twenty lawyers.

Though purists may declare that the Old West was a thing of the past in 1892, it lingered in memory at the time of Fiorello's boyhood as a period of pleasant excitement. Even the ritual of bugle calls—guard-mount, drill calls, sick call, stable call, call-to-arms, each as different as the day's activity it elicited—lingered in one's thoughts as more than a melodic clock for posts under scorching desert suns.

This fantasy, a prettying up of the white man's conquest of the Western frontier, flavored Fiorello's early years; it had nothing to do with Thoreau's frontier—"wherever a man fronts a fact." According to the facts—the kind that would deeply concern Congressman and Mayor La Guardia—the forty-six forts established between 1849 and 1896 in what is now the area of Arizona were not primarily concerned with bugle calls and their peripheral beauty. At first, they took care of those headed for California and its gold; then the emphasis shifted to caring for those who settled in communities. This meant killing Indians. And to kill a single, solitary Indian—according to one probing estimate—cost the government a million dollars. An outrageous expense! Thus simple accounting indicated it was better to transform the red man from nomad to farmer, and this became the government's avowed—more economical—purpose.

But how could they ever change the Indian's taste for buffalo, for the gustatory delight of that shaggy grotesque's hump and gut, to a preference for steer, the flesh of which the red man regarded as stringy and without flavor? Indian agents, generally, lacked the subtleties of understanding and compassion that might bring about such a transformation. As adjuncts of a corrupt Indian Bureau, "utterly unworthy of a free and enlightened government," they supplied their charges with moldy beef—a staple, used at a later date by the War Department, that would drastically change La Guardia's life.

In spite of the million-dollars-per-Indian cost, cavalry in gay yellow, guidons whipping in the breeze, eradicated hostiles. Colonel J. M. Chivington—a minister turned army man, and always a realist—decreed on one occasion that Cheyenne children, like adults, were to be killed and scalped. He gave this order—and its justification—a metaphoric turn: "Nits," he said, "make lice."

As it turned out, the method that really worked—slaughtering the buffalo to near extinction—hadn't been planned. There could not have been a more efficient, inexpensive procedure. The buffalo, after all, provided the Indian with food, clothing, shelter and fuel. Eliminating one eliminated both.

Morality, obviously, did not enter into the thrust westward, for, as an officer's wife put it, the Indians "are, after all, neither Christian or white." Naturally, young Fiorello was more aware of his physical environment than of this amoral milieu, an environment presumably made secure in the year of his arrival in the Arizona Territory by the army's adoption of a repeating rifle—the Danish Krag-Jorgensen—which held five cartridges and dispatched them as needed.

His home held security too; his father, as bandmaster of the Eleventh Infantry, appeared more musician than soldier. A family-at-home portrait emphasized the importance of music to the La Guardias: young Richard, born in 1887, on the floor with a drum; Fiorello held a cornet and his sister Gemma, about two years older, a violin; and on the piano stool—the piano behind him—sat bearded, aristocratic Achille. It was also a home with a cow and chickens. Carpeting, with a magnificent, swirling pattern, graced the floor.

The world, however, intruded. In heavily accented English, Achille informed his children in no uncertain terms that no Italian was to be spoken in his home—only English. Though he was white—not the oppressed red, black or yellow—an immigrant might still feel the stigma of being a member of a minority and subject to the discrimination of quotas. As for Fiorello, his father had decided that he would one day be a "second Sousa," for no one was more American than John Philip Sousa and his "Stars and Stripes Forever"; surely an approximation of this popular artist would approach his Americanism. (Achille somehow managed to overlook the fact that Sousa was the son of German and Portuguese immigrants.)

A desire to live vicariously through his son may also have entered into the goal that Achille set for Fiorello. He, after all, had not become a "second Sousa." As an accompanist and arranger for Adelina Patti—the protégée at seventeen of Leonard Jerome, Winston Churchill's grandfather, and one in an illustrious line of great coloratura sopranos—Achille had been merely, frustratingly, in the vicinity of fame.

Understandably, this bandmaster off in a desert wilderness—giving music lessons to officers on the post, accompanying Gemma and Fiorello on the piano when they played benefits in Prescott—would regard Sousa, the March King, whose career was linked with presidents of the United States, as the pinnacle of achievement. Before coming to Fort Whipple, Achille had only a mustache—though a full one, with a sullen droop. To it, trimmed, he added a beard. Together they looked strikingly like the mustache and beard that John Philip Sousa sported.

When Achille instructed Gemma and Fiorello and they made a mistake, he would shout his displeasure—as though their error had irrevocably doomed the "second Sousa" ambition. Gemma would cry, but Fiorello seemed pleased rather than pained, for he begged, "Keep on screaming, Papa; in this way, I'll learn."

As a child in Foggia, Italy, where he was born, Achille also had an indomitable spirit. It had caused him to flee from home and southern Italy, the locale of a traumatic, humiliating experience. It started with his having put a sharp object on the seat of his teacher—a priest—who obliged by sitting on it. The punishment that followed had been worse than a flogging; Achille had to get down on all fours and trace a cross on the floor with his tongue. Wild with fury, he ran to his parents with an account of his humiliation. They not only believed the priest had done the right thing, but threatened to punish their son in the same way the next time he needed punishment. He reacted by running away from home, vowing never to return or to enter a Catholic church.

His flight lasted twenty years, took in all of the world, and included a study of music—composition, arranging, a mastery of the cornet. In addition to playing all over Europe, he was a musician on the Hamburg Line and served as a bandmaster in the Dutch East Indies. He then went to the United States and joined Adelina Patti's popular tour.

When he was thirty-one, he returned to Europe for the express purpose of finding a wife and bringing her back to the United States, where he had decided he wanted to live. All went as planned. At a dance in Trieste, Austria-Hungary, Achille met Irene Coen—twenty-one and a descendant of two eminent Italian-Jewish families, Luzzatto and Coen. And in spite of the cold, calculating premeditation of it all, love blossomed.

Irene's father was Abramo Isacco Coen, a merchant. Her mother—Fiorina, meaning little flower, after whom Fiorello was named—was a Luzzatto. One of her family, Luigi—"dark-skinned, hook-nosed, burning-eyed" and with a voice "like thick gruel"—championed numerous reforms. He introduced the cooperative movement into Italy. He served as counselor of the crown, secretary-general of the Ministry of Agriculture, head of the postal and telegraph system, president of the budget commission and the Minister of the Treasury. In 1910, he became prime minister. And, in that year, he dined with Theodore Roosevelt, who was on a visit to Rome. The idea of a prime minister being a Jew amazed Roosevelt. He felt that although Luzzatto was upright, in sympathy with liberal and progressive ideas and anxious to do justice, he lacked the force that was essential in a leader. If this was actually a flaw in Luigi Luzzatto, a relative of his, Fiorello La Guardia, who was beginning a dynamic career as a lawyer in the year of the Roosevelt-Luzzatto meeting, would supply more than enough force for all his kin.

This relative of Luzzatto's spoke his mind—forcefully—on all things, including genealogy. During his first term as mayor, he wrote a letter —which was not sent, for obvious reasons—to a Mr. John M. LaCorte of Brooklyn: "I am sure you are quite mistaken in the genealogy of my family. I have never had time to look this matter up myself. In fact the only member of our family that I know who has a real pedigree is our little Scotch Terrier known as Mac, who is a son of McIntosh, who is a son of Dundee, who is a son of Glasgow, but with all of that is only a son of a bitch. Very truly yours."

Six months after Achille and Irene met, they were married in a civil ceremony. Shortly afterwards, they left for New York and settled in Greenwich Village. In 1881, Gemma was born; on December the eleventh of the following year, Fiorello arrived at the La Guardia home at 177 Sullivan Street. Three years later, Achille joined the United States Army, and after a few reenlistments, he found himself bandmaster of the Eleventh Regiment of Infantry in the Territory of Arizona.

Achille's son would naturally have some curiosity about his antecedents, but his prime concerns were those of all youngsters, those that frequently got him in trouble. Whether the school staff was three or four—or five or six later on—as an adult, he realized that he had been a headache to all his teachers. An unforgettable one meted out punishment with a ruler that left black and blue marks on the calves of the recalcitrant's legs. Fiorello questioned authority. And his physical solidity emphasized—visually—a characteristic obstinacy.

Once in a fight in the school yard, with a boy who was frustratingly too tall for him, Fiorello ran purposefully into the school, sprinted back with a chair, clambered up on it and proceeded to throw punches. He fought not only for whatever had caused the fight, but also to prove that his lack of size—which would always be a touchy matter—was definitely not a handicap.

The usual boy-growing-up sensitivities plagued him. At about the age of ten, he experienced his "first glimpse of racial feeling born of ignorance." The appearance of an organ-grinder and monkey in town caused boys to whoop, as they circled Fiorello, and demand, "Hey, Fiorello, you're a dago, too. Where's your monkey?" Fiorello's father made the matter even worse by forgetting his Americanism credo. He appeared, spoke in Neapolitan with the organ-grinder and then—horror of horrors—invited him home for a pasta dinner.

In part because he thought he was what his peers had called him—a dago—he could more readily identify with the immigrant laborers, mostly Mexican and Italian, who worked in constructing the railroad that was heading from Prescott to Phoenix. An injury meant the loss of a job. And if you were killed, no one would even be notified, because records that would make notification possible weren't kept. This was patently unfair; common sense, decency, told you that. And once when

17

he bit into an apple, he saw hungry Indian children watch him with pain in their eyes—and in their stomachs—and he knew that they had been deprived of food by the slick, immoral Indian agents who got their jobs "because they were small-fry ward heelers" and were therefore called politicians. Consequently, he regarded politicians, from then on, as the lowest of the low.

Being in the "that's unfair" stage of childhood, he experienced the heroics of idealism and its singular satisfactions. Immoralities even struck at his father and mother. When an obviously crooked lobby in Washington attempted to arrange a commission for Achille—and other men at the fort—at a fat price, Fiorello yelled, "Swindle!" and persuaded his father not to fall into the trap. In his mother's case, the stakes were only a weekly dime or quarter for a lottery ticket, but because of the principle involved, Fiorello, with characteristic vehemence, showed her—after he had gone into the mathematics of it—that she couldn't possibly win.

His reaction to events indicated a precocity, a hypersensitivity, to the understanding of injustice; the discovery that injustice also existed outside the Territory of Arizona came as a result of reading Pulitzer's *World*. Though the Sunday *World* reached Ross's drugstore in Prescott tardily—on the following Saturday or Sunday—Fiorello was on hand, waiting. It catered strictly to the child in him with a comic strip called the "Yellow Kid," printed in yellow ink, one of the gimmicks of an ebullient, warring journalism to attract readers, and responsible for the pejorative term *yellow journalism*. But the *World*, whatever its motivation, presented an idealism to which he was akin. It fought the corruptions of Tammany and its boss Richard Croker. And it also brought to an incredulous Fiorello, through its coverage of the seventy-four investigative sessions of the Lexow Committee of the State Senate, his first awareness that police and politics could be in league for crooked objectives. "They've got us," said tall and handsome Police Captain Schmittberger. A few days later, in full uniform, he stood up on the witness stand and told all—"frightful revelations about commissioners, inspectors and captains." And the crusading Dr. Parkhurst proclaimed that those responsible for the municipal government of New York City were a "lying, perjured, rum-soaked and libidinous lot."

Fiorello, at twelve, displayed a similar understandable naivete concerning the Pullman Strike of 1894, a strike—in depression times—against an impossible wage cut. That federal troops confronted workers with fixed bayonets disturbed him, for he could not understand why the soldiers did not assume a comparable bellicose stance before railroad company officials. He must have arrived intuitively at the justice of this childish view. It was as though he knew that George M. Pullman—chin-bearded, inventor and manufacturer of the sleeping car, owner of that "model" company town, Pullman, Illinois, in which paternalism reached noble heights of larceny—had declared dictatorially that there was "nothing to arbitrate" and had hired a small army of Pinkerton detectives "and got Winchesters ready."

In young Fiorello's attempt to be completely fair, he placed himself in a dilemma. Although he was on the side of the strikers, he also felt that President Grover Cleveland's injunction against them was justified on the grounds that the United States mail had to be kept moving. The boy, of course, did not know that the railroad employees had agreed to keep the mail trains running and that "austere, unbending and un-genial" Cleveland—generous only in avoirdupois—had blatantly ignored this concession in order to have a basis for his strike-breaking injunction.

It was just a matter of time until La Guardia would become aware of all the finely honed techniques and strategies of politics—not just for breaking strikes, but for the attainment of a variety of ends, noble and otherwise.

CHAPTER THREE

AT FOURTEEN, FIORELLO LA GUARDIA DECIDED HE would be a musician when he grew up—a child's concession to a parent. Prior to this decision, he had flitted from one yearning to another: to become a jockey, a newspaperman, a pugilist. Nonetheless, in the year he became fourteen, a presidential year, he took a great interest in the McKinley-Bryan campaign, that furious battle of words between the agrarian and commercial sections of the country. Although residents in a territory could not vote in a national election, they did have a delegate in the House to represent them. Therefore there were oratorical crusades for this office—and for local offices—and La Guardia found it all very exciting.

Two years later, the *World*—accurately equated with Pulitzer—would make Fiorello a newspaperman pro tem. The Pulitzer and Hearst perennial battle for journalistic supremacy continually intensified. Axiomatically, since wars sold papers, Hearst—who created scandals effortlessly, and without compunction, to enliven his papers and thus increase their sales—determined to produce a small war. This small war would be in Cuba and against Spain; ostensibly, solely to free the oppressed Cubans.

This, after all, was an era in which staple virtues were extolled in simple, unsophisticated terms. Thus, as the nineteenth century ended, an editorial in the *Youth's Companion* could decry the outrage of boys throwing snowballs at girls—and, incredibly, in sight of the American flag, which, the editorial pointed out, "means fair play, equal chance, protection to the weak and honor to women."

Hearst played this fine, upstanding theme, too, orchestrating it for a vast mass readership. On February 12, 1898, his *Journal* ran a story with an arresting headline: "Does Our Flag Protect Women?" The shocking implication of this question was that our flag certainly did not.

An attempt at eroticism—by Frederic Remington, of all people, known only for his portraiture of horses, cowboys and Indians, painted in his New Rochelle, New York, studio—compounded this sensational disclosure. His appalling picture covered a full half-page. Its center of interest was a three-quarter backside view of a nude woman, standing in a ship's cabin and spotlighted by illumination from a porthole. Around her, Remington had skillfully positioned three men so that they did not obstruct a view of the sketched nakedness; at the same time, by means of stereotypes, he made it clear that these men were Spanish and lascivious.

The story came from the Hotel Inglaterra in Havana, from the type-writer of handsome, dashing Richard Harding Davis, the greatest foreign correspondent extant, who earned a reputed salary of $3,000 a month. Davis cabled the *Journal* that as the American steamship *Olivette* was about to leave for the United States, Spanish police officers—the vile foreigners sketched by Remington—had searched three Cuban women for insurgent dispatches. From this intelligence, Davis's paper arrived at an inescapable conclusion, one that it felt compelled to pass on to its readership: "War is a dreadful thing, but there are things more dreadful than even war, and one of them is dishonor."

Three days later, Whipple Barracks experienced great excitement over a report that the *Maine* had been blown up. (The fort was too remote to know of the speculation that Hearst had arranged the deadly explosion to make certain he got *his* war.) "The Postal Telegraph operator in Prescott," La Guardia recalled in his autobiography, "pasted up Associated Press bulletins on the *Maine* disaster as soon as they came in, and along with the other children of Army men, as well as the parents, I watched and waited eagerly for the latest news. We expected war momentarily, especially after the news came that two hundred and fifty American lives had been lost."

But war could not come that fast, because both a cry for war and opposition to it had arisen with equal shrillness in Congress. Senator Redfield Proctor, head of the largest marble-producing company in the world, declared with a sincerity that touched the nation's heart, "To me, the strongest appeal is not . . . the loss of the *Maine,* but the spectacle of a million and a half people, the entire native population of Cuba, struggling for freedom and deliverance from the worst misgovernment of which I ever had knowledge." This flood of oratory did not move Tom Reed, Speaker of the House, ponderous, bald, so sharp of tongue that he could impale two individuals at once with: "They never open their mouths without subtracting from the sum of human knowledge." Reed had in mind the marble quarries in Vermont that Senator Proctor owned when he pointed out, "Proctor's position might have been expected. A war will make a large market for gravestones." (A few decades later, insurgent Congressman La Guardia would be making comparable trenchant comments. For example, as though emulating Reed's caustic thrust and vivid style, he challenged the financial genius of the millionaire Secretary of the Treasury Andrew W. Mellon, maintaining that it did not equal the skill of a woman in a tenement "raising six children on a weekly envelope containing $30.")

But yellow journalism empathized with Senator Proctor. Hearst, for one, virtually paraphrased the senator's views through an appeal addressed to *Journal* mothers by the wife of Senator John Mellen Thurston of Nebraska. With purple apostrophe, she proclaimed, "Oh! Mothers of the Northland, who tenderly clasp your little ones to your loving hearts! Think of the black despair that filled each [Cuban] mother's heart as she felt her life-blood ebb away, and knew that she had left her little ones to perish from the pain of starvation and disease."

Most readers responded to this soulful outpouring as Hearst planned: Cuba must be freed of the Spanish oppressor. The Cubans were indeed in precisely the same tyrannical trap as our forefathers in 1776. We must hold our heads, and our flag, high . . .

Congress, in fulfilling its function, had to reflect the will of the people; it therefore subjected President McKinley, "a kindly soul in a spineless body," to enormous pressure.

It was therefore little wonder that, about ten days after the sinking of the *Maine*, orders arrived in Fort Whipple to get ready for war. (Achille La Guardia's regiment was better prepared than others, for it had those modern Danish Krag-Jorgensen rifles.)

Still McKinley held on to peace—though his grasp was growing ever weaker as the country's cry became "Remember the *Maine!* To hell with Spain!" Spain wanted peace desperately, too. In fact, the queen's government made every possible concession, "and a cause for war no longer existed," but the concessions were clearly granted to a country that, as the anti-imperialists pointed out, was bent on expansion.

War—the more anticipated, because delayed—finally was declared on April 25. And the men at Fort Whipple welcomed it, because they had feared McKinley had dallied too long for war ever to become a reality. Fiorello recalled, during the last months of his life, that Bucky O'Neil, the first man in the Arizona Territory to enlist—who had been an editor, lawyer, judge, sheriff and his special Spanish American War hero—gave a talk in Fiorello's school after war had been declared, on the war's meaning. "And when we had won the war," O'Neil said, "no other nation would again attempt to dominate territory in the Western Hemisphere." Obviously, this justification for the war by his hero was good enough for young Fiorello.

Achille La Guardia's regiment proceeded to Jefferson Barracks, just south of St. Louis, where U. S. Grant had come as a young lieutenant and from which point troops had gone off to fight in the Mexican War and the wars against the Noble Savage. This time, troops left—leaving their families behind—for Mobile, Alabama, first stop on the way to action in Cuba.

At fifteen, Fiorello hungered with adolescent fervor for excitement and great causes. That year, the United States was no older than Fiorello in its outlook. Its flag was "the flag of the free"; its patriotism innocent, uplifting and unbounded. It sang two songs: "There'll Be a Hot Time in the Old Town Tonight" and "The Stars and Stripes Forever," which, with blaring brasses and a pounding of drums, pointed out in its opening words:

> Let martial note in triumph float
> And liberty extend its mighty hand;
> A flag appears mid thunderous cheers,
> The banner of the western land.

The *Washington Post* tried hard to fathom what had happened to the United States: "Ambition, interest, land-hunger, pride, the mere joy of fighting, whatever it may be we are animated by a new sensation." Speaking for those who hadn't succumbed to martial airs or sensory novelties, Mr. Dooley—Senator Tom Reed with a brogue—stated eloquently, "We're a gr-reat people. An' the best iv it is, we know we ar-re."

Such cynicism could not possibly touch Fiorello at fifteen; he would, naturally, pick Bucky O'Neil, chaser of outlaws, over such spoilsports as the anti-imperialists. Having been left behind, for his attempts at joining the army had failed, Fiorello felt frustrated and restless. The recruiting office had found him lacking in weight, height and years. Of course, they had no requirement for such subtle and really significant qualities as doggedness, gall, self-confidence.

When he went to Pulitzer's *Post Dispatch,* those three elements in his makeup obtained what he wanted, a job as a correspondent from Mobile. There would be no salary, the editor who had succumbed to his sales pitch reminded him, but his expenses to Mobile would be paid. Of course, Fiorello's objective was not remuneration, but to catch up with his father and the Eleventh; merely working for Pulitzer of the *World,* even without compensation, must have been deeply satisfying. When Joseph Pulitzer had bid for the bankrupt *Dispatch*—later uniting it with the *Post*—and acquired it, as the only bidder, for $2,500, he fashioned its platform along idealistic lines that were pure Pulitzer and latter-day La Guardia. This was also true of the specific ways in which the paper's goals were to be implemented: "a drive to clean up abuses in city government, an expose of wealthy tax dodgers, a successful crackdown on the lottery racket and vigorous advocacy of a park system and other municipal improvements."

Fiorello's first bit of reporting, in the form of a letter to the editor, appeared on May 18. It had a misspelled by-line—F. Guardi—the introductory headline "The *Post Dispatch's* Youthful Correspondent Heard From" and a picture of La Guardia holding a cornet. Prefatory remarks by the paper stated that their correspondent was bright and an exceptional cornetist. Proof: on the night that a fire raged in the Jefferson Barracks, he ran into the burning building for his cornet in order to blow the fire call. Fiorello's initial story radiated optimism and patriotism: "They are a nice lot of good spirited boys and the right sort of men to defend their country." And they were all eager—perhaps the Youthful Correspondent imagined himself in their place—"for the orders to go to Cuba."

No evidence indicated that Tampa affected his high spirits adversely, although as an embarkation point, its only merit was its nearness to Cuba. However, Tampa was a long nine miles from the port, a port that could be reached only by a single-track railroad. Theodore Roosevelt—vigorously being a boy once again—happily described the city as "a scene of wildest confusion." Loaded trains clogged tracks, and no one had the slightest knowledge of what the various cars contained.

Broad humor arose spontaneously from such a muddle. Choices had to be made as to what should be put aboard the transports, for they proved too small to take everything. As between mules and horses, mules won out, because in the jungle pack animals are a sine qua non, even though cavalry without horses is as paradoxical as battles without ammunition.

Thoroughgoing ineptitude and first-rate bungling went on and on, giving the war a uniformly farcical quality. General W. R. Shafter, sixty, a Civil War gold medal winner, three hundred pounds of corpulence, whose gout compelled him to wear a gunnysack on one foot instead of a boot, could obviously not lead a saber charge to meet the epic, heroic requirements of the *World* or *Journal*. This did not stop Hearst from writing, "He is a bold, lion-headed hero and massive as to body—a sort of human fortress in blue coat and flannel shirt." (He might have mentioned the general's sun helmet, a desperate attempt to negate the heat of the heavy blue, wool winter shirts that had been issued to men at war in a torrid jungle summer.)

Captain Woodbury Kane was plagued by a different sort of problem, singular, personal. As president of the American Tobacco Company and a millionaire, it seemed only fitting that he wear a sword, but the sword persisted, disrespectfully, to get between his legs and trip him up. Finally, he carried the ornamental weapon over one shoulder while in action, and brandished a six-shooter with his free hand.

As for former Confederate officer General Joseph Wheeler, it must have been the excitement of battle in the Santiago campaign—not failure to identify the enemy—that caused him to shout to his troops, "Give it to the Yankees!"

Black gunpowder—issued along with woolen shirts for tropic wear and cumbersome swords and canned roast beef that harbored ptomaine—could be deadly for those at either end of a gun. This was simply because the puff of smoke that followed the firing of a cartridge containing black gunpowder pointed out the position of the soldier who had fired the shot. Men, in short, died; and the war's ludicrous aspects turned poignant, and Richard Harding Davis romanticism appeared no more tenable than a fairy tale.

And when it was all officially over, welcoming martial airs could not conceal that the returning heroes were "yellow, haggard fellows, too weak and tired to smile." And Fiorello's hero, Bucky O'Neil, had remained in the torrid Cuban jungle, because in the charge on San Juan Hill, a bullet struck O'Neil's body and made the sound *chug*, which a correspondent observed was the invariable sound made by a bullet striking a body.

Tins of beef, which came to be known as "embalmed beef," also made a sound related to death when they swelled and popped open—in the oven-hot hold of a ship or in unmitigated jungle heat. This war's fatalities were also related to an egregious statistic: of the 6,472 who died, most were casualties of unsanitary conditions. And Achille La

Guardia would become an anonymous digit in that statistic. (Fate was far kinder to the man he wanted Fiorello to emulate. John Philip Sousa was stricken with typhoid fever, just as he was about to get into the conflict; by the time he had recovered, the war was over. What's more, the "Stars and Stripes Forever" netted him approximately $300,000.)

Understandably, "The *Post Dispatch's* Youthful Correspondent" no longer "radiated optimism and patriotism." His father had become ill as a result of eating diseased beef which corrupt contractors supplied to the army.

Pulitzer had also been disillusioned by the war. He had once said quite casually that "he had rather liked the idea of a war—not a big one—but one that would arouse interest and give him a chance to gauge the reflex in his circulation figures." As it turned out, this war's sole virtue had been brevity. With cables between New York and Cuba sometimes costing $2.12 a word, Pulitzer could not have afforded a longer war.

Tom Reed, as disillusioned as Pulitzer and as bitter as La Guardia over the war's corruption, also figured cost; the cost, not of cables, but of killing an individual in the Philippines, to which the "splendid little war" spread. In writing to the clerk of the House Committee on Appropriations, he complained that it cost thirty dollars for each yellow man left dead in the bush. (A bargain, considering how expensive the death of a red man had been.) Reed therefore wanted to know, "Why didn't you purchase him of Spain F.O.B. with definite freight rate and insurance paid?"

La Guardia did not strike back at the war's fulsome inanities—specifically as they related to his father—until he became a congressman.

CHAPTER FOUR

ACHILLE LA GUARDIA'S ILLNESS LED TO HIS DIS-
charge from the army on August 22, 1898, because of, among other
ailments, "disease of stomach and bowels," a circumlocution for the
condition caused by eating spoiled canned beef. This entitled him to
a munificent eight-dollars-a-month pension. (The government, after
all, was still burdened by a million Civil War pensioners, a burden in
1890 of $106,000,000.)

Backed against the wall physically, emotionally and financially,
Achille sought escape. He took his family to New York and then to
Trieste, where they lived with his wife's family, and he struggled in a
variety of unsatisfactory ways to make a livelihood. Then in 1904, just
as the ailing Achille appeared to have latched onto a possible success,
a hotel which he had leased and developed into a growing business, he
died.

Four years earlier, Fiorello had obtained a job in Budapest, through
a friend of his father, as a clerk in the American consulate. Eighteen,
hair parted precisely in the middle, energetic, wiry, he still suffered
from a restlessness that would not countenance routine. The consul,
Frank Dyer Chester, twelve years La Guardia's senior but an infinite
distance from him in family, education and connections, had also received his appointment through influence, the influence of Senator
Henry Cabot Lodge. Chester, La Guardia later recalled, "was not a
politician. He was a scholarly gentleman who had won honors at Harvard. . . ." In spite of all their dissimilarities, Chester, observing that
young La Guardia was "ambitious for promotion," felt compassion.
Still, he told Fiorello quite candidly that since he lacked a Harvard
degree, he "would never get any higher than the menial position of

clerk in the American foreign service." Encouraged by Chester to study languages—Italian, German, Croatian, a South Slavic language—as a way of sidestepping this dreary fate, Fiorello also worked hard at history and kept abreast of what was happening back in the United States by reading, as he later recorded, "every newspaper and magazine I could lay my hands on."

Chester, however, continued to detect flaws in his clerk—other than lowly birth, non-Harvard education and ambitions beyond his station. One of La Guardia's duties in the typewriterless consulate was to act as the consul's—in Chester's dearly loved word—amanuensis. But an amanuensis whose penmanship was illegible was a flagrant affront, and Chester, with a prima donna's annoyance, reported this failing to Washington. One other deficiency that Chester had observed in his clerk, which he did not mention in his report to Washington, was Fiorello's lively interest in pretty girls. Chester, however, disliked women. This led Fiorello on one occasion to hand him a gun and ask, "What do you have to live for?"

As a dedicated misogynist, Chester took it upon himself to save La Guardia from women—actresses in particular—who passed through the consulate. When one bleached blonde, notorious as a blackmailer, appeared, Chester warned La Guardia and another clerk that should they go out with her they could consider themselves fired. "That was enough for us," La Guardia recalled. La Guardia and the other clerk took the dangerous woman, appropriately, to the Folies Bergeres. Knowing La Guardia as he did, Chester, out for blood, also went to the theatre, saw his clerks escorting the forbidden woman and promptly fired them. But through the vice-consul's plea in their behalf, they managed to get their jobs back.

La Guardia—not yet twenty-one—craved more than a clerk's job. He moved up to being a consular agent in Fiume, operating out of a two-room office, in one of which he lived. (The bathroom facilities were in the hall and were shared.) The eight-hundred-dollars-per-year salary went far in supplying the young bachelor with the good things of life—music, beautiful women, lazy evenings in beer gardens, soccer at the Austrian Soccer Club, swimming in the blue Adriatic. Romantic derring-do also came along, for the culture of that time and place offered and fostered it.

La Guardia was amused by this, but he also had a hostile view of the country, the most reactionary and aristocratic in Europe. Because this "scrappy grotesque little ball of fire" would not stand for the injustices with which he came in contact, he became—at least according to one State Department official—"the worst headache in the history of the Department."

Single-handed, he took on the Cunard Steamship Company. He saw the inhumanity of making immigrants pay for their passage to the United States only to be rejected at Ellis Island for trachoma, the scourge of the time, or because of some other disease. On one occasion, he boarded a Cunard Liner packed with immigrants and ready to sail; instead of bearing a signed bill of health, he brought a doctor to examine the passengers. All immigrants, La Guardia said adamantly, had to be examined at this end of the trip, and the steamship line would pay for the examination. Indignant, the company sent a protest to Washington, through Chester. It proved to no avail, for the State Department ruled that La Guardia had not exceeded his authority.

La Guardia even dared to oppose Her Imperial Highness, the Archduchess Maria Josefa of Austria. When she arrived in Fiume on a visit, all Hungarian officials outdid one another to please her. This included the presentation of an embarkation of immigrants—a contemporary pastime—for her entertainment. But La Guardia would not consent to an immediate performance by the Archduchess's peasants, for this meant that after they had marched up the plank on display, they would have to remain in the hold of the ship for three days and nights, until the ship was scheduled to sail. La Guardia would not be mollified when Her Imperial Highness invited him to have tea with her and view the embarkation. He turned down the invitation, vehemently refused to set aside regulations and declared, "Tell the Archduchess that she may boss her own immigrants, but she can't boss the American consul."

La Guardia also went to the captain of the ship and made it clear that if passengers were taken on three days before sailing time, he would not grant the ship a bill of health, without which a ship could not enter New York's port.

When La Guardia returned to his office, entreaties and threats continued to bombard him. He therefore took cover from the storm in the home of a friend; his hostess provided an early tea, played the piano and chatted entertainingly. His hostess was the wife of the officer of the port, who was frantically searching everywhere—except in his own home—for the vanished American consul.

The furor eventually died down. And La Guardia summed it all up with an offhand "I did miss meeting Her Imperial Highness."

La Guardia found life in Fiume too easy. A few hours constituted a workday, and his income made too many luxuries possible. Besides, men who had been in the service for decades found that they had not been advanced and were without security. Afire with ambition, Fiorello knew a promotion in Fiume was not possible. He required action. He therefore left his brother and sister and mother—though she pled with him to stay—and worked his way to New York on a British ship, as an interpreter and by assisting a doctor vaccinate the eighteen hundred immigrants who were aboard.

CHAPTER FIVE

U PON ARRIVING IN NEW YORK WITH A TWO-HUN-
dred-dollar grubstake, Fiorello obtained a job through the man who
had helped him get into the consular service. The job, however, meant
living hundreds of miles from New York, in Portsmouth, Ohio, and
working for a company that made fireproof bricks. Fiorello gave it up
after a try of only a few weeks, because, as he explained, "In Portsmouth I would have no opportunity for the kind of schooling I
needed." After all, when he tore himself away from the entreaties of
his mother, he had argued that he simply had to go to the United
States to make something of himself.

Fiorello had not been more specific then, but toward the close of his
life, he stated: "I had a definite plan worked out in my mind for my
future. I wanted first to complete my education, get admitted to the
bar, and then enter public service." This chronology suggests that he
would become a lawyer simply because a political career required it:
an obvious, pragmatic sacrifice, because he felt lawyers and scoundrels
were one. He referred to lawyers as "semi-colon boys," those, in short,
who used even punctuation marks to trip up the unwary and mulct the
naively innocent. But he had no more respect for politicians, for the
dastardly Indian agents of his childhood still lurked in his mind. He,
of course, his rationalization ran, would be a different type of both
lawyer and politician—which he proved to be, with a pyrotechnic
vengeance.

To go to law school, he had to earn the money this required. His
struggles—at least in their variety—recapitulated those that his father
had endured during the last few years of his life. He progressed from a
ten-dollars-a-week wage in the employ of the Society for the Preven-

tion of Cruelty to Children, translating that part of the French penal code that related to the legal status of children, to twice that amount as stenographer for Abercrombie and Fitch Sporting Goods. (He had mastered shorthand in a month; the course that made this possible had cost seven dollars and fifty cents.)

Since he required an even better wage than stenography offered in order to attend evening classes at New York University's Law School, he took a civil service exam for interpreter at Ellis Island. Because he knew Italian, German and Croatian, he appeared high on the eligibility list. When accepted, he received a salary of twelve hundred dollars a year. This meant that he would now be able to study law, though he would have to do it at night, after a full day of work. But an unexpected obstacle arose: the certificates that La Guardia had received from the schools in Arizona were not acceptable. He therefore took regents' exams, after attending the New York Preparatory School, which, he said, "poured the stuff into us as fast as any individual could absorb it." Finally, he entered law school in 1907—nicely timed with the arrival of a panic, which brought hard times that ran into 1908.

His life during this period could not have been more strenuous. Study followed long, laborious days on Ellis Island; and because immigrants were arriving at a daily rate of 5,000, he had to endure a seven-day workweek. He found the downtrodden arrival subjected to all sorts of legal paradoxes. "It is a puzzling fact," he pointed out with characteristic fury, "that one provision of the Immigration law excludes any immigrant who has no job and classifies him as likely to become a public charge, while another provision excludes an immigrant if he has a job!"

A full-to-the-brim schedule didn't keep him from writing letters about such matters, scathing letters, to Congress. Of his stay on Ellis Island, La Guardia said in retrospect: "I never managed during the three years I worked there to become callous to the mental anguish, the disappointments and the despair I witnessed almost daily." (He also noticed that the Immigration Service victimized him. In a straight-from-the-shoulder, detailed brief, he stated that his salary should be raised, because he received $1,200 while those less qualified received $1,400.)

His last year as an interpreter widened his experiences of the grimmer aspects of life. He had been assigned to night court and cases dealing with aliens engaged in vice. This assignment, however, had advantages: it freed him from daily time-consuming trips to Ellis

Island and he could devote his days to study. Now, at first hand, instead of through Pulitzer's *World,* he learned about the corruption of the police and the venality of judges and the lengths to which lawyers would go to make a fee.

Andrew Tedesco, the inspector in charge of the White Slave Division of the Immigration Service, was "unkempt and unprepossessing in appearance." But his advice to save the young interpreter from a dishonest life had a straightforward, incisive ring. "You can get experience in this job or you can make a great deal of money," he told La Guardia. "I don't think you'll take the money. But, remember, the test is if you hesitate. Unless you say 'No!' right off, the first time an offer comes your way, you're gone."

Graduated from New York University's Law School with just passing grades and over the hurdle of bar examinations, La Guardia opened a law office. He embarked on this career even though he felt "that too many lawyers were being turned out like so many sausages every year," and even though his capital consisted of sixty-five dollars, the amount he earned in two weeks on Ellis Island.

The opening of his office consisted of acquiring space, at a cost of fifteen dollars a month, in the law offices of McIllheny and Bennett, located at 15 William Street, on the tip of Manhattan, just a few blocks from City Hall. Fiorello also purchased letterheads and second-hand furniture. However, no such simple direct way existed for acquiring a passion for the practice of law. In his very first case, in the Municipal Court, he learned that justice can be dispensed "in a hell of a way." He lost the case, even though he had presented it so well that the judge congratulated him.

"Well if I did so well," La Guardia asked, "why didn't you decide in my favor?"

"Oh, young man," the judge replied, "I'll give you a break some other day."

Five years before La Guardia had this experience, Louis D. Brandeis said, "We hear much of the 'corporation lawyer,' and far too little of the 'people's lawyer.'" La Guardia was a people's lawyer, and unlike most lawyers who viewed their profession as synonymous with business. In a very unbusinesslike way, especially since "clients were few and far between," La Guardia would turn a client away if he "thought the client had no case or did not need a lawyer, but could settle his differences himself." And La Guardia to the amazement of his colleagues never took on a case unless he was convinced of the rights of his client. Equally odd, his fees covered the gamut of nonexistent to small.

La Guardia entered politics—like law, not known for its idealism—by toiling in the 25th Assembly District. Usually those who worked in the political vineyards expected a sizable portion of the harvest. George Washington Plunkitt, "the Sage of Tammany," expressed this view in prose destined to live: "I seen my opportunities and I took them."

Since Democratic Tammany was evil personified on a grand scale, Fiorello had no alternative but to be a Republican. Besides, Tammany embraced the Irish, not the Italians. And very likely, with calculating, subconscious stirrings, La Guardia knew that only by being an irregular Republican could he avoid the anonymity of serving as just another cog in a machine. But irregularity sprang reflexively from his extravert makeup, and his behavior as a lawyer matched perfectly his ways as a politician. His work in both areas, moreover, concerned itself with immigrants. He spoke their languages—with an accent, but he spoke them—and was belligerently, impatiently sympathetic to their needs.

Tammany proceeded along related lines. The boss could remain in power by having "jobs for the faithful and jobs for everyone." What's more, for a politician not to know his constituents was tantamount to suicide. Henry H. Curran made graphic use of this axiom while running for Congress. Upon concluding a campaign speech, he would take a dollar bill from his pocket and say, as he waved the bill before his audience, "Here is a dollar bill, a new green dollar bill, and it is yours on one condition." This invariably made all his listeners pay close attention. "It is a reward," he continued, "to anybody here—man, woman or child—who ever saw my opponent in this district! Did you ever see him here once? Did he ever trouble to look you up, to come around and see what you want and need? Did he ever do anything but draw pay and pass you up? Here is the dollar—do I hear an answer?" No one, Curran pointed out, ever claimed the dollar.

La Guardia's approach to law tied in with being seen and known by potential voters. He joined the garment workers, most of whom were immigrants, in their battles against deplorable sweatshop conditions. Upon arriving in the land of opportunity, they had no choice but to accept whatever employers offered them. And the laws and those who executed them were on the side of the employer. One magistrate, in sentencing a girl striker to the workhouse, said, "You are on strike against God and Nature, whose law is that man shall earn his bread by the sweat of his brow. You are on strike against God."

With but few exceptions, La Guardia's friends were Italian and for the most part in the arts—the sculptors Attilio Piccirilli and Onorio Ruotolo, the great tenor Enrico Caruso, the flutist Giovanni Fabrizo. There they were in the midst of millions of poor, struggling immigrants, clearly being exploited. Their art—though it was not politics—encompassed this vast agony.

A strike in 1912 by men garment workers followed one by women. The union needed a lawyer not only to fight picket cases—for picketing could be termed illegal, if this served a powerful interest—but also to explain union matters to Italian workers who could not understand English. (La Guardia, who had learned Yiddish while in the consular service, was also able to pacify feuding Italian and Jewish workers by speaking Italian or Yiddish as required.) Few lawyers dared engage in such activities, for fear of offending the establishment.

La Guardia even joined the picket line. And he let the police know of his presence by defying them to arrest him. They didn't oblige. He also served on a committee of three who negotiated with employers after an unsatisfactory try by leaders of the United Garment Workers; this negotiation led to a shorter workweek, fifty-three hours, and a pay increase, one dollar a week.

All of his strike activities brought him to the conclusion that he could better economic conditions and bring about "less favoritism to special interests in the administration of law" by becoming a congressman. His motivation was not completely altruistic; as always he had his eye on the next rung. It even crossed his mind that he would have a better chance of being elected to Congress if he went out West and established residence there. But he remained in New York, in the 14th Congressional District, which encompassed the entire tip of Manhattan up to 14th Street, a district in which Tammany had never lost an election. And he served as treasurer and election district captain. Obviously, he was someone starting at the bottom.

La Guardia's big chance came at the end of summer in 1914; a Horatio Alger hero in the right place at the right time. La Guardia was in the club rooms of the 25th Assembly District, where "the boys were filling out petitions for the nomination for Congress."

"Who is the candidate for Congress?" someone hollered.

As he came from his back-room office, Clarence Fay, the leader of the district, shouted, "Who wants to run for Congress?"

"I do," La Guardia said, eagerly seizing the opportunity.

"Okay, put La Guardia down," Fay said.

Just as La Guardia thought he had the nomination, felt all the elation of such a situation, someone asked, "Hey, La Guardia, what's your first name?"

"Fiorello."

"Oh, hell, let's get someone whose name we can spell."

La Guardia didn't give up. He spelled his name carefully and slowly —still his given name came out "Floullo" in the official manual of New York State—and argued successfully that he be put down in the petitions.

This babe in the political woods had much to learn. As the nominee, he expected to be heard when he attended his first political meeting in a district clubhouse, for it was advertised "that all the prominent candidates would talk." Speaker after speaker spoke, and each time the chairman said "And now we will hear from a young and promising candidate," La Guardia, who knew he was young and considered himself promising, started to rise only to find that he wasn't the one being introduced.

When the meeting concluded, La Guardia approached the chairman and said, "How come?"

This caused general laughter. And everyone told him what amounted to: "Why, Fiorello, you haven't a chance of winning. We've never elected a Republican to Congress from this district. Now, what you should do is go out and campaign for the state senator and assemblyman, help elect the ticket. That is all you can do."

La Guardia, still intent on becoming a congressman, pleaded, "Could I try?"

"Oh, no, don't be foolish," they told him. "You just go out now and help the others, and some day you may get a nomination for an office you can win."

Ignoring this advice, La Guardia bought a secondhand Ford, plastered it with signs proclaiming his political intentions, and went about the business of defeating the formidable saloon keeper, President of the National Liquor Dealers Association and Congressman, Michael Farley. He had the help of young and clever Harry Andrews and of Louis Espresso, a stocky, gravel-voiced political pragmatist. He spoke on street corners, verbally shanghaiing those leaving political meetings.

He made a house-to-house canvass, "storming up and down" tenement hallways, talking with persuasive passion to immigrants in their native tongues. He said precisely what he thought of Michael Farley—that he was neither a good saloon keeper nor a decent congressman. He distributed handbills bearing a handsome picture of himself and a picture of Farley that made him look crude and undesirable.

La Guardia's campaigning proved effective. Even though La Guardia lost, Farley won by only 1,700 votes, and prior to that election, the Democratic majority had never been less than 16,000. The short dark-haired man who had never been permitted to speak at political gatherings was now viewed with respect by both Republicans and Democrats, and he himself was sufficiently encouraged to start working immediately for a victory in 1916.

In the meantime, the Republican Party rewarded him by appointing him deputy attorney general of the state of New York. This was not much of a gift, for the real work of this office was done in Albany and not in New York City. In fact, the New York branch "served only as a clearing house for minor matters and a storeroom of forgotten cases."

Shortly after La Guardia took the oath of office, a young woman obtained a job as secretary in the attorney general's office. Blonde and blue-eyed, reticent, of a staid German Lutheran family and freshly graduated from high school, Marie Fischer approached her first job with timidity and uncertainty. She could not help but be impressed—overawed—by the energy and assurance of one of the deputies, Fiorello La Guardia. He took his job seriously; unlike the other deputies, he put in a full day. He paced his office, raving, waving his arms. Because Miss Fischer was new and could be imposed on, La Guardia's excessive chores were given to her.

Three cases came La Guardia's way that caused him to dash madly about in a customarily tranquil office. For a number of years residents on Riverside Drive in New York City had been subjected to the fumes of industrial plants across the Hudson. (Staten Island had a comparable problem.) When La Guardia was given the case and told vaguely "to do something," he did—with his customary drive and enthusiasm. He struck the telling blow when he went to Washington and filed seven complaints by the state of New York against the seven corporations in New Jersey that were responsible for the unhealthy, disturbing fumes. "Imagine my surprise," La Guardia said, "when I got a good calling down for proceeding so precipitately." The mystery cleared up quickly; La Guardia found out that Charles S. Whitman of New York, who had risen to the governorship via the district attorney's office, yielded to the pressures of the companies who didn't want the enormous expense that would be involved in changing manufacturing processes in order to eliminate the objectionable fumes. (Years later, in what might be construed as a most magnanimous gesture, the changes were made.)

Though he had been a lawyer for five years, such manipulations continued to amaze him. Among routine chores, from legal work for the State Department of Agriculture to exploring unpaid mortgage taxes, he received a case which involved a violation by Long Island fishermen—the harvesting of scallops under a year old. Invariably, juries had failed to indict.

To get to the bottom of the matter, La Guardia questioned jurors and received a frank answer: "Why don't you go after the big oyster companies? We are not going to convict these little fellows. The big companies do the same thing day after day and are never bothered."

La Guardia immediately questioned the conservation officials about the matter.

"Would you prosecute one of the big companies?" they asked.

"Of course I would," La Guardia shot back. "It's a violation of the law, isn't it?"

"Yes, but—"

That was all La Guardia had to hear; he went out after one of the big oyster companies, represented by a prominent lawyer—and a wily one, as it turned out. La Guardia's opponent asked for and received one adjournment after another. When the case finally came to trial, the oyster company's lawyer drew a telegram from his pocket which he'd received from Governor Whitman, informing him that the law about scallops had been changed the night before.

"Now, if Your Honor please," the lawyer said, grinning, "inasmuch as this had been changed, I submit it would be hardly worthwhile to continue with this trial. Clearly the legislature has seen the fallacy of such a law."

"Oh, yes, Counselor," the judge said, "I quite agree."

The law had been changed in a simple, clever, effective way. "In public waters," just those three words, had been inserted. It was in those waters that the little fishermen fished, but the big companies— curiously enough—fished only in leased, *private* waters.

If La Guardia hadn't yet learned all the sleight of hand of special privilege, that year involved him directly with yet another one of its tricks. According to a new Weights and Measures Law, the weight of all food and containers had to be printed on the item. Many large packing companies failed to comply with this stipulation, "misstating the weights on hams and bacon," and they were brought to trial in the Magistrates Court of the City of New York. State Senator James J. Walker—who would be La Guardia's opponent fourteen years later in the New York mayoralty race—represented the defense. He pointed out that he was the author of the law and that the ham and bacon in question, since they were not wrapped, were not subject to the law. The true weight had to be shown only on containers.

The Tammany judge, a friend of Walker's, immediately dismissed the case. And as La Guardia protested, he realized the futility of his protest; all the more so, when the judge and Walker invited him to have a drink.

"Jimmy," La Guardia said, "how in the world can you possibly appear in a case to defeat your own law?"

Walker shook his head despairingly. "Fiorello," he said, "when are you going to get wise? Why do you suppose we introduce bills? We introduce them sometimes just to kill them. Other times we even have to pass a bill. Why are you in the Attorney General's office? You're not going to stay there all your life. You make your connections now, and later on you can pick up a lot of dough defending cases you are now prosecuting."

As Walker spoke, the judge smiled and nodded agreement with everything that Walker said.

La Guardia persisted. "But a lot of little storekeepers have been fined for selling the same kind of hams in wrappers."

"Fiorello," Walker said, "you stop worrying about those things. What are you in politics for, for love?"

La Guardia reported all this in the attorney general's office, expecting shock, outrage, but found only indifference. After all, an old story, after many repetitions, does indeed pall.

The far bigger fight, the war in Europe, intrigued La Guardia. Because he wanted to participate in it as a member of the air corps, he decided he would learn to fly. Though he was thirty-three and believed flying was for the young, he apparently felt this dictum did not apply to him.

His thought of getting into the war—aside from an innate love of conflict and a taste for uniforms—related to a romantic attachment.

During a garment strike, just as might have happened in a love story in the *Delineator,* he met and fell in love with a young dress designer. Thea Almerigotti was blonde, beautifully fragile, and Italian. Because she hoped for the emancipation of Trieste, her birthplace, from Austrian rule, La Guardia felt that it would be a nice romantic gesture to free Trieste for her.

La Guardia's work, flying lessons and idyllic dates with Thea did not eclipse his interest in getting into Congress. That his first try had led to defeat only served to intensify his resolve, to make the challenge more engrossing. He immediately set about the business of making valuable contacts, and because he had no other way to learn the ins and outs of Congress, he "read the Congressional Record religiously."

Potholes filled La Guardia's road to Congress. Once again, his opponent was saloon keeper Farley, rich in ineptitudes and therefore worthy of strong backing, because of an understanding between the Republicans and Democrats that this perfectly malleable nonentity should continue in office. And while La Guardia's surprisingly good showing in 1914 made his chances in 1916 appear even better, it also made the nomination—and its possible fruition into victory—valued by others. Apparently, La Guardia didn't realize this, for when he heard that he hadn't been picked, he was thoroughly shocked. But it was for his own good, they all said, like a desperate parent resorting to cliché. To be licked twice, they all pointed out, as though from the same script, would be detrimental to his political career.

La Guardia heard exactly the same story when he went posthaste to see Fred Tanner, the Republican state chairman and a "prominent lawyer, scholarly and gentlemanly." But then Tanner let drop the real reason for La Guardia's not having been picked. Friends of Hamilton Fish, Jr., would contribute a sizable amount of money to the Party if Fish were the candidate from the 14th Congressional District—despite the fact that he lived in Putnam County.

Though a gentleman, Tanner then made a single error in judgment. He offered to reimburse La Guardia for the expenses he had incurred in filing a petition for the nomination. La Guardia blew up. "Go to hell!" he shouted and hurtled out of the office.

"Fiorello, hold your horses," Tanner called after him. "Damn it, if you want to run, go ahead and do it. Don't blame me if you're licked again."

La Guardia took Tanner's advice; he ran. And when he found himself unopposed—by Fish or anyone else—he claimed that he was surprised. He may have been. Nonetheless, in subsequent elections, he used the very same technique of threatening to run independently in order to get a nomination. He also managed to obtain the nomination of the Progressive Party, a very important acquisition, for it eliminated a candidate with views on labor, immigration, and education that were identical to his.

Again, as in the campaign of 1914, Andrews and Espresso worked for La Guardia. And Marie Fischer, the blonde young woman whom La Guardia had guided during her first job, in the state attorney general's office, volunteered her services.

Understandably, La Guardia continued to amaze those who worked for him. He set an example of dedication and an unending expenditure of energy. He always put on a show "not excelled in Maurice Schwartz's famous Yiddish theatre around the corner." Mike Farley, or "the sitting Congressman," as La Guardia referred to his opponent, never appeared in his district—and when he did come to his saloon, he "forgot to treat the boys." Farley also turned over his campaigning to others, and La Guardia enjoyed annihilating these men who substituted for Farley on the stump. He also marched down to Farley's saloon, shook his fist melodramatically at the structure and challenged the saloon keeper to emerge and debate the issues.

La Guardia offered more than just a good show. The Irish accepted him, for he knew more about the history of Ireland than did Michael Farley who, from an Irishman's point of view, was also not sufficiently hard on the English. Irish volunteers therefore came to La Guardia's side.

In addition to all this support, Fiorello stood to profit simply by running for office in a presidential year in which the popular Charles Evans Hughes opposed Woodrow Wilson. Because of Hughes's popularity in New York, many voters would vote the straight Republican ticket, and thus vote for La Guardia.

In spite of all the elements that tended to encourage La Guardia, there was an inescapable bête noire: a Republican had never won in his district. Anything that might make a victory more likely could, therefore, not be overlooked. The Monday night before the election, La Guardia and his forces worked until two o'clock in the morning. Then, after a few hours' sleep, they rushed off to the district's flophouses, and before Tammany could get to them, roused the eligible voters, nourished them with coffee, doughnuts and Republican ideology, transported them to the polling place and hoped—after all this effort—that they would vote Republican.

Finally, La Guardia had the onerous job of seeing to it that the election would be an honest one. Voting was by paper ballot, and ballots could be disqualified by being marked—easily done with lead shaved from a pencil and concealed under a fingernail. A ballot that represented a voter's choice could be substituted, with the alacrity of magic, by one that didn't. Polling places had to be watched, and La Guardia's watchers represented every profession from schoolteacher to longshoreman.

Fiorello himself picked a tough district on the waterfront, one that especially needed constant, careful scrutiny.

"What are you doing here?" Charles Culkin, a Tammany Hall leader of the district, asked. "You shouldn't be here. Everything is all right."

"Everything is not all right," La Guardia told him, "and what is more, Charlie, you sit here and help me watch the count, and, if not, someone is going to go to jail, and I mean you, Charlie. You stay here and protect your own district."

Culkin did what La Guardia advised.

When the vote in that district was counted, a district in which the Democrats usually won five to one, La Guardia was the winner, though by only a few votes.

Amazed, Culkin shook his head in bewilderment and asked La Guardia if he was satisfied with the count.

La Guardia said, "Yes, as soon as the certificate is signed and turned over to the police."

The extreme care he exercised was incorporated in the instructions to the La Guardia watchers: they were to "remain on duty until the count was entirely completed, the returns officially signed, and the ballot boxes sealed."

At four o'clock the next morning, the final count showed that La Guardia had won, but by only 357 votes.

Elated by his victory, La Guardia expected widespread, unrestrained Republican rejoicing.

"I particularly thought," La Guardia commented years later, "I would get a riotous reception in my own home district. I never saw such gloom anywhere. The hangers-on at the club hardly nodded to me. Someone was on the telephone in the rear office, assuring the Democratic leader of the district, who was supposed to be his rival, 'No, Joe, we didn't double cross you; we didn't do anything for this fellow. You just can't control him.' An apology for my victory is what I heard instead of congratulations!"

The next day, La Guardia expressed a tearful regret: if only his mother, who had died the year before in Budapest, had lived to see his victory, won on his own, without the help of the machine.

CHAPTER SIX

COMPARED TO NEW YORK'S CROWDED PUSHING, noisy, odoriferous 14th District—when La Guardia arrived in Washington, as a congressman-elect—Washington had a bucolic air. A few hundred farms were contained within the Capital's limits. Dust rose in the perfumed late-autumn sunlight from unpaved, tree-lined streets. And when rain settled dust, a Reo or electric could become mired to the hub in mud, and the automobile's owner might hear guffaws that accompanied the cliché of the time, "Get a horse!"

La Guardia's inner fires made him dash off to this somnolent, pastoral Washington, for he was unable to wait until he started working there. He went quite frequently—between his having been elected and the time the 65th Congress convened—"under the rule of courtesy by which members-elect were permitted on the floor." He said, "I liked Congress from the very first day." He liked it because the Hall of the House of Representatives was an oasis of bedlam in Washington's serenity; its excitement-charged atmosphere an extension of his temperament. "Frantic confusion" described the scene—which certainly did not appear to be appropriate for the deliberations of a legislative body. Members came and went, with no more apparent purpose than scurrying ants. Conferences dotted the floor, informal, spur-of-the-moment affairs. And there was—one of a congressman's privileges—"extraordinary freedom of speech." This merely removed one element of conflict from La Guardia's habit of speaking his mind.

It seemed natural that such a body would have the ever-changing quality of a kaleidoscope; thus every two years, a fourth of its members were replaced, and the replacements were not always an improvement. Once the wife of one congressman observed caustically that the

44

wife of a "new one" was given to elocution. Brash, thirty-four, with forceful ideas of his own, La Guardia had displaced a saloon keeper who played politics for what it was worth to him. Some, as a consequence, viewed La Guardia as a "sawed-off wop," usurping the place of a to-be-relied-upon mick pol.

For these reasons and others, La Guardia did not suffer the usual fate of newcomers to the House—anonymity. That he was the first Italian-American to be elected to the Congress of the United States helped him stand out in the 435-member crowd. He had also been elected on the Republican ticket in a strong Tammany district. He accentuated his lack of height—even more noticeable now that his wiry frame had been taking on weight—with on outsized black hat. He looked far younger than his age. Ancient Uncle Joe Cannon, who had been disposed as Speaker a few years before in a bitter fight and who worked hard at being a wit, stalked up to La Guardia one day, and after addressing him as "boy," asked him to go on an errand for him. Then, as though suddenly realizing his error, he laughed with feigned embarrassment and said, "Oh, excuse me, I am not in the habit of seeing youngsters here as members."

But in spite of his nationality, appearance, inexperience, young La Guardia had to be taken seriously right from the start—another reason for his being noticed. The Republicans and Democrats were evenly divided in the House, and La Guardia's vote as an Independent—for he had run on the Progressive as well as the Republican ticket—might be decisive in the election of the Speaker. For this reason and because of his Italian ancestry and socialistic tendencies, which included championing labor, the old members who were deep-rooted in conservatism's rut regarded him obliquely, suspiciously.

They also shook their hoary heads at the way this abbreviated upstart ignored congressional custom which, together with innumerable rules and precedents, constituted the very foundation of the House. They ignored or were ignorant of the fact that congressional customs were not eternal, that La Guardia had not been the first iconoclast among them. After all, members had worn red carnations on January 29 to commemorate the birthday of William McKinley of Ohio, whose favorite flower was the carnation, for only a bit more than fifteen years. And hadn't the custom of wearing hats in the House gone in 1837, and smoking in 1871? Even congressional gestures of respect for the dead were not eternal. At one time when a member died, his desk was draped, and his fellow members wore crepe on their left arm for thirty days. But wearing crepe had its shortcomings and was given up in 1884. And the removal of desks in 1913 proved a grand excuse for doing away with the desk-draping custom.

In 1917, however, every member knew that it still behooved a newcomer to tiptoe to a seat in the rear and maintain a respectful silence during his initial term. Surely such a custom, based as it was on an innate necessity in man to dominate others, would never topple. But when the House convened on March 5, 1917, La Guardia's short, sturdy legs, moving busily, took him up front; and he then plumped himself down between two prominent Republican leaders. One was none other than James R. Mann of Illinois, almost twice La Guardia's age, "the greatest parliamentarian of his or any other period," and—more significantly, considering La Guardia's untoward behavior—known to be "pretty hard on Young Members."

Just a few days later, on March 21, "all the glories of spring could not blot out the knowledge that war was very near to the United States." And on that very day President Wilson summoned Congress to a special session at twelve noon on April second. Nor could spring's glories divert one from the President's purpose—the "serious, very serious, choices of policy to be made, and made immediately. . . ."

Inevitably, that historic day in April had a tension-charged atmosphere. Even the sunny plaza in front of the steps of the House—with squirrels and robins busy in its new grass—appeared blighted by the paradox of numerous policemen. In late afternoon, there would also be belligerent pacifists—young, fiercely idealistic and determined to block President Wilson's entrance into the Hall of Representatives. It was as though all they had to do was prevent Wilson's War Message from being uttered and their country's involvement, magically, would not happen.

Inside the House Office Building, keyed-up individuals jammed corridors. Mail and telegrams poured in, in unheard-of volume. Individual items made clear, forceful statements; but en masse they merely led to the realization that there were as many opinions, for and against the United States' entrance into the war, as there were individuals. And although a congressman should answer the mail of his constituents—even if it were no more than a penciled scrawl from a constituent's child, requesting a theme for a school paper on Thomas Jefferson—La Guardia could see at a painful glance the impossibility of taking care of his rising flood of communications.

La Guardia moved on to the chamber of the House; its atmosphere, too, was one of emotion and impending great and irrevocable deeds. By eleven, the gallery was packed. Some visitors were therefore compelled to sit on the steps of the aisle, and they had brought their lunch in anticipation of a long, not-to-be-missed stay. On tenterhooks, anything could set them off. Thus the entrance of Jeannette Rankin of Montana, the first congresswoman, caused even more of a stir than had the arrival of the first Italian-American congressman. Males applauded her, their applause a blend of condescension and welcome. She carried a bouquet of yellow and purple flowers that had been given to her that morning at a suffragists' breakfast in her honor; on that occasion, she had said that the campaign had been worthwhile for "women had learned solidarity." Still she appeared to be self-conscious about being both new to Congress and a woman, for—unlike La Guardia—she took a seat far back on the Republican side.

At exactly twelve noon, the clerk, Mr. South Trimble, called the House to order. At long last, the historic day was really under way.

The chaplain, Rev. Henry N. Couden, D.D., offered a prayer to "God of the ages," asking with the solemnity of an organ's tones for blessings on Congress called in "extraordinary session under extraordinary conditions which calls for extraordinary thought, wise counsels, calm and deliberate legislation. . . ."

The first order of business followed: the election of the Speaker. La Guardia was one of five independents who would decide the election, since the 65th Congress was locked in an equilibrium of 215 Democrats and 215 Republicans. Out of party loyalty La Guardia voted for the Republican candidate, James R. Mann. The weight of the remaining independent vote favored Champ Clark, a Democrat, who had lost the nomination for president in 1912 on the forty-sixth ballot because William Jennings Bryan had shifted his support to Wilson.

Addressed as "Mr. Speaker" as soon as he was sworn in, Champ Clark, who resembled the late President William McKinley in features and bearing, swore in Fiorello La Guardia, Jeannette Rankin and the other new members of Congress. This "gentleman," who was "always delightfully interesting and decidedly human," then went on to give the fledgling legislators advice, benignly—like a father to his children. Of all things, considering the precarious state of the world, his lecture concerned how they should assess the communications they would receive from their constituents. Letters were "propaganda." They should also be regarded as representing only two percent of the voters of a district. Congressmen must also represent the ninety-eight percent who did not write letters . . . .

Such matters could not be listened to with any degree of concentration; this, after all, was a War Congress. Still rules and procedure required roll call voting for the various officers of the House: clerk, sergeant-at-arms, doorkeeper, postmaster. . . .

On and on, drearily on, the voting went. The air by now had become heavy with the odor of the sandwiches in the gallery. When would President Wilson arrive? This all-pervasive question—and even the tedium, the boredom of waiting—added to the suspense. It was not until 7:47 that the House finished organizing itself.

By eight o'clock, an April rain had started; and the President—escorted by a troop of cavalry, protection against those pacifists on the plaza—approached the House. Years later, his son-in-law, Secretary of the Treasury William G. McAdoo, would recall "the pouring rain, a soft fragrant rain of early spring; the illuminated dome of the Capitol stood in solemn splendor against the dark wet sky."

The question as to the precise time of President Wilson's arrival was about to be answered. The swinging doors of the Hall of Representatives swung open and in trooped the senators, headed by Vice-President Marshall, whose somber mien indicated that now the country needed much more than a good five-cent cigar, and each man, with but three or four exceptions, carried a small American flag, like schoolboys on parade. The President followed to the insistent beat of Speaker Champ Clark's gavel and his announcement, "Gentlemen, the President of the United States!"

The reception by the Cabinet, justices of the Supreme Court, diplomatic corps, both Houses of Congress, those jamming the gallery, went on and on. President Wilson, meanwhile, ascended the speaker's platform, fidgeted nervously, as he held his typed "communication concerning grave matters" with both hands, while resting his arm on the green-baize-covered desk.

In the tense quiet that followed the clamor, the President began. "I have called the Congress into extraordinary session because . . . American ships have been sunk, American lives taken. . . . It is a fearful thing to lead this great peaceful people into war. . . . The world must be made safe for democracy. . . . America is privileged to spend her blood and her might for the principles that gave her birth and happiness and the peace which she has treasured. God helping her, she can do no other."

In the stillness that followed these last words of a speech over a half hour in length, only the patter of rain could be heard on the glass roof. Then "a roar like a storm" erupted which knew no partisanship; Democrats and Republicans had fused, become one. And though it is axiomatic that Congress is diminished to the extent that it does not oppose the President, is nothing if it merely follow him like sheep a shepherd, at this moment even La Guardia—and on the very day he was sworn in as a congressman—lost his truculent individualism.

The next morning, a topical, provocative advertisement appeared in the *New York Times:* "Whatever Congress Decides! Franklin Simon & Co. are ready to take immediate orders for Hand-tailored Khaki Army Uniforms for officers and privates $16.00."

At the very start of the war, La Guardia felt with the certainty of inescapable logic that the United States would get into it. Therefore, in true Theodore Roosevelt fashion, he forthwith studied flying with one of his Italian friends, aviation pioneer Giuseppe Bellanca. When the United States entered the war, he wanted to be in its air corps.

On March 21, 1917, the day the President summoned Congress to a special session at the beginning of the following month, La Guardia rushed to New York, bent on making the most of the eleven days before the special session convened.

He delivered patriotic speeches—of the most blatant Fourth of July vintage. Though he was a Progressive, and even considered himself a pacifist—in 1923 he would introduce a resolution outlawing war—like Wilson, he found moral justification in this war that would liberate the people of Central Europe from the Hapsburgs. His love for Thea—and her love for her birthplace, Trieste, which she longed to see liberated from Austrian rule—was a factor in his complex motivation. Being prowar also made him, an Italian-American, feel more American, even though he still remained a hyphenated American.

And so he rushed about the Lower East Side proclaiming, "These are days when we must renew our love for the land and the flag that flies over us." Pulitzer's *World*—still engaged in boosting circulation—sponsored such patriotic addresses and happily reported that "Congressman La Guardia, young, enthusiastic and energetic, stirred the audience wherever he went."

He also stirred many of his constituents to anger, and at the same time, bewildered and puzzled them. With the exception of his incomprehensible prowar stand, he and the socialist, liberal, bohemian 14th

District were kindred spirits, and he could therefore represent it effectively.

Then, on April 3, La Guardia introduced a bill in Congress, his first. In a way, it might be considered atonement for his part in the overwhelming approval given the President's War Message the night before. HR 345 also indicated that in spite of all his recent patriotic orations La Guardia had not completely forgotten that "splendid little war" and that it had taken his father's life. His bill demanded imprisonment during peacetime, and death when a war was in progress, for anyone engaged in providing the army or navy with faulty equipment or spoiled food.

This was undoubtedly personal, emotional legislation, the sort of House legislation which the Constitution wanted poured into the senatorial saucer to be cooled down to objectivity.

The following day, after thirteen hours of debate, the Senate voted on the war resolution. Only six senators—who belonged to the group whom Wilson had denounced as "willful men"—stood in courageous opposition to the eighty-two who favored war; two of them, Norris and La Follette, were to become very close friends of La Guardia. They suffered the punishments of taking an unpopular stand. And they merely listened—dutifully, tolerantly—to those who argued against their indulging in a fine gesture, a hopeless gesture, one that would negate their future usefulness as legislators.

Senator George W. Norris of Nebraska, his strong, craggy countenance eroded to gauntness by inner turmoil, pondered what the attitude of a congressman should be. "Should he always follow what he believed to be the majority sentiment of his district, or should he obey his own conscience even when, in doing so, it appeared he was voting against the wishes of a majority of his constituents?" And Norris knew, without wandering over the circuitous labyrinths of intellectuality, that "conscience was the guide."

In the swearing-in ceremony, Speaker Champ Clark might more profitably have directed his counseling to the role that a congressman should play. In La Guardia's case, the junior congressman faced the same problem with which Senator Norris had to wrestle. His constituents—unlike Norris's—were antiwar. And he knew that if he didn't represent their pacifist view, he would be placing his career in jeopardy. Conscience was his guide, too. He felt that you were obliged, duty-bound, to reward someone who voted for you with "total ingratitude." And, of course, national interest came above district interest, for obviously the country as a whole was of more value than any of its parts. So he would repeatedly fight for "what seemed remote and irrelevant causes for a New York congressman to excite himself about." This approach meant having something more substantial in your head than thoughts of what would help you be reelected; one's reelection should hinge solely on competence in amassing the facts and being able to act more wisely on them than the electorate.

But with what wisdom should the individual congressman evaluate the facts that led teacher, political scientist, dyspeptic, dour, presbyterian Woodrow Wilson to his evaluation: "the world must be made safe for democracy"? Heated, bitter debate on the declaration of war raged on and on in the House, three and a half hours longer than had the debate in the Senate. Any member could take the floor; "no member was gagged." The members made one hundred speeches.

When one, "talking in opposition to the draft," ordered all congressmen to stand who were going to enlist in the war that they were so eager to declare, La Guardia popped to his feet like a jack-in-the-box, along with four other congressmen who felt as he did; and to make sure his lack of height did not keep him from being seen, La Guardia waved his hand furiously above his head. Unlike Wilson, he did not have to wade knee-deep through the perspiration of indecision—armed neutrality, "too proud to fight," neutrality of thought as well as of deed . . . Fiorello was still the Fiorello who—at sixteen, as a *Post Dispatch* war correspondent—followed Hearst and Pulitzer's troops to their singular glory. Speaker Clark gaveled for La Guardia and the four others to come to order so that the talk on the floor could continue.

"I believe," Mr. Sinnott of Pennsylvania said, "every American citizen of German birth or extraction will exclaim in the language of the poet:

> Though my father's father
> Felt hale German blood
> Course through his veins,
>   A satisfying flood;
> Yet as for me,
> Strong-limbed and free,
>   I'll face the war a man;
>   Not alien, but American."

Poetry and prose eventually ran out. And words could not continue to put off the inevitability of the vote—and the certainty of its outcome.

Around 3:00 A.M., the roll call vote started. There had been levity during the debate, but now responses echoed eerily in a solemn silence.

La Guardia voted yes.

In the course of the roll call, Jeannette Rankin entered. When her name was called, she remained silent. This started a buzz of comments on the floor and in the gallery, but the clerk went on with the roll call.

When the clerk called Miss Rankin's name for the second time, she still remained silent. Finally she rose, and though her voice broke under the pressure of her friends and brothers to desert her cause, what she said could be heard distinctly in the silence: "I want to stand by my country, but I cannot vote for war. I vote no."

La Guardia was later to say concerning the question as to whether or not Jeannette Rankin was crying when she voted, "I do not know, for I could not see because of the tears in my own eyes."

Though the emotion he clearly felt suggests an ambivalence, the decision of the House was unequivocal. The slip containing the count—at the completion of the roll call—was handed to Speaker Clark. A bang of his gavel produced complete, immediate silence. "On this motion," the Speaker said, "The Ayes are 373 and the Noes are 50."

Though this overwhelming verdict for the United States' entrance into the war was based on a variety of motivations, one factor sealed the decision: the belief of over sixty percent of the congressmen, which stemmed from incredible naivete, that no American boys would be sent overseas as combatants. Had this majority known that of the 4,791,172 who served in the armed forces, 2,084,000 would go to France, they might have voted differently.

La Guardia believed that getting into the war meant much more than providing the Allies with needed supplies. It meant sending men. Without delay, he sounded out his constituents on conscription. He sent a postcard—for their reply—along with a letter that said, "This country is at war and needs every available man. Shall we have a volunteer army? Or an army composed of all citizens of military age? I think conscription is needed and I am trying to educate the people up to it. It is up to you to respond; don't blame me if you don't like the way I vote." In short, he believed that as a legislator, he was leading them in the right direction—the way he was determined to go—not simply representing their uninformed, mistaken wishes.

He voted for the Draft Bill, which passed on April 28, a mere three weeks after war was declared. But before he voted for the bill, he fought a clause in it that would have exempted congressmen from being conscripted.

At the same time that he was battling for conscription, he furiously opposed the Espionage Bill, which endangered free speech and would stifle the press. The bill also gave President Wilson far too much power. Wilson's statement that he would not make use of the powers given to him by the bill failed to pacify La Guardia. "The law admittedly makes the president a despot," he pointed out sardonically, "but with the comforting assurance that the despot about to be created has the present expectation to be a very lenient, benevolent despot."

Just as La Guardia would not permit himself to be overawed by his constituents, he opposed the domination of the chief executive by brandishing the disrespectful club of irony. And he felt obliged to get the war profiteers. This required having a press that was free to reveal individuals who were "willing to turn America's blood into gold and sell rotten corn beef, wormy beans, paper shoes, defective arms for our American boys." And he reminded the House, "On the second day of this session, I introduced a bill providing death punishment for dishonest contractors. I hope the Committee on the Judiciary will report it out." (As fate would decide, it languished and died there.) "I will tell you more on that subject when the time comes. I had better not get started on that now." (He continued not to present the humility expected of a freshman congressman.)

La Guardia kept up his hectic, belligerent pace through his first few months in the House. It was not enough, he maintained, to send men overseas and protect them from profiteers; Congress must also supply the Allies with the money that they needed—three billion dollars. That this "loan" would be repaid in its entirety, he viewed with a cynical realism that the future justified. Still, he told the House that if the loan brought about "a happy termination of the war, and a permanent peace for our country, it will have been a good investment."

As he rose on the floor of the House—working on committees wasn't for him—he alienated his colleagues by his aggressive behavior, and they began to speculate as to whether or not this short, dark-complexioned Republican from a Tammany district was a loyal American. His reiterated defense of the individual with a low income seemed downright socialistic: the war should not serve to make the rich richer; the rich should bear the war's financial burden. Those who made less than $1,500 a year should be exempt from taxes, and instead of raising postal rates, bank checks should be taxed. He also proposed a Constitutional amendment for a food control bill, "giving power to the National Government at all times"—instead of just during war—"to regulate and control the production, conservation and distribution of food supplies." And he told the House, "It does not take a professor of political economy to know that with what food there is available prices are out of all proportion to the ordinary rule of supply and demand; that somebody is taking advantage of the situation, amassing great fortunes at the expense of the health and happiness of the American people." (He also disagreed with Mann of Illinois that aeronautics was still in the experimental stage, and insisted that the use of planes was essential in an army.)

Then what happened on July 25 made the suspicions of La Guardia's disloyalty untenable. While Major Benjamin D. Foulois recruited men in the Southern Building in Washington, a short, stocky man approached him and said that he knew how to fly planes.

"Your name?" the major said.

"Fiorello H. La Guardia."

"Any relation to the congressman?"

"Not exactly," La Guardia said. "You see, I *am* the congressman."

La Guardia's enlistment may have confounded the politicians, but nothing could have pleased Thea more. When he went to New York to show her how grand he looked in a uniform, she responded as though he did indeed look grand. (Love must have been an influencing factor, for the more objective view of a biographer, writing a dozen years later, revealed that "his uniform seemed to have been designed for a stable orderly," and that he didn't wear Bond Street riding boots, but "bulging puttees.")

In Thea's eyes, the uniform went beyond the sartorial; it meant that Fiorello was going to fight to free her birthplace, inhabited by Italians but in the grasp of Austria since the Austro-Prussian War.

Up to this point in his life, the concentration on and demands of politics had kept him from marriage. Now a haze of factors—including the immediacy of Thea's beauty and favorable reactions to his having joined the army—led La Guardia to ask her to marry him.

Thea answered that she wouldn't marry anyone while Trieste was Austrian territory, that he might ask her again when this was no longer the case.

So Captain Fiorello La Guardia went off to war, with this additional, personal, romantic objective. He took a photograph of Thea with him, in which she appeared "frail and delicate-looking, as fair as an Illyrian spring."

CHAPTER SEVEN

I T WOULD HAVE FIT LA GUARDIA'S TEMPERAMENT TO
make a San Juan charge and capture Trieste; then whirl and, at a
gallop, return to claim his bride—beautiful, patriotic Thea.

Complex, inflexible reality does not countenance such satisfying
fantasies. How surmount the fact that the Hapsburgs had been the
ruling house of Austria since 1282 and that Trieste had been its possession since 1382? But Trieste remained a mere possession, rather than
an integral part of Austria, because its inhabitants were Italian and
could not be coerced into becoming Austrians, no more than the proud
Indians could be shoehorned into the American mold. Any change in
Trieste would continue to be superficial, as long as subjugation failed
to extinguish its Italian spirit and erase memories, traditions and
enmity for Austria.

Trieste's inhabitants also kept alive in Italy the history of what had
been done to them by the bestial Austrian. And though Italy, by
joining Austria and Germany solely for defensive purposes, formed the
Triple Alliance, its antipathy was not diluted by this fragile tie of
words on paper. Italy had remained neutral at the outbreak of the war,
primarily because Austria occupied Italian territories. And when
Austria attacked Serbia, this aggression released Italy from its obligations as a member of the Alliance. Eventually, Italy joined the Allies—
who had had its sympathy all along. Besides, "the Allies had promised
Italy all Austrian territories peopled by Italian subjects."

In escaping to the United States from a century's entrenched
tyranny, Thea Almerigotti brought with her Trieste's longing for identity, for autonomy. She therefore, without a suggestion of inner
struggle, put her personal happiness in the balance by asking La
Guardia to go to Trieste's aid.

Just a few days after La Guardia told Major Benjamin D. Foulois that he knew how to fly planes, he received the commission of first lieutenant. (In short order, he became a captain.) On September 1, 1917, he reported to post headquarters at Mineola, Long Island.

The flying cadets put in his charge—volunteers for service overseas—were to be transported to Italy for training there. Some had been to college; some had even graduated from college; all knew very little about flying, even less than La Guardia; few had ever been up in a plane.

Before they left for Italy, a noteworthy private arrived. Albert Spalding, the celebrated violinist—whom Captain La Guardia described as a "smart-looking, young gentleman" and who, La Guardia also noticed, wore a tailor-made uniform—had not had the patience to wait for a commission. He became La Guardia's aide. And Frank Giordano, a Greenwich Village barber and longtime friend of La Guardia's, joined the men as a cook. A slight case of favoritism: La Guardia had seen to it that Giordano was accepted for the job, although he exceeded the maximum age at which married men were accepted for military service and was flat-footed. ("He was a mighty fine barber," La Guardia eventually admitted, "but not much of a cook.")

In mid-October, La Guardia found himself not only in charge of the first large detachment of flying students, but also—by strange, unfathomable coincidence—in Foggia, birthplace of his father, home of generations of La Guardias. Trieste, which he must free from the trap of cruel tyranny, lay a mere three-hundred-mile flight from Foggia's position above Italy's elongated heel. The flight would be north, on a slightly westerly diagonal across the Adriatic.

But that seemingly benign route was as pocked with potholes and pitfalls as a winter road. Flying in Mineola, La Guardia soon realized, had been playacting compared to the bruising reality of war flight. Examples abounded. That summer about fifty huge Caproni bombers, three-engine affairs, had struck an Austrian naval base at Pola, just south of Trieste. Though this Italian flying edifice generated an impressive 600 horsepower, it had the decidedly "bad habit of catching fire when throttled down for glides or descents." One of the Capronis in that raid on Pola had struggled to stay in formation, but simply couldn't attain sufficient altitude or speed. As a consequence, being below and behind the other floating hulks, it stood alone, dark against luminous blue, a perfect target for enemy gunners.

The hazards of such flight were compounded by the dubious instruction of the Eighth Aviation Center School of Foggia, a school blessed only by its location—southern Italy offering consistently ideal flying weather. La Guardia had been assigned to the school as an instructor, but his work proved to be administrative, for he, too, had to learn to fly. (He assessed his flying ability with unalloyed objectivity: his difficulties, he said, were merely concerned with taking off and landing.)

Italian aces instructed all students. Aces though they may have been, they did not speak English—or very little—and therefore had to convey their special wisdom through an interpreter, a plane, or a motor mechanic, and much, if not all, meaning was lost en route. To impede the acquisition of skill still further, Italian instructors acted on the belief that a trainee could absorb only ten minutes of in-flight instruction a day. Therefore La Guardia would go up in a dual-control Farman biplane and—after a few gyros to the left and right, or some other maneuver—down he would come to find out what he had or had not done correctly.

Another equally serious problem was an insufficient number of training planes. The United States couldn't solve this problem for two insurmountable reasons. Being removed from the scene of battle, it could not know—clearly, or intimately—the totality of that scene, and such knowledge was necessary in the creation of an effective plane, which also entailed constant aeronautic changes. During the war the belligerents turned out eighty-three different types of pursuit planes, in striving for perfection: a safe plane from which to deal out death. This unending flux made standardization in far-off factories impossible.

Italy therefore received an order from its American ally for 500 planes—a new type of plane, naturally, one that offered greater speed and efficiency. But the planes weren't delivered, in spite of the urgency of their need. La Guardia, finally, found out why: in flying this very latest type of plane, test pilots had been killed.

When the first delivery was at long last made, La Guardia took a look at the glorified gliders and knew at once that "they might come apart in the air." Without permission, he rushed off to the purchasing headquarters in Paris; and, a mere captain, he complained like a general about the plane's weak structure.

"They demanded," La Guardia related afterwards, "what in hell *I* knew of 'stresses' and 'strains.'"

Then, choosing the pleasure of imperiousness over the practicality of compromise, they ordered him back to Foggia and to flying planes rather than criticizing them.

La Guardia went up—per that order, in a practice session—and flew straight into a storm. While the plane was tossed about, its underpowered motor expired. In the resulting crash, the plane somersaulted twice as it landed in a camp of Austrian prisoners near the Foggia flying school. When La Guardia was taken to a hospital, the doctors there found that in addition to numerous bruises, his spine had been injured.

The next morning, one of La Guardia's men, Lieutenant Marcus Jordan of Washington, D.C., paid a call. Jordan kidded La Guardia about busting up a plane and landing in a hospital bed—all light banter, evidence of compassion, meant to be therapeutic. No more than two hours after he left, La Guardia heard that Jordan had crashed in one of the new Italian planes and had been killed.

Instead of taking comfort from "I told you so," for the plane had "come apart in the air," just as he was sure it would, La Guardia scrambled out of bed. On crutches, brushing aside a blur of pleading and admonishing doctors and nurses, he fled from the hospital and was driven to the plant where the plane that killed Jordan had been manufactured.

First of all, as he stood leaning on his crutches, he identified himself. How he did this was important. Neither Congressman La Guardia nor Captain La Guardia would do; so "he announced that he was the Commanding Officer of the American Air Forces in Italy." Then, as the Commanding Officer of the American Air Forces in Italy, he cancelled the order for the 500 flying coffins.

With a speed bred of near hysteria, the Inter-Allied Purchasing Commission frantically summoned La Guardia to Paris. Still on crutches, he faced an array of top brass—the silent tableau radiating menace, anger.

A general said, "Just who the hell do you think you are, Captain? Where the hell did you get the authority to cancel a $5,000,000 order?"

"By the authority in me vested to take every precaution to safeguard the lives of my men!"

"Will you go back to Italy and direct the manufacturers to continue production?"

La Guardia fidgeted on his crutches. "I cannot do that."

"Well, then, will you go back to Italy and attend to your own business?"

"I don't see how I can do that either."

The argument went on and on, with heated threats on both sides that led to dead ends. Eventually, La Guardia won out, for Italian aces—independent of his action—came out as vehemently against the planes as he had, and even said they'd resign their commissions before they'd fly them.

This episode stemmed from the same compulsions that had, during La Guardia's consular period, made him paternally solicitous of immigrants. Now, in addition to safeguarding the lives of his men, he saw to it that their cuisine was familiar meat-and-potato American rather than alien Italian. When they went off at Christmas to Rome and its women, he arranged for a mobile prophylaxis station to keep their bloodstream free of microscopic intruders. He also saw to it that Spalding, his adjutant, didn't receive flying training, for, as Spalding conjectured, La Guardia wanted to be sure that when peace came his protégé's "fiddling fingers" would be around to fiddle. But La Guardia gave other reasons. He spoke of Spalding's advanced age, his late twenties. La Guardia also flatly stated that flying was for the young only, neatly ignoring the fact that he was six years older than Spalding and that at an "advanced age" *he* was flying.

La Guardia's love of music, rooted in paternal indoctrination during his Arizona childhood, made Spalding's talent very special. He therefore respected the man, enjoyed being in his presence, wanted his company on a particular bit of derring-do. (This dangerous mission was undoubtedly welcomed by the stereotype soldiers in camp who suspected the violin of being effeminate; besides, the practicing done on it disturbed their poker games.)

The whole adventurous project had been La Guardia's idea. He had the uncanny ability of grasping all the factors of a difficult situation and coming up with an answer—all done with the astounding speed of a sleight-of-hand card trick. The plane factories of Italy were not operating at maximum capacity—in the south, the Ansaldo works; in the north, Fiat, Isotta Fraschini and Caproni. They lacked raw materials—copper, steel, ash wood for propellors, all of which the United States was supposed to be supplying them with, but was sending instead to Great Britain and France. La Guardia spotted a solution, pounced on it. Nearby Spain was a perfect source of material. He would go there, make the arrangements and speed up production of Italian planes.

Though authority—especially of the bureaucratic variety—irked La

Guardia, he obtained permission for his venture. (Another proposal of his—to foment revolution in Hungary and thus get her out of the war—had been turned down by President Wilson himself, as a plan that "could be very unwise and dangerous.") He and Spalding were to go to Spain, dressed in civilian clothes, armed with letters of credit. Final authorization, however, had to come from Commander-in-Chief John J. Pershing. This might take as long as ten days. The wait—and two obeisances to bureaucracy in a row—were just too much for La Guardia.

"We leave tomorrow night," La Guardia told Spalding. "Tickets, clothes, orders, those are your affair. I didn't specify what kind of orders. You have an imagination—use it! Any kind of orders that will do the trick. They'll be O.K. by me."

Apprehensive and far from sure of himself, Spalding managed to fake orders, which stated they were carrying out "the instructions of the Commander-in-Chief," that would get them by "the eagle eye of the military police, through the cordon of French vigilance." He had far less trouble picking out a civilian suit for La Guardia, for Spalding knew La Guardia "would be unconscious of anything short of the most outrageous misfit." He based this on the appearance of La Guardia's uniform, which "always looked as if it had been made for someone else."

In the meantime, La Guardia scurried about obtaining passports and letters of credit to the extent of five million dollars.

Once they had circumvented a very difficult M.P. sergeant, apparently capable only of glaring and asking questions, they relaxed on a train headed for Barcelona. "La Guardia talked about home, about the girl to whom, once the war was over"—and Trieste, presumably, free of Austria's domination—"he was to be married." And when he showed Spalding Thea's picture, Spalding thought that one "could not imagine two greater opposites" than the lovely, gentle Thea and "the volcano of vitality at my side."

After arriving in Barcelona, La Guardia said that if they were to pass as tourists, they had better see a bullfight. "It's one of the sights," he added. "No doubt we shall be watched, and not by friendly eyes, either."

But before attending this obligatory bullfight, La Guardia had Spalding search through two years of newspapers to find out which shipping company had suffered the greatest losses at the hands of the Germans. As it turned out, a delicate weighing of losses in arriving at an answer was unnecessary, for the Taja Line "had lost more than all the others put together."

La Guardia and Spalding paid a call on Señor Taja—squat, round-headed, slow of gesture, soft-spoken, the father of an only son who had been the victim of a German torpedo and, as a consequence, a thoroughgoing hater of the Hun. Without hesitation, eagerly, Taja became an accomplice.

Understandably, they felt like characters out of an E. Phillips Oppenheim thriller, participants in a roman à clef of intrigue; for they were shadowed, and their hotel room was searched. They saw Taja as infrequently as possible. But this aura of fiction had a substratum of reality; eventually, a million and a half dollars' worth of vital materials reached Italy in Taja's ships.

Their job done, La Guardia and Spalding relaxed at lunch with General Armando Diaz, who had reorganized the fragmented Italian army after Caporetto. That same day, they had dinner with the king of Italy himself, Victor Emmanuel. Before he entered, a voice announced, "Sua Maesta, il Re!" Nervous steps brought the diminutive king, attired in a gray-green uniform, into the room. At first he spoke in English, but he switched to Italian when he learned that his guests understood it. La Guardia actually towered over the king and, according to reports, called him "Manny." In the course of the bonhomie which this first-name relationship suggests, La Guardia told the monarch exactly what was on his mind: though His Majesty's war industries were progressing nicely, their capacities could be improved; and, he believed, "the days of monarchies were numbered."

Ironically, when La Guardia reported the mission's completion to the embassy in Madrid, he received orders from Pershing, which had been sent to the embassy, giving him permission to go ahead with the mission.

Important as the successful adventure in Spain had been, it did not completely satisfy La Guardia. He wanted to fly. Like his boyhood hero, Theodore Roosevelt, his singular chemistry had to have the thrill, the heroism, of unflinchingly facing Death by War.

La Guardia therefore squirmed restlessly in fulfilling other behind-the-lines obligations—vital though they, too, might be. At the request of Ambassador Thomas Nelson Page, he became the spokesman of the United States government in raising the morale of the Italian people after the catastrophe, on a rainy, foggy October 24, 1917, near Caporetto—"a little white town" with a fine fountain in its square—which had taken the lives of 180,000 men who had been rushed from farm and factory, "inadequately trained and badly equipped" to stem the Austro-German drive.

An Italian soldier in Hemingway's A Farewell to Arms reflected the mood of real soldiers, a mood of defeatism that La Guardia had to transform, with the magic wand of oratory, into a belief in war's effectiveness:

War is not won by victory. What if we take San Gabriele? What if we take the Carso and Monfalcone and Trieste? Where are we then? Did you see all the far mountains to-day? Do you think we could take all them too? Only if the Austrians stop fighting. One side must stop fighting. Why don't we stop fighting? If they come down into Italy they will get tired and go away. They have their own country. But no, instead there is a war. . . . Everybody hates this war.

La Guardia's oratory surprised, shocked, entranced, inspired the Italians. For a six-month period, he let it flow at night—after an arduous day spent in training to fly. Accustomed to an "oily redundancy" style, the Italians found themselves bombarded by La Guardia's terse, hard-hitting, colloquial use of their language. On one occasion, when he made a passionate plea for the redemption of Trieste, no one in the wildly cheering, patriotic audience could possibly have known that his plea was related to a woman in distant New York.

La Guardia was also on Italy's side in its contention over the dispersal of pilots trained in Italy. The Italians wanted these pilots on the Italian front, but the United States felt it had the right to ship them to France, or wherever they were needed most. La Guardia went to work to acquire bombardment pilots for the Italian front.

In late spring of 1918, events happened to mesh: Pershing gave his okay on the plan to have pilots complete their training by engaging in combat on the Italian front; and La Guardia went to a bombing school in Malpensa, where he got his diploma after nursing a patched-up tri-motor Caproni, whose crankshaft had splintered in midair, safely into a swamp. (With La Guardia off to the Italian front, Spalding had a chance at last to take up flying. Of La Guardia's reaction, Spalding said, "From Fiorello came a letter affectionately and passionately profane about what he termed my insanity—a characteristic document.")

On August 5, 1918, Captain La Guardia became Major La Guardia, exchanging the silver bars on his shoulders for golden oak leaves. (Forever after, he liked best of all to be addressed as "Major.") On

September 14, he took part in a big raid over enemy lines. Afterwards, his report—typically terse—stated: "Enemy fire intense and accurate. Plane hit twice in left wing."

In addition to hitting the usual targets—munition dumps, bridges, crossings, cantonments—American pilots on the Italian front landed "far behind the Austrian lines to deliver propaganda material, carrier pigeons and supplies for Italian agents." A note of defiance was also dropped, which told the Austrians, tauntingly, that they might try to down a big Caproni biplane, christened "The Congressional Limited," because its crew included Congressman La Guardia and a member of the Italian Parliament, Pietro Nigrotto. The Austrians did indeed try—but without success.

During that summer of 1918, with the Second Battle of the Marne, the turning point for the Allies arrived. And in the fall of that year, the character of the conflict in Italy changed. Before, the Austrian army had contested every inch. However, on October 24, picked by the Italians inasmuch as it was the anniversary of their defeat at Caporetto —and an attack on that day would inspire the Italian soldiers "with a burning desire to wipe out the memory of that unhappy day"—an offensive was launched (the Battle of Vitorio-Veneto) which ended with the Austrian army in flight and whole regiments surrendering to General Diaz. Italian troops had no difficulty then in occupying Trieste, eight days before the Armistice. Thus Italy's dream was realized; Trieste was "once more within her maternal protection."

Thea kept her promise. At the end of winter of the following year, she and Fiorello were married. The wedding took place on Madison Avenue in New York, in the office of the Cathedral College. Thea wore a gown of white lace, La Guardia his uniform. A breakfast in the Hotel Netherlands, and then the ineffably happy couple left on their honeymoon.

CHAPTER EIGHT

I

T WAS AT THE END OF OCTOBER, JUST TWO WEEKS
before the Armistice, that Major Fiorello La Guardia had returned to
New York and a hero's welcome. Tanned, handsome in a uniform
resplendent with Italian medals—the *Croce di Guerra,* the *Commen-
datore*—and with gold service stripes on his arm, La Guardia could not
have offered more as a candidate. The exuberant welcome by his
party was paradoxically both sincere and politically motivated.

Six years earlier, socialism—in the person of Eugene Victor Debs—
had shown surprising strength; in his bid for the presidency, Debs had
received six percent of the total vote. Obviously, socialism, which had
been "an exotic plant in this country," had taken root. Now, because of
all the war's dislocations, Democrats and Republicans alike viewed
socialism as a threat that had to be stamped out "as one stamps out a
forest fire." They equated socialism with opposition to the war—"an
inescapable aspect," in socialism's dogma, "of competitive capitalist
imperialism." And this opposition had brought together quite a few
disparate elements: German-Americans loyal to Germany; some trade
unions; Jews, "fresh from the other side," imbued with socialism's
dream; Irish-Americans, naturally against the British and therefore
against the war, but whom Charles Murphy of Tammany ordered into
line with "this is not a time for partisanship or prejudice."

This inflammatory situation made fusion between the Democratic
and Republican parties not only possible—for the first time in history—but imperative. By agreement in July of that year, both parties
were to back candidates in all districts in danger of being engulfed by
socialism. They had no choice but to go to this heretofore unconscionable extreme.

La Guardia became a key figure in this sudden, patriotic, urgent joining of forces. Not until September of that election year had he known of the Tammany-Republican fusion. (To be suddenly in league with Tammany, a concept hated since childhood, could be justified by the all-important end of defeating socialism and its dread bugaboos.) And it wasn't until the following month—a mere few weeks before the election—that La Guardia returned to the States to form new squadrons that would fly Caproni planes built in America. Since the war was clearly nearing its end, the order that brought La Guardia home was probably a pretext to have him on hand to fight the Socialists for his seat in Congress.

The *New York American* reported La Guardia's having "slipped into port last evening as quietly as if he had glided over the Austrian lines in his bombing plane." This simile was pure euphemism. It ignored the farcical, typically La Guardian aspect of his arrival. While the welcoming party waited for La Guardia at one pier, he arrived at another. Expecting a welcome home and receiving none, La Guardia, disappointed, headed for the Brevoort Hotel. It was there that his welcomers finally caught up with him. At the time, La Guardia was in his hotel room's lavatory. Desperation plus sudden inspiration led one of the party to act decisively. He put his shoulder to the door and warned La Guardia that he would not allow him to leave the lavatory until he heard him promise that he wouldn't say anything to reporters.

Granted that in politics silence may at times be golden, saying the right thing at the right time may be of even greater value. Thus, when reporters asked La Guardia what he thought of Scott Nearing, his Socialist opponent, the Major not only asked who Nearing was, but confused him—as in a slapstick routine—with Upton Sinclair. He then went on to say that when he met Nearing, he would ask him what regiment he came from.

The next day's newspapers played up this remark with lip-smacking relish. Regiment, indeed! Why, Nearing had been indicted for his opposition to regiments, charged "with writing a pamphlet which might interfere with recruiting and enlistment in the armed forces of the United States."

Having determined precisely what stimulus would elicit this response from the press, La Guardia, with somber seriousness, now told newspapermen, "The question of patriotism must not be introduced into this campaign." (Wouldn't wearing his uniform, heavy with medals—as he stumped for office—obliquely suggest love of country and the individual's duty to it?) "Scott Nearing must have a fighting chance," he went on magnanimously. "I did not know that he was under indictment, but remember this—under the laws of this country a man is innocent until he is proved guilty."

Almost everyone enjoyed La Guardia's scenario, from "Who is Scott Nearing?" to his plea that Scott Nearing be treated fairly. But at the beginning of that year, discontent had flourished in the 14th District and had developed into a shrill demand that La Guardia be unseated. The slogan Let's Be Represented expressed his constituents' grievance. (The *Philadelphia Record* saw a few truths from a cynical height: "Congressman La Guardia, absent to fight for his country, is absent little more than some Congressmen during the baseball season. Why raise a fuss over him?") And when La Guardia heard of the slogan, which was also the title of a petition with three thousand signatures asking for a special election to determine who would take his place, he observed with sardonic amiability, "If any signers of the petition will take my seat in a Caproni biplane, I shall be glad to resume my upholstered seat in the House."

Though Marie Fischer, La Guardia's secretary, was shy and reticent, she wrote extravert letters to newspapers in her employer's defense. Editorials in favor of the fighting congressman proliferated like the luminous bursts of a Roman candle. And La Guardia's Republican friends in the House spoke out for his renomination, for his reelection. All this struck down the movement to unseat La Guardia; and then— slowly, but inevitably—the hullabaloo it had made subsided.

Forthwith, La Guardia began his speechmaking, indoors and out— 2nd Street, Stuyvesant Place, Second Avenue . . . His audiences loved him and all the patriotic clichés he symbolized and unashamedly expressed. He could ask Scott Nearing why he didn't go to Russia to try out his beautiful theories, because "go back to Russia" sentiment was flourishing in the United States and the Palmer Red Raids were already waiting in the wings. Therefore, he could also say that it was color blindness "to call an American socialist a red, for they were not red; they were yellow." But all these performances were a prelude to his debate with archsocialist Scott Nearing. Their campaign managers had arranged it; each side, obviously, hoped to gain supporters by the confrontation.

Cooper Union, a brown sandstone, five-story structure on Fourth Avenue at 8th Street, was the setting for the debate. In its vast Great Hall, rendered both ornate and impressive by Doric columns, Abraham Lincoln on a snowy February night in 1860 had asked an audience of fifteen hundred if the South, because it thought slavery right, could be placated. "Thinking it right, as they do," he went on, "they are not to blame for desiring its full recognition, as being right; but thinking it wrong, as we do, can we yield to them?" On the night of November 2, 1918, La Guardia and Nearing were to pose questions that also dealt with matters of principle and how they should dictate behavior.

By coincidence, and fittingly, as La Guardia and Nearing came up on the stage, a pillar on which were the concluding words of Lincoln's February 1860 speech separated them: "Let us have faith that right makes might, and in that faith, let us to the end do our duty, as we understand it."

The two men about to lock horns would have agreed to Lincoln's plea—and therefore not be in agreement on a single issue of the campaign. Both in their middle thirties, their appearances were in sharp contrast: Nearing blond, slender, in mufti; La Guardia swarthy, bull-stocky and attired in ennobling khaki. Nor could their outlooks have been further apart, for one was a war hero and the other a conscientious objector—one, moreover, whom both the University of Pennsylvania and the University of Toledo had dismissed on the grounds that as an economics professor he was entirely too radical.

La Guardia spoke first, the blows of his gestures matching the impact of what he said. With studied care, he avoided the expected. Instead of opposing socialism, he pointed out that the Socialists of Europe supported the war. (Nearing maintained, his gestures "airy and graceful," that the majority of Socialists in Europe did indeed support the war. But was the majority always right? If you believed that there was a possibility of the majority being wrong, at times, then La Guardia's point was not wholly convincing.)

Angry cries arose in the crowd—evenly divided between backers of La Guardia and Nearing—as first one and then the other stated his views.

La Guardia did not disagree with Nearing on the virtues of pacifism. He pointed this out with a pleading, disarming candor. He, too, wanted peace, a permanent peace; that was why he had gone off to war. Cheers battled with hisses in the packed auditorium, as La Guardia's excited falsetto penetrated all sound, declaring, "I said: I went to war to fight against war, in order to end war. I don't think we can end war by merely talking against it on East Side street corners."

The implication stood out as plain as a message on a billboard: pick the hard-hitting, practical politician on the ballot, not the theorist with high-flying ideas which were incapable of being brought down to earth.

In concluding, La Guardia gave one final thrust with an observation on Nearing as a professor of economics: "It's a mistake; he's a poet."

A half century later, with that much time's perspective, Nearing pointed out that idealist, rather than poet, "would probably have been a more correct descriptive term." And if La Guardia had used the word *poet* in a slightly derogatory way, he didn't mind, for "in political debate, you don't worry about slightly derogatory remarks."

Right after the election, however, Nearing—and Socialists generally—could not have been this genial. The fearsome growth of socialism had been checked by a blast of nationwide Republican victories, expressing the electorate's desire for a change from a war president and his administration. As for La Guardia, the coalition with Tammany had made his victory possible. He received 14,208 votes; Nearing 6,168.

A week later the Armistice was signed, and the very next day La Guardia resigned his commission. Then, as he put it, "I got the old suit out of camphor and returned to the House."

His colleagues gave him a back-slapping welcome. One spectator in the gallery, his secretary, "watched it with shining eyes."

Into the huge, square Office Building with its wide corridors and high ceilings came an endless flow of letters. La Guardia found them to be as varied as they were numerous; most cried for help of one sort or another. Samuel Oliver, a ten-year-old of Brooklyn, 432 Ashford Street, began his entreaty with: "I am writing to you because you are a good man, a friend of the Jewish people. God bless you for that, Mr. La Guardia." Then he asked ingenuously for advice. Should he become a pugilist or a congressman?

La Guardia had no form letter for this or any other troublesome situation. But he would undoubtedly have given the very same answer—in his eyes, the unmanipulated truth—to any child who had asked that question: ". . . when they fight in the ring they must conduct themselves according to set rules and fight clean and fair. In the political game there are no set rules. . . ."

Back in the House, La Guardia slashed away verbally—as though the political game had no set rules—to gain vital postwar objectives. The set rules, the facts of political life, were irritants which he tried to ignore or wave away as one would the persistence of gnats. Fact: a congressman was made a congressman. His cast of mind, volubility, et cetera, resulted from continuous congressional service; one could therefore say that "once you have become familiar with the species, it is as easy to pick out a congressman as it is to distinguish a dandelion in a bed of tulips." Another fact: eminence in Congress was usually achieved neither by ability nor by dedication, but by the inalienable blessing of seniority. To reach the heights, therefore, a congressman need only be capable of so contriving the affairs in his district that he remain continuously in office. Frederick H. Gillett of Massachusetts had managed to stay in for thirteen consecutive terms and thus became speaker of the House for the 66th, 67th and 68th Congresses. And since the House did its business through some sixty standing committees, choice committee assignments—synonymous with power, influence and position—had gone to Mann, Mondell and Moore simply because they had been around the longest. La Guardia, too, had been touched, though lightly, with seniority's wand. By regaining his seat, he had taken another step down the long road to seniority and its largess.

Seniority, bred of patient waiting rather than legislative creativity, rubbed La Guardia's temperament the wrong way. After all, the war had left the country with grave problems requiring his immediate, unrestrained, passionate, effective attention. It had been Wilson's war, fought to end all war. This objective La Guardia had taken as literally as a fundamentalist would view Adam and Eve; any other interpretation would be subterfuge of the lowest order. At Cooper Union, he had said, "I am against war, and because I am against war, I went to war to fight against war." And now, on the floor of the House, he said, "If you will consult the two million American men who fought overseas, you will find no difference of opinion among them. They are all absolutely for an arrangement—I do not care what you call it, a League of Nations or anything else—which will make impossible another world war."

This pro-Wilson view antagonized most of his colleagues, for in 1919 the legislature was Republican and the executive branch of government Democratic. With political forces thus aligned, "flint strikes upon steel and sparks are inevitable." And a Republican congressman with a "clearly delimited cast of mind" would fight the administration on every single issue, would do nothing that did not contribute, in some way, to winning the forthcoming 1920 election.

To party-loyal regulars, La Guardia proved a nettlesome enigma, favoring as he did Wilson's League, while opposing his million-man peacetime army, fighting it, in fact, so unrelentingly in the Military Affairs Committee and on the floor of the House that the standing army was reduced from 500,000 to 200,000. He was simply unpredictable. Who, for example, would have guessed that this celebrated war hero would now become one of that La Follette, Norris, Frear pacifist group? This, after all, was a time when reaction was in the saddle and rode government. According to Norris, "every executive official is afraid for his life if he undertakes to even be friendly to such men as myself."

Before too long, because La Guardia managed the paradox of being consistently unpredictable, no stand that he took surprised. The "eminently conservative and safe and sane type" of congressman, like Speaker Gillett, would say as little as possible about the Prohibition issue simply because it was believed—inasmuch as the Eighteenth Amendment had been accepted by both Houses after a minimum of debate—that most voters back home favored it. But La Guardia on the floor of the House repeatedly assailed the Volstead Act, which would implement that amendment.

As spare of words as he was of flesh, cadaverous Republican Congressman Andrew John Volstead from Yellow Medicine County, Minnesota, had only one apparent vice—the chewing of tobacco. This stained the fringes of a mustache that was so wide it virtually concealed his lips, which must have been thin, judging by the intense, fixed gleam of his eyes. A lurid past consisted of an occasional nip, justified by the comforting axiom "one drink never hurt nobody." Now he believed in the regulation of morality by law, simply because, in his words, "Law has regulated morality since the Ten Commandments."

Although this lanky, humorless individual had sixteen years of seniority, La Guardia showed him no deference, gave him no quarter.

Once, during a debate in the House, when Volstead asked La Guardia if he would relinquish the floor, La Guardia shot back a belligerent "Certainly not."

"Just for a brief statement?" Volstead asked.

"Not for a statement; for a question."

"I just want to explain—"

"The gentleman can explain on his own time," La Guardia broke in brusquely, with a flurry-of-arms gesture. "I have only ten minutes."

And on that same day, La Guardia told the congressman from Minnesota *his* view of law and morality, speaking with the fury and omniscience of a prophet: "I maintain that this law will be almost impossible of enforcement. And if this law fails to be enforced—as it certainly will be, as it is drawn—it will create contempt and disregard for law all over the country. . . ."

Then—for even a prophet knows the value of comic relief—he reveled in a bit of genealogy: "Now I do not say that excessive drinking of whisky is good. I don't know anything about that. As I told you, none of my ancestors had that failing. I have traced them way back, and the only one I could find who drank to excess was a certain 'Nero'—and he got the habit from his mother, who was born on the Rhine."

In the beginning, Volstead's Act decreed that a beverage was intoxicating if it contained one half of one percent alcohol. This ruled out of existence the workingman's staff of life, a cold, psyche-nourishing growler of beer.

The wage earner was being victimized in many other ways. "When I got back to the House," La Guardia said, "I certainly found the profiteers buzzing around the capital." These vultures were circling over war surpluses.

La Guardia arose angrily on the floor to point out that copper companies received surplus copper at a ridiculously low price, the very same copper which originally they had sold to the government at a very profitable high price. And that wasn't the extent of their arrogance, their gall; "the copper people were even to get fees for selling the government's copper to themselves."

While in this mood, La Guardia lambasted the head of the Bureau of Supplies, who made the outrageous salary of $25,000 a year and who claimed that he could not sell surplus foodstuffs to Americans because the surplus corned beef and roast beef were packed in six-pound cans and "no family in this country could use six pounds at a time."

"Evidently," La Guardia told the House, "the corps of experts are not familiar with vital statistics or appetites of families."

La Guardia let it be known that when he asked "this $25,000 beauty" what he planned to do with the meat, "he said he thought he might find a market in Rumania or Bosnia or Herzegovina or some other country like that. The gentleman does not know that those countries never used canned beef. They use very little, if any, meat. That you could not find a can opener in all of Rumania."

La Guardia, with a terrier's grip on this hapless $25,000-a-year expert, continued to worry him. He revealed that the man had offered to sell bacon to the Salvation Army—of all institutions—for he apparently wasn't aware that it "specialized in doughnuts and not in bacon." La Guardia therefore expressed surprise that the bureau head "had not offered that bacon to some Jewish synagogues."

Congressman La Guardia may have enjoyed flailing away with derision, but this did not in the least lighten his antipathy for war profiteers. Thoughts of his father's death, hastened by the greedy of an earlier war, surfaced frequently. He tried again to get the bill through that would punish—with imprisonment, and with death during wartime—those who sold spoiled food or faulty equipment to the armed forces. A world at war had produced millionaires; by 1919, the United States had amassed 42,000 of them. The war also accounted for a concomitant increase in the cost of living and more hungry bellies than usual in the country's large cities.

That so many of La Guardia's fusillades were directed at big business did not sit well with conservative Republican legislators. After all, his party was now crying: "less government in business and more business in government"; enough of Wilsonian idealism; let there be an economic boom. But instead of being sensible—synonym for practical—and keeping his eye on the prosperity target, La Guardia aimed at problems all over the map. He had concern for the satisfactory employment of 4,000,000 returning soldiers—and their adjustment, after adventures in hell, to the innocence and humdrum of the old hometown. His raillery against the discrimination that the Negro suffered was not delicate. He had the audacity to ask Southern congressmen, "The Negro soldiers fought alongside us, did they not?" He battled other forms of discrimination, taking a tough, unwavering position on outbreaks of anti-Semitism in Poland—which brought them to a halt; and continued to oppose the Espionage Act, being used then to prosecute mere radicals.

All such behavior—highly individual, in the view of the regular run of Republican—brought him party invitations. After all, an oddity gave spice to a social event, and he could be "so amusing." A puritanical nonwaster of time, La Guardia turned down all invitations, except those to government functions.

When his good friend from Brooklyn, Senator William M. Calder, insisted that he go to a dinner party with him, La Guardia made an exception.

During cocktails that evening, La Guardia was engaged in a conversation about Croatia and Dalmatia with a man to whom he had taken an instant dislike.

"What do you know about Croatia and Dalmatia?" La Guardia asked belligerently. "I've lived in that part of the world for three years, and I know what I'm talking about."

"I'm the Serbian Ambassador here," the man answered haughtily, indignantly.

La Guardia sidled away from that contretemps and barged squarely into another, in the dining room. The conversation with the lady on his left, about Liberty motors and airplanes, proved to be one he never forgot. "I sounded off," he recalled, "and told her how rotten I thought they were, and tore into General Motors in particular. I soon learned she was related to one of the big shots of that great organization."

Following dinner, La Guardia went—innocently enough—into the men's room.

A man there asked, "How do you like the party?"

"Why, I never saw such a bunch of nuts before," La Guardia answered. "I'm going. Want to come along?"

"I can't," the man said. "I'm your host."

That evening of unmitigated gaucherie led La Guardia to the conclusion that he wasn't cut out to travel the society circuit. As it turned out, he related afterwards, "the same host and hostess wanted to give a dinner party with me as the guest of honor, on the grounds that I had been 'so amusing.'" He, however, wouldn't "submit to that one."

This lack of the social graces and his dogged, zealous efforts in behalf of minority groups—both characteristics indigenous to his personality—might very well turn out to be invaluable political assets. So shrewd New York Republican boss Sam Koenig and other worldly-wise pols came to think. They proceeded, rather than jumped, to the conclusion that the half-pint Italian might possibly be able to win the election for president of the Board of Aldermen, an office that had been made vacant by Al Smith's election to the governorship.

When a reporter confronted Congressman La Guardia with a copy of the *New York American* of May 20, which stated that La Guardia had been selected by the GOP to make the run, La Guardia played coy, humble, unambitious.

Features awash with innocence, he said, "This is the first time I have heard about being selected to run for President of the Board of Aldermen of my city. It is indeed very kind and complimentary to mention me in this regard." A show of embarrassed squirming and a shuffling of feet. "I really have not given the matter any thought. I am too busy with my congressional work to think of any other position at this time." He listed all the chores in Washington that needed doing. Then, "Don't you think there is enough to be done here to keep any Representative busy without looking for other jobs? Of course, the campaign will be exciting and interesting, but the job I believe is too inactive. . . ."

The job, he knew full well, was second only to being mayor. It would mean heading a 65-man board, or legislative body, everlastingly dominated by Democrats; it would mean serving as acting mayor in the mayor's absence. Because La Guardia yearned so fervently to be mayor, even this role of stand-in had tremendous appeal. After all, New York City had a few dozen congressmen, but it had one, only one, mayor.

Finally Koenig and other bosses summoned La Guardia from Washington and offered him the nomination. He didn't grab it, like a sucker going for bait; instead, he spoke dispassionately about the unlikelihood of his being elected. (Naturally, in the "climb to the top of the greasy pole"—Disraeli's apt metaphor—one must employ footholds of evasiveness and deviousness.)

"Besides, I like the House," he said, with a final flourish of simplicity, equanimity, "and I don't want to leave it."

CHAPTER NINE

LA GUARDIA CONTINUED TO BE "RELUCTANT" TO accept the offer to run for president of the Board of Aldermen. With a vehemence meant to pass for sincerity, he placed public service high above personal ambition. As for the machine, it had one unencumbered motive: La Guardia's running for office could help in building an Italian vote that might contribute to a Republican victory in 1920.

Then "folksy, homespun" Will Hays, chairman of the National Republican Committee, approached La Guardia about the matter. Hays was "thin, dark, energetic," and one's attention wandered, in speaking with him, from what he was saying to an amazed awareness of his rabbit ears and chipmunk teeth. But imagery concerning rabbits and chipmunks hadn't kept La Guardia from hearing precisely what he'd said. Hays—who stood on his very own platform of "faith in God, in folks, in the nation, and in the Republican Party"—promised, unquestionably promised, that if La Guardia were elected aldermanic president, he would receive the Republican Party's nomination for mayor in 1921. The magical word *mayor* transformed La Guardia's uncertainty to decisiveness; galvanized, he accepted the GOP offer.

Like the stereotype immigrant who lands in the United States with only a dollar in his pocket and parlays it into a fortune, La Guardia—possessing only thirty-five dollars, because setting up housekeeping with Thea in the Village had drained his resources—set out for the mayoralty by way of the aldermanic presidency.

La Guardia had another resource: Paul Windels, in the capacity of campaign manager. Windels was just a few years younger than thirty-seven-year-old La Guardia, but he differed radically in all other respects. Blonde, blue-eyed, willowy-tall, Windels practiced law with ingenuity and wisdom. (As a politician, he had done poorly; in his only race, for the vice-presidency of the Philexion Society at Columbia University, he had lost out to Joyce Kilmer, who had gone on to fame by insisting that only God could make a tree.)

What La Guardia lacked in campaign funds, he made up for with the sine qua non of a future mayor; unrelenting, determined drive. Another unquestionable asset was his Democratic opponent: Robert L. Moran, a sickly Bronx florist, completing the aldermanic presidency of Frank L. Dowling, who had died in 1917 with two more years to serve. Because Moran lacked the strength—and heart—to campaign, ads presented his case to the electorate. They stated: Moran knows the city and its needs. Moran's record is his platform. (By "record" was meant his perfect attendance at aldermanic meetings.)

Instead of hurling invectives at Moran, too ill to hurl them back, La Guardia bustled unceasingly about New York City proclaiming that Mayor John F. Hylan's budget for 1920 had been "conceived in the bowels of darkness." (La Guardia had to strike out at someone, but Hylan was really no more worthy an opponent than Moran. When Hylan was appointed a judge of Children's Court, a New York columnist pointed out that it was now possible for children to be tried by their peer.)

"Mayor Hylan runs to the Bronx," La Guardia exclaimed with a fluttering of arms that burlesqued the Mayor's frenetic activity, "and makes a political speech on the one question of which he knows absolutely nothing—that is the traction question." (Evidently, La Guardia did not regard Hylan's having once been a locomotive engineer on the old Brooklyn Transit as pertinent, and perhaps he didn't because Hylan had been fired for almost running down his boss, the superintendent of the transit line.) "Mayor Hylan's blundering is responsible for the 10¢ and 15¢ fare in New York City today. . . . I am absolutely in favor of a 5¢ fare if that is possible. I feel that is possible by intelligent handling of the situation, and by an economical administration of the transit companies. . . . Mayor Hylan, despite what he says, is really the best friend the traction trust has in this city today. . . ."

No, the Mayor countered, La Guardia was the traction trust's best friend, and it was therefore "working hard to defeat Robert L. Moran and to elect Fiorello La Guardia as President of the Board of Aldermen."

The *New York Times* came to La Guardia's defense editorially, concerning another vital municipal matter. It denounced the Board of

Estimate as "wrangling, quarrelling, impotent, a board worthy of Gilbert-Sullivania." To check, to restrain, their comic-opera finance—romping gayly with a budget of nearly $275,000,000—La Guardia was desperately needed. And the Committee on City Affairs of the National Republican Club agreed. It also wanted to see the election of another major, Major Henry H. Curran—forty-two, a Yale man and graduate of the New York Law School, formerly an alderman. The office for which he was running—president of the Borough of Manhattan—provided two votes in the Board of Estimate. And since the president of the Board of Aldermen had three votes, La Guardia and Curran together could exercise some control of the city administration.

Though the Republican powers wanted to woo the Italian vote, for this election and for the presidential one just ahead, and do it through La Guardia, they could not have anticipated one of La Guardia's direct approaches. He shouted at an audience: "Any Italian-American who votes the Democratic ticket is an Austrian bastard!"

But La Guardia could also be subtle. A circular had been issued by the Committee of Real Workingmen, an organization that backed Moran, which maintained that both Moran and La Guardia were worthy individuals and should be kept in the jobs that they held at that time. After all, "numbers of Italian Americans who have none of their nationality in Washington desire that he, La Guardia, stay where he is. . . ."

La Guardia contacted the head of the committee—William Waller, obviously a Real Workingman, for he was bridge tender of the Willis Avenue Bridge. "It was delightful to read the high regard which your committee has of me," he wrote, "and the appreciation of my services as a public servant. . . . Your circular is so flattering that it occurred to me that perhaps my Committee will be able to assist you in the distribution [of circulars], so if you will send me a few hundred thousand of this circular, I will see that they are properly placed. . . ."

Subtlety in no way characterized his eloquent exposures of Tammany's civic immoralities. During a block party on North 8th Street, between Bedford and Driggs Avenues in Brooklyn, he charged, "Oysters that menace health and endanger life are being sold in New York City with the official approval of the Tammany administration." Tammany's Health Department should stop their sale at once. And Tammany's Health Department should do something about the fifty million gallons of filth that were dumped daily on the oyster beds in Jamaica Bay.

There were other perils—all Tammany-inspired. One made La

Guardia's voice especially shrill, and his gestures speeded up, became two-fisted, harder-hitting. Children occupied firetrap school buildings all over the city; they were overcrowded tinderboxes. The city had to make a genuine effort—at once—"to wipe out this danger to its most precious human possession."

And while La Guardia raced about New York City, making fifteen, sixteen, seventeen speeches before going out for his evening stint of speechmaking, concern about campaign costs nagged at him.

Every time he asked Windels about badly needed money, Windels told him to handle his own business and that he would take care of finances.

Thea worried over her husband's worry; his indebtedness, after all, had grown to $30,000. Tensions weren't eased by the betting odds, which favored Moran over La Guardia two to one.

Then Frank Munsey—owner of the *New York Sun*, who on occasion fancied himself a liberal—offered to bet the La Guardia camp, not two to one, but three to one, that Moran would win. Thea felt a tormented desire to chance all the money she possessed, $1,050. With the winnings, she reasoned, she could help pay off the campaign deficit. She turned away from one extremely important possibility: that her husband might lose. By the Saturday night before the election, however, a self-induced confidence gripped La Guardia's followers. Not only did Thea place her bet, but $9,000 more was raised and added to it. If they won, the campaign money problem would be solved, and—all-important in La Guardia's eyes—he would have much more chance of becoming what he so avidly wanted to be—mayor.

The polls opened at six in the morning on Tuesday, November 4. It was expected that the vote would be heavier than it had been the preceding year, when an influenza epidemic, "which had taken more American lives than had the Germans," kept voters at home.

Thea, her beauty enhanced by a fur neckpiece and dotted, full veil, accompanied her husband to a polling place in a tailor's shop, one flight up, at 66 East 12th Street. Before dropping his ballot in a padlocked box, La Guardia held it poised over the aperture until the photographers had the picture and then, still unusually cooperative, he told the press what it expected to hear: he was confident of victory.

And when the polls closed, after having been open for twelve hours, New York City's first "dry" election night began. Wet election nights had tended to be boisterous, the carryings-on of both elation and despair; this night, by contrast, brooded with a heavy, ominous quiet. But the strain of sobriety erupted in some understandable violence, some angry expressions of frustration—for example, the smashing of an empty bottle against a stone wall. In front of the Forward Building, police rescued Jack Weinstein, eighteen, of 18 Rutgers Street, from a cluster of punching, grabbing, infuriated Italians determined to right a wrong: a remark by Weinstein that disparaged La Guardia.

There was no lack of evidence that La Guardia's Italianate backing seethed with emotion: at his headquarters—the Imperial Hotel, 31st and Broadway—as election figures were marked up, Italian supporters shouted, "Viva La Guardia!" One of them, La Guardia's barber, stood on a chair and shrieked, while shaking both hands high over his head, "I shave him for two years."

Their wild excitement implied victory, but as the candidates came to the wire, they ran in a close pack. La Guardia would be ahead, by just a few votes—and briefly; then the same would be true of Curran.

This nerve-wracking, volatile situation called for extremely careful supervision at the polls. At one point, La Guardia spirited Windels off in an automobile, with stealth worthy of a Machiavellian plot. Then he smashed this aura of intrigue; a mundane statement did it: he'd heard a rumor that some monkey business had been going on with votes in the Bronx.

La Guardia next resorted to metaphor, for vividness, for accuracy. "My military training," he said, "teaches me not to take my eyes off the enemy until it is all over. So I am still counting the votes."

Midnight arrived; the race continued nip and tuck. One bright spot appeared. Major Michael Kelly, whom Tammany had rejected, was running to get revenge, as a candidate on the Liberty Party's ticket. Though Kelly's name did not appear on the ballot, write-ins indicated that he was actually splitting the Irish vote with Moran. And the Irish still had substantial voting power, even though the Irish flag hadn't waved over City Hall on St. Patrick's Day since 1886. But all the Jewish vote and all the Italian vote—as expected—were going to La Guardia. Still, the outcome remained far from certain. (Was anything in 1919 fixed, immutable, to be everlastingly relied on? Well, William Wrigley, Jr. at this time was telling America, not as yet recovered from war, that the price of a package of Wrigley's gum was five cents before the war, during the war and *now*. Then, in a blare of commercial summation, "Both flavor and price last.")

Eventually, La Guardia took his eyes off the enemy. He and Thea were awaiting election results in a room at the Hotel Brevoort; at four in the morning, a call came from Sam Koenig. Because of the way Koenig couched his message and spoke it, there was no doubting it. "F. H.," he said to La Guardia, "You're in."

A *New York Times* banner headline the next morning declared, with wording that appeared to harbor a shade of elation, "This Election Near a Collapse for Tammany."

Koenig's elation, unlike the *Times*'s, knew no bounds. He savored the extent of Tammany's defeat; in it, he saw a solid foundation for the 1921 mayoral campaign, in which the Republicans' candidate would run on a straight Republican ticket.

Thea, of course, had been overjoyed from the moment she heard the good news at the Brevoort. It meant at least two things to her, both wonderful: her husband's victory cancelled that worrisome campaign debt; and now that Fiorello had become president of the Board of Aldermen, "she was Second Lady of New York."

La Guardia had a realist's view of his victory; qualifications therefore took the luster from it. First of all, he was in by the slim margin of 1,530 votes. (And Curran's win had been close, too. Still, it gave the Republicans five invaluable votes of the Board of Estimate's sixteen.) La Guardia also could not overlook two elements that made his having been elected possible. He would definitely have lost if it hadn't been for Kelly's premeditated division of the Irish vote with Moran, and there was also the devastating Republican sweep due to the general, unequivocal opposition to Woodrow Wilson. Why, that sweep had overwhelmingly reelected the governor of Massachusetts, even though Silent Cal was an individual who said little, governed less and had indeed led a life "as placid as that of a man in a convent."

Something else took the edge off of La Guardia's victory. When Will Hays promised La Guardia the Republican Party's nomination for mayor in 1921 should he win the aldermanic presidency, he didn't stipulate that the win had to be a landslide. And yet, like an ominous foreshadowing, talk in Republican circles centered on Henry H. Curran as the most likely choice for mayor; it pointed out his "considerable experience in municipal affairs as a member of the Aldermanic Board." (They overlooked, through ignorance or design, how much experience La Guardia would have by the time 1921 rolled around.)

Curiously, of all people, it was Richard Croker, that boss of Tammany who had shouted during the Mazet inquiry of 1899, "If you can show me where I have taken a dollar from this city you can cut that right arm off," who inadvertently gave La Guardia a degree of comfort. After the election, he told La Guardia—as it turned out, with confusing prophetic accuracy, "Some day an Italian and a Jew will be mayors of New York, and the Italian will come first."

CHAPTER TEN

I
N NEW YORK, THE YEAR 1811 MEANT THE OPENING OF its City Hall, which had $35,000 worth of West Stockbridge, Massachusetts marble as a facade, for show, and prosaic brownstone in the rear to make up for the extravagant marble expenditure—and, by this economy, though this was not intended, a symbol of political strategy and compromise was incorporated into the City Hall's very structure. Eighty-eight years later, a new charter converted New York City into a metropolis of five boroughs, with a population of almost three and a half million—a fantastic increase of two million. To make the most of a sliver of priceless land at 23rd between Broadway and Fifth Avenue, there arose in 1902 a building in the shape of a flatiron which reached the unheard-of height of twenty stories, an accomplishment made possible by ingeniously bolting a steel frame together. The first subway rumbled along its labyrinthian murky path in 1904; surface trains appeared a few years later in the new $125,000,000 Pennsylvania Terminal, regarded as one of the wonders of the world, and then at Grand Central, equally expensive and even more complex.

The swearing in of La Guardia as president of the Board of Aldermen by Justice Philip McCook—who would one day administer the oath of mayor to him—deserves a place beside these momentous events and edifices. This was true even though the Board of Aldermen had accomplished little if anything since its creation in 1901. In Tweed's day, it was referred to, with justification, as the Forty Thieves. Riddled with sinecures, too—including the effrontery of eleven sergeants of arms! And one day, the power that the Board of Aldermen exercised would go to the Board of Estimate.

This history of thievery and impotence didn't bother La Guardia in the least. In his opening address to the Board of Aldermen, he said,

"The financial condition of the City requires care in the spending of money and the utilization of property." He looked to the future, to the goal of becoming mayor of New York City. If he glanced back at all, he might have drawn encouragement from John Purroy Mitchel's having become mayor after serving, a decade ago, as president of the Board of Aldermen. This position as head of the board, after all, taught one eager to observe and assimilate, all the rudiments of running New York City. (This was highly specialized expertise, for New York is a unique municipality. And though this city might be thought of as a few Philadelphias in size, it would be erroneous to consider it merely an immense Philadelphia.)

A Republican less strong-willed than La Guardia might have been disturbed by Tammany's perennial domination of the board. But "he had no intention of being a figurehead."

La Guardia's independence exploded even before he took office. He threatened Congress in mid-December with not resigning his seat, with not going off on January 1 to become president of the Board of Aldermen of New York City, if the subcommittee considering a bill for the creation of a separate Air Service did not cease its "petty politics and get together." "I told the committee this yesterday," he said, "and I still hold to it. However, I have good assurance that the bill will be reported out after the holidays."

The bill was indeed reported out, and La Guardia sent his resignation from Congress to Governor Al Smith of New York and at once began shooting off his special verbal fireworks. Two days before Christmas, not affected one iota by that holiday's spirit, he let fly at Mayor Hylan, charging he "has changed the makeup of committees of the Board of Estimate, fixing them so that Major Curran and myself will have but little voice in the preliminary consideration of legislation affecting New York City and the expenditures of its $275,000,000." And that wasn't all, La Guardia screamed. Mayor Hylan had set out to deprive him of the chairmanship of two important committees, a flagrant act because Robert L. Moran, the retiring president of the Board of Aldermen, had held those committees. Then a few days before the New Year arrived, La Guardia made a statement to the public in which he outlined in detail what he expected to fight for when he took office, sounding more like the mayor he hoped to become than a mere alderman.

If New York City is to maintain its supremacy on the Atlantic seaboard, it simply has to have more pier and warehouse accommodations.

The City Charter must be revised. Why, it's so out-of-date that it forbids a New Yorker to "drive cattle, sheep, swine, pigs or calves through the streets and avenues of New York."

The Transit Question has to be tackled, has to be answered, without a moment's delay.

It's imperative that harmony between the Department of Education and the City Administration be established, because nearly 40,000 children are not properly housed and aren't getting the instruction they should get.

On and on La Guardia went, pointing out flaws, his statements charged with urgency. And on the day Robert L. Moran introduced him to the members of the board, they eyed him speculatively and with varying degrees of apprehension; in addition to all his eccentricities, he was the first Republican in twenty years to be president of the Board of Aldermen.

On January 1, a brand-new gavel was presented to the brand-new, thirty-eight-year-old president of the Board of Aldermen. He wasted no time in making the gavel a secondhand one. In calling one individual to order, he told him, "Every member present must behave as a gentleman, and those who are not must try to."

This call for gentlemanly behavior made the abrasive, querulous, petulant, ungrammatical, profane La Guardia appear to be in favor of such behavior. He was in favor of it. For the other guy!

You didn't handle Tammany with social amenities; even La Guardia's conservative colleagues might have regarded this as an inescapable truism. But they couldn't countenance radicalism. And as soon as La Guardia assumed the aldermanic presidency, he came to the aid of five Socialist state legislators who, after having been charged with disloyalty, were removed from office. As if that weren't enough, he made a statement that smacked of pure bolshevism: "With grain, eggs and oatmeal becoming luxuries in the average family, these Socialists, along with the general public, are right in demanding a radical change of conditions."

Still, the boss Republicans overlooked such poor political behavior, remembering how La Guardia had fought Wilson and helped Harding and Coolidge defeat the Democratic ticket of James M. Cox and Franklin D. Roosevelt by corralling and turning over the Italian-American vote. The bosses also knew that he had been pleased when the Harding landslide had swept Nathan L. Miller into the governor's mansion at Albany.

But La Guardia's delight with Miller—an able politician, a believer in government by the few, a first-rate maker of enemies—proved short-lived. Miller had not been in office a month when La Guardia tore into him savagely over his Transit Commission Program. (The governor, in league with traction looters, wanted to raise the five-cent trolley and subway fare. Naturally, La Guardia agreed with the intent of an anonymous poet: "Our Boss who art in Albany, Miller be thy name. Thy orders come, thy will be done in New York as it is in Albany . . . for thine is the State, and the County and the City forever.")

La Guardia ignored, or didn't appear to be at all aware, that this internecine scrapping with the Republican Old Guard in New York State was pulling out the underpinnings of his hope of becoming mayor. He couldn't stomach Miller's dislike of immigrants because they were foreigners; his being for Prohibition and against direct primaries. Still, La Guardia's behavior—which should have been molded somewhat by expediency—seemed a political death wish.

His behavior included contempt, which usually focused on Comptroller Charles Craig—as bald and chubby as a cherub, but without even a trace of geniality. Craig was pompous, a City Hall martinet. He was in the habit of using long, legalistic sentences and of quoting learnedly from the Charter, giving chapter and verse, to support his stands. On sight, Craig and La Guardia became mortal enemies.

Craig called La Guardia's actions "blackguardia"; each called the other a liar. Once at a hectic Board of Estimate meeting, during which Craig and Hylan were fighting, La Guardia tried to get a word in. This infuriated Craig, who shouted to Mayor Hylan, "Will you hit that little Wop over the head with the gavel!"

Hylan might have obliged—but not to please Craig. He had heard —just a few weeks after the installation of the new president of the Board of Aldermen—that La Guardia had proclaimed that he was going to undertake an investigation of the Hylan administration.

Hylan brooded over this, until the evening they met at the 69th Regiment Armory, where a reception was being held for De Valera, president of the Irish Republic.

"Good evening, Mr. Mayor," La Guardia said.

Hylan's response clearly lacked cordiality, and La Guardia—with an air of monumental innocence—asked him what was wrong. Hylan told him that his statement about investigating the administration had not been justified. To prove it, he would give him any records that he wanted and would help him get at the facts.

"La Guardia, any time you think there's anything wrong," Hylan went on, "you come to me first, and if you find I'll not cooperate with you, or that I will stand for anything not right, you may go the limit!"

"Do you mean it, Mr. Mayor?"

"I do," Hylan told La Guardia.

They thereupon shook hands. And this verbal agreement could not have been made by a more incongruous pair, for Hylan's six foot of brawn, towering over La Guardia, was topped by flaming red hair. Hylan wasn't called Red Mike without reason.

The pact Hylan and La Guardia sealed that night also united them in their mutual distaste of Comptroller Craig. However, it didn't set well with the big, important cogs in the Republican machine. Why should a Republican—and La Guardia vociferously claimed to be one —come to an understanding with Hylan? (Even Tammany hadn't picked Hylan for mayor of their own free will; they wanted Al Smith. After all, Hylan had a reputation—far and wide—of having very little gray matter under his red hair. Al Smith had said of Hylan, "If he has helped the Albany situation in the slightest degree, he has helped it by going to Palm Beach for a month every winter." But William Randolph Hearst liked Hylan; his taste in art also sometimes ran to the bizarre. Hearst therefore promised Tammany chief Charles Murphy—whose words, though spoken slowly and gently, had the power of God—that he would back Hylan if Hylan were the mayoralty candidate.)

La Guardia continued to irk his fellow Republicans, in small as well as more serious ways. Why, Mayor Gaynor would don his silk hat just to go from his first-floor office to the Board of Estimate on the second. But La Guardia wore a khaki shirt at Board of Estimate meetings to protest a Tammany punishment: all members of the board—but him— had received a salary increase. And his interests ranged too far afield for a president of the Board of Aldermen, from thoughts on daylight saving time to urgings that the Military Academy not reduce its four-year course to three. And he ignited Board of Estimate meetings. The Citizens Union—Republicans banded together to uncover irregularities and establish civic virtue—complained that La Guardia was "an active participant in the disgraceful brawls that featured the sessions of the Board." But La Guardia believed, and let it be known, that "the Board of Estimate is not government according to Hoyle, but according to the rules of the Marquis of Queensberry."

What happened during a session in early summer of 1920 proved how true this was. It started with La Guardia ordering Craig to bring up a matter that he had failed to bring up.

Craig snapped, "You say that again, and you will get what you deserve."

Instead of complying with Craig's request, La Guardia started a punch aimed at Craig's disgruntled features; it didn't land, for Curran grabbed and held on to La Guardia.

When Charles L. Kerrigan, Craig's secretary, stepped behind La Guardia, La Guardia spun around—in spite of Curran's hold—and shouted, "If you try to start anything with me, you'll go out of that window, you bootlicking valet!"

"I'm no wop!" Kerrigan yelled.

"What's that you say?" La Guardia went for Kerrigan this time; again, Curran restrained him. "What's that you say?" La Guardia's fury made him keep asking that question. "What's that you say?"

Virtually each day detonated a new facet of the Craig-La Guardia antipathy. La Guardia boiled over because Craig was determined to exempt over one hundred jobs in his department from civil service. He let Craig know exactly how he felt about this attempt to get rid of many competent persons, who had been in the city's service for years, and substitute "riffraff who could not pass the civil service test." La Guardia pointed out that "faithful and able employees"—under civil service—"really keep the work going [in the Department of Finance], in spite of the Comptroller."

Craig took his turn at attacking, accusing La Guardia of sending $390 worth of personal telegrams which he included in his bill to the city for business telegrams. Craig's accusation of the theft was one of petty larceny compared to what La Guardia discovered in connection with the construction of the New York County Courthouse.

La Guardia therefore rushed off to Mayor Hylan.

"Mr. Mayor, you remember what you told me that night at the 69th Regiment Armory? Well, this Courthouse business stinks—it's ROTTEN; you can't stand for it."

Hylan, whose mistakes were not of the heart but of the head, said with the greatest of naivete, "What do you mean?"

"Mr. Mayor, you look into it as much as I have, and you will find that the city is being robbed! The price of the limestone is ridiculously high, and not only that, but the specifications call for about 300 cubic feet more than they need!"

Hylan, finally, got around to asking, "What do you want me to do, Mr. President?"

"I want you to have anyone you select look into this matter. If I am wrong in anything I have said, or off in any of the estimates I have given, I will publicly state that I have been wrong. But, on the other hand, if you find that I am right, for goodness' sake, protect the city!"

The commissioner of accounts investigated, and as a result con-
tracts—over Comptroller Craig's objections—were rescinded.

"You are not only saving the city millions of dollars," La Guardia
told Hylan, "but you have set an example that the day of looting on
public improvement is past!"

Though this blow smashed solidly into Tammany, Republican big-
wigs disapproved. They argued that La Guardia should have let the
crooked bids for the County Courthouse go through, for he would
then have had a great campaign issue—the dishonesty and incredible
wastefulness of Tammany.

But it went against La Guardia's grain to play it smart, by using the
crooked bids for political gain, by behaving himself while president of
the Board of Aldermen, by being innocuous—and thus a perfect
mayoralty candidate. He also made the mistake of crossing Governor
Miller and of alienating Republicans by his unorthodox political ways:
"his tendency to go whooping off the reservation, his fiery antics, what
they regarded as his radicalism and demagoguery."

By nature combative, La Guardia was exhilarated and immeasur-
ably satisfied by these confrontations. Bruising conflict is also an integral concomitant of leadership, and he'd been a leader from childhood.
His sister Gemma, in reminiscing, recalled proudly, "He would always
play the 'leader,' and Richard and I always had to follow him."

In 1920, La Guardia's City Hall skirmishes and pitched battles were
also a joyous extension of a private jubilation. During the spring of
that year, Thea's pregnancy neared its culmination. The thought of
being a father, at last, at thirty-eight, sent him into raptures. Not only
did he exhibit the caricature behavior of a late-in-life father, but he
was also an individual who had an innate love for children—and now
he was to have a child of his own. And he looked forward with joy—of
equal intensity—to the fulfillment of that promise Will Hays had
made. Not only would he be a father, but the next mayor of New York
City.

After the birth of a daughter—named Fioretta Thea, for her father's
maternal grandmother—Thea, young—only twenty-five—became ill.
Chalk-yellow pallor. Coughing—dry, deep in the throat, somehow
ominous. And tiny Fioretta Thea was sickly. La Guardia blamed the
city; in despair, he had to strike out at something. New York's air
equalled stench, germs, disease . . .

The course he must take was obvious; La Guardia and his wife and

child would leave the city. A series of moves followed, each a scurrying, frantic search for health. It was after they had settled in Huntington, Long Island, their first new residence, that La Guardia learned
that Thea had tuberculosis.

Stunned at finding out the nature of Thea's illness, La Guardia
placed his baby in a New York hospital and journeyed with Thea to
Saranac Lake, New York, in the rugged, lake-spotted Adirondacks.
Here Thea could receive the open-air treatment, a therapy developed
by Dr. Edwin Livingston Trudeau, who in attempting to cure his
brother of tuberculosis had contracted the disease. Trudeau had found
Saranac's air, purified and cooled by the Adirondacks, to be perfect for
treating diseased lungs.

But La Guardia couldn't remain at Thea's side and at the same time
carry on his battles for the people of New York. He had to be in City
Hall, just as Thea had to be in Saranac. Thea, however, also needed
her husband's presence—as the continuation of her life required the
healing essences of mountain air and sun. After all, they had been
married only a little over a year—and TB meant death; in cartoons it
was represented as the Grim Reaper, wielding a wide, inescapable
scythe.

Since Thea wouldn't remain in Saranac without her husband, they
decided on a makeshift compromise—finding a home in the Bronx,
where, according to the *Bronx Home News*, "it is believed a higher
altitude and purer air than circulates in the traffic congested Village's
39 Charles Street will be conducive to her recovery."

Not only did the purchase of the two-story stucco house at 1820
University Avenue take every penny that La Guardia possessed, but it
made borrowing necessary. To supplement the Bronx's salubrious
higher altitude, he added a sun porch to the house to provide Thea
and his infant child with the sun's therapeutic rays. When their nurse
became ill, he took over—cooking, doing the housework—and he told
the press his experiences as a child in Arizona now came in handy. In
their home in the Village, La Guardia had also cooked—especially for
friends, among them the Bellanca brothers, August and Giuseppe, and
the sculptors Attilio Piccirilli and Onorio Ruotolo—and he boasted
extravagantly about his spaghetti sauce.

Those happy days had become mere memories. One could hope for
their return, and for all the promise of his marriage to Thea, but out of
despair rather than with confidence. A politician, La Guardia knew the
hazard of ignoring facts: his wife and child were not recovering—the

sun of the sunporch and the Bronx's altitude notwithstanding. At night, he walked the floor with his baby. He sat at Thea's bedside. And at City Hall, with the added ferocity that his personal problems engendered, he fought Craig and Albany—in Miller's clothing—and didn't give a damn as to the consequences.

Then tragedy closed in. On May 3, Fioretta was rushed to Roosevelt Hospital, and six days later she died of spinal meningitis. She hadn't lived even one full year. Thea was too ill to attend her child's funeral; La Guardia went alone.

Disconsolate, La Guardia received yet another shattering blow. His life consisted of his work and his family; and suddenly both were in jeopardy, for on the second of August he heard incredible news: Curran had been picked to run on a fusion ticket against Tammany's mayoralty candidate. What of the promise Will Hays had made? What of the promise given at a meeting of the Republican State Committees? Boss Koenig denied such a promise had ever been made; without authority, if it had been. Those who had attended that meeting could not recall a promise having been made. One person did say, "My recollection is that Senator Calder said, 'If this little wop does not run for Mayor this city will go to hell.'"

Infuriated by such obvious treachery—and by the senseless death of his infant child—La Guardia made a glaring mistake, on the very next day, the third of August. Two of his employees, upon questioning, said they weren't supporting La Guardia in his race for mayor, so he fired them. The press made a great outcry: La Guardia, who had always fought Tammany, was now engaging in "Tammany Practices." The press should have been aware of differing motivations, should have known of La Guardia's overwhelming anger at a cosmos that would snatch life from a mere infant, and was therefore an anger that would flare up at anything that confronted it.

La Guardia and Thea talked. Not of their irrevocable, heart-searing loss, or of her illness, for words on those subjects were futile, meaningless, painful. La Guardia consulted with Thea. What did she think about his running as an independent? Her weak smile was ambiguous. But might it not be wiser, La Guardia pressed on, to face Curran in the primary? Yes, they agreed it would be; the Republican voters in a primary, not the leaders, should pick the nominee. And their conversation also struggled to be a diversion, to make this political problem appear their only problem.

In La Guardia's first campaign speech, on June 3, he declared he would give to thinking Republicans an opportunity to protest against reactionary legislation and the unfair action of the upstate administration. He stood for Home Rule, because rural legislators in the north had no conception of New York City's problems or how they might be solved. Home Rule would make the five-cent fare possible. And this was vital, because as the *Philadelphia Public Ledger* pointed out, "so large have American cities grown that you cannot get to work without the trolley. You cannot get home without them. You cannot hold a job or earn a living or do the day's shopping without the incidental help of the street cars. . . ." And to accomplish sovereignty, La Guardia prepared for New York City to secede from New York and become the forty-ninth state.

Even though La Guardia said that if Miller's domination were not broken, Hylan would be reelected, he was linked by his opponents with Hylan—and with Hearst. He insisted pitifully that he was a Republican, not a Democrat. "No one expects that I will be nominated for mayor by the Democrats. I am a Republican."

Then all the trials and tribulations of Job descended upon La Guardia. Curran, who had restrained him from punching Craig's lackey, who had a fat little mustache pasted under his nose, who never crossed the party's powerful ones—this man defeated La Guardia. Devastatingly: 103,000 to 37,000—almost three to one. Following this defeat, Thea's condition worsened; all her symptoms intensified.

Fate's scenario followed the Book of Job. Like Job, La Guardia had lost a child. Job had also been smitten with boils, and his wealth vanished. And so it came to pass that when Thea needed her husband more than ever, unendurable back pains brought La Guardia down. The doctors at Roosevelt Hospital found that he had an abscess at the base of his spine—an aftermath of the injury he'd suffered in the Foggia plane crash.

Instead of undergoing the operation that had been prescribed, La Guardia journeyed to the sanatorium in Croton, New York, to which Thea had been taken. He stayed with her, not wanting to leave her; but finally pain drove him back to the hospital.

While he was recuperating from the operation, which had been a success, thieves, using a jimmy, entered through a second-story rear window of his home, which had been unoccupied for eight days. They made off with 220 pieces of sterling silver bearing the monogram *LaG* and with a briefcase containing valuable papers, including a record of La Guardia's war service. (The silver and briefcase—

stripped of the papers—were recovered in a few days' time.) To spare La Guardia, his physicians kept all word of the robbery from him.

But the very next month he had to withstand far greater shocks. First, he had to endure the result of the mayoralty race in which he had expected to run and win. Though all newspapers—with the exception of Hearst's and the *Daily News*—had fought Hylan, Hylan was "re-elected by a prodigious plurality."

The press struggled to understand Hylan's victory. Perhaps, the *Baltimore Sun* said, New York is "corrupt and contented." The *New York American* turned to narration.

Once upon a time, as they say in fairy-tales, a lot of traction looters got together and decided they would drive a mayor out of the City Hall. This was because he wouldn't let them charge more than a nickel for a ride in the people's subway. But the mayor, who happened to be John F. Hylan, kept up his fight to keep the carfare at five cents, and the people made him mayor again by a fabulous figure. And the traction looters lived unhappily ever after.

Boss Charles Murphy had other views about the matter. For the first time in a New York mayoralty election, women had voted; and they are "a great moral force and their votes have shown it." And the overwhelming Democratic victory makes it seem "foolish for our enemies to charge that there is nothing good, but everything corrupt, in Tammany."

So the Tammanyites could gather in the Wigwam on 14th Street and gloat that their purity had brought them a deserved victory, while La Guardia knew only black despair.

Two days later, Thea died.

Rumor had it that La Guardia—a completely broken man, with a past he could not forget and a future that held only a promise of pain—took to drinking.

After Thea's funeral, Craig—knowing no mercy—bombarded La Guardia with: "The trouble is that he wanted to be Mayor and the people gave him their answer. Now he is sore. He's the 'late lamented La Guardia'!"

CHAPTER ELEVEN

I T APPEARED THAT LA GUARDIA COULD NOT POSSIBLY
rise again from the political defeat and personal losses he had suffered.
Although this had not been his first loss at the polls—there had been
1914—the *Westchester Globe* wrote his epitaph, with a self-righteous
air and a Republican view of history and human destiny: "The Republican Party will live on, while individuals drop out of sight."

After Thea's death, La Guardia spent the last two weeks of his term
as president of the Board of Aldermen in Havana—needing to be away
from New York. Piccirilli accompanied him, to serve as an individual
to whom he could turn for comfort. And it was Hylan, whose inadequacies were his reputation, who did possess the sensitivity and compassion to send La Guardia a letter, a surrogate to strengthen—and
heal—through appreciation: "I could not let this, your last day at City
Hall, pass without writing you how sorry I am that you are leaving,
and particularly that the people of this city are losing your services.
. . . There is no office in the gift of the people that is too good for
you."

Inevitably La Guardia found himself alone in the house he and
Thea had shared. The bright winter sunlight that lay with steady
intensity on walls, floor, ceiling of the sunroom, a room meant to have
curative powers, was mockery now. Thea and his infant daughter were
gone—a euphemism, and a lie, for *gone* included the possibility of
return. Friends came to provide solace, if they could, by their presence. The depth and outrage of his pain were evidenced by the outcry
he made to Zoe Beckley of the *Evening Mail:* "New York is the richest
city in the world. But until every child is fed and every home has air

93

and light and every man and woman a chance for happiness, it is not the city it ought to be." The reporter, while noting "the black tie, the somber band upon his sleeve," asked him if he could provide all this with the city's million-dollars-a-day budget; La Guardia's response sprang from irreparable torment: "Could I! Could I! Say—first I would tear out about five square miles of filthy tenements, so that fewer would be infected with tuberculosis like that beautiful girl of mine, my wife, who died—and my baby. . . ."

The hard blows of reason quickly blunted the edge of his suffering. By inclination and habit a hard worker, he turned naturally to activity and it served to help him forget. He began the new year by starting to practice law again, as a member of the newly formed firm of La Guardia, Sapisky and Amster. (In 1910, upon beginning his practice of law, he had changed his middle name from Enrico to Henry to dilute Fiorello and La Guardia with anglicism. Now he had no comparable simple device to help him adjust once again to being a lawyer.)

A newspaper story in February stated that La Guardia—whom it felt the need to identify as the former president of the Board of Aldermen—had entered the movies. Though newsworthy, this item was a bit misleading. A movie company had been started by Deloris Casinelli, an actress who had gained national recognition for her role "in the great war picture *Lafayette We Come.*" This company had as its objective the creation of "artistic pictures for art's sake," and La Guardia was to serve as its general counsel. He also represented the Free State of Fiume and New York City in its fight to obtain a thirty-foot ship channel in Jamaica Bay. He came to the aid of Sacco and Vanzetti in their life-and-death struggle, joined the Fraternal Order of Eagles in their efforts to gain old age pensions . . .

In addition to contributing a therapeutic busyness, his legal work provided him with essential income. Still, he felt what appeared a compulsive need to engage in political activity. Revenge might also have been a factor, getting even with Nathan Miller, of the broad, strong face and narrow, cold-blooded mind, whom he blamed for keeping him from becoming mayor of New York, and attacked as "a political liability of the Republican Party."

If a vendetta motivated La Guardia—and there were those who were sure it did—it began just a few months after Thea's death, the night the League of Italian-American Clubs was formed and La Guardia realized the potential of a million Italian voters.

La Guardia's plot to return to Congress—ingenious, rather than sinister—meshed perfectly with the uncertain state of the nation in 1922.

That year began with a frigid January which dumped twenty-nine inches of snow on Washington, another irritant to the Capital's psyche. It kept President Warren Gamaliel Harding from knocking practice golf balls all over the south grounds, and his Laddie from retrieving them. And so the man—whom those in a smoke-filled room had picked to be president, because he was the best of the second-raters—had more time to dwell on his inadequacies. A war-weary electorate had put him in office with a seven-million majority simply because he looked like a president and had offered it a tranquil, relaxing, euphoric goal: normalcy. Now, in a postwar depression, there was 11 percent unemployment. The President didn't know what to do about this—or the threat of coal and railroad strikes. Being a poker player, he simply couched his predicament in poker terms: he had been dealt a bad hand. And he knew that his vice-president couldn't tell him what he ought to do. (At a dinner one night, a woman seated next to the Vice-President told him that she had made a bet that she could get him to say three words in the course of the evening. According to the story— apocryphal or otherwise—Coolidge snapped, "You lose." And fantasy reported that on one occasion Calvin Coolidge opened his mouth and a moth flew out. H. L. Mencken was even less kind to the silent Dr. Coolidge, preferring Dr. Harding, who at least had "the courage of his hypocrisies.") And Harding could not turn to Congress for counsel, for it—with good reason—had come to be known as the "do nothing Congress."

But a ray of hope appeared: an upswing in the economy. (The upswing would continue up and up for seven years, until 1929, until a "Black Thursday" in October of that year.)

The upswing failed to elicit jubilation among Progressives, those wild believers in the panacea of governmental controls. La Guardia was one of them; in 1922, he stated flatly, unequivocally—most unusual for a politician—"I am a Progressive."

Since the practice of law could use up only a fraction of his energies —and not completely bury the substratum pain of his personal tragedies—in March he formed the League of Italian-American Voters. Two months later, he proclaimed that if the Republicans picked arch-conservative Miller to run for governor of New York, he would run as an independent. Then to further startle the Old Guard, he issued a pamphlet that presented the forty-one planks of his platform—a thoroughgoing radical, well-nigh socialistic platform. The eight-hour workday. Equality of opportunity for women. Unrestricted immigration. The outlawry of war . . .

The following month, June, William Randolph Hearst played his card. Practical joker, art collector, yellow journalist, lord of a $40,000,000 castle, Hearst was also an individual who ached to be president of the United States. To attain that office, he was even willing to use lesser positions as stepping stones, and that was what he considered the governorship of New York. The most satisfactory approach to Albany—and perhaps, in the end, the shortest—was by circumlocution. He let it be known that he wanted a progressive governor of New York. The Republicans should therefore nominate La Guardia, and Hylan would be the proper, progressive Democratic nominee. This arrangement insured a progressive governor; whether he be Democrat or Republican—as far as he was concerned—made no difference whatsoever. Of course, Hearst kept his real intention to himself: to split the Republican votes by having La Guardia enter the lists, and thus make it possible for Hearst—eventually given the nod by the Democrats—to be the next governor of New York.

To beat the progressive drum even louder, Hearst invited La Guardia to write for his newspapers. La Guardia, who could not help but see through Hearst's scheme to capture the governorship, pounced on this opportunity to use Hearst as Hearst was using him. Throughout the summer and fall, in passionate progressive-radical prose, he expressed himself on the issues in Hearst's papers.

As in a smoothly functioning comedy of errors, while Hearst was scheming to get the governorship, La Guardia maneuvered stealthily to get back into Congress.

When Koenig appeared one day, he let it be known that as a representative of the Republican Party, he had a deal to offer. If La Guardia would give up his plan to run for governor as an independent, he would be chosen to run for Congress from the 20th Congressional District. (Koenig couldn't offer the 14th, for Tammany had acquired it.)

La Guardia knew he didn't have to grab this offering with the speed of hunger and gratitude. Yes, he would accept. But on one condition: he would run on *his* platform, not on the Old Guard's.

Koenig winced. With reluctance, however, he agreed, having no alternative.

La Guardia hurled himself into the campaign, still struggling to escape painful personal memories; besides, only two months remained in which to defeat Karlin, the Socialist, and Tammany's Henry Frank, a Jewish lawyer who had never held office.

As soon as La Guardia established a base of operations in an empty store at 1677 Madison Avenue, he issued a statement of clarification. Yes, he was a Republican. But no, he wasn't running on the Republican platform. "I stand for the republicanism of Abraham Lincoln; and let me tell you now that the average Republican leader East of the Mississippi doesn't know any more about Abraham Lincoln than Henry Ford knows about the Talmud." (La Guardia was certain Ford knew next to nothing about the Talmud, for that body of jurisprudence stemmed from Jews, who, Ford believed, were "the source of almost every American affliction, including high rents, the shortage of farm labor, jazz, gambling, drunkenness, loose morals and even short skirts.")

"I may as well tell you," La Guardia went on, "for it wouldn't be fair to put it off until after I am elected, that I don't fit in at all with the average so-called 'Republican' in the East. I am a Progressive. I want to work with such men as Senator Borah, Senator Johnson, Senator Brookhart and Senator La Follette."

In giving talk after talk after talk, he raced around the streets of the district he wished to represent; it extended from 99th to 120th Street, from Central Park to the East River and, like La Guardia himself, was part Italian, part Jewish. He viewed each street corner as an opportunity to speak his mind.

In discussing his Socialist opponent with a newspaper man, he said, "To secure to each laborer the whole product of his labor (or to do that as nearly as possible) is a worthy goal of any good government. That is my platform. But when the average Republican leader in the East hears it, he thinks that I am quoting from Karl Marx. I quoted it from Abraham Lincoln." (And, in so doing, he was enunciating the Progressive credo, the word of Jefferson as well as of Lincoln, the belief that the State had a responsibility for the welfare of the individual.)

Speaking from trucks and under the light of flares, he berated Prohibition and its Volstead Act, which "makes it possible for the rich to buy and use imported liquor of choice vintage while the poor are drinking poison hooch made out of denatured alcohol obtained on permits issued by the U.S. government." And an unenforceable law corrupted law enforcement agents. A cartoon of that year told the story:

Drunken law enforcement agents at a table in a speakeasy. One says, "Less have 'nother round o' evidence."

The opposition accused La Guardia of being a carpetbagger, of invading Manhattan from the remote fastnesses of the Bronx. This charge was so mild it suggested the possibility that Karlin and Frank had no real ammunition, that they had to fire blanks just to be doing something.

But support for La Guardia kept coming in. Hylan remained constant, even to word choice. "There is no office within the gift of the people that's too good for him. Now that he is running for Congress, I hope that all my friends in Harlem, regardless of party, will vote for him."

The press—including the Hearst papers, of course—supported La Guardia. It was no more surprising that Progressive Hiram Johnson of California, as short and solid as La Guardia and as forceful, should let it be known that the country would be needing congressmen like La Guardia in the years ahead.

Conservatives tried to persuade Johnson to make an about-face; he answered with a wire that concluded, "And if I had one thousand votes in his district I would cast them all for him."

What really troubled Frank—Karlin could no longer be considered a threat—was Edward Corsi's support of La Guardia. Corsi, Italian-born, very popular, a lawyer-journalist-social worker, might be instrumental in La Guardia's capturing the Italian vote. (La Guardia even had Italian women on his side; they had formed an organization, the Daughters of Italy, 350 strong, whose members went from door to door and did their determined best to sell La Guardia.)

This turn of events transformed the comedy of errors into straight farce—with more than a full dipper of venom.

Fearful that he had lost the Italian vote, Frank went all out to snare the Jewish one. On Rosh Hashanah—the Jewish New Year, which came along quite conveniently—he sent cards to the Jews of the district. Tammany noted the pleased response of the recipients of the cards—a minority savoring crumbs of recognition. Having softened up the Jewish electorate, Frank's campaign workers created a few paragraphs of vilification which, after pointing out that "the most important office in this country for Judaism is the Congressman," gave the salient feature of each of the three candidates. *Atheist* was the word for Karlin. (Good God, everyone knew Atheist and Socialist were synonymous!) As for La Guardia, he was "a pronounced anti-Semite and Jew-hater." Therefore, "be careful how you vote. Our candidate is Henry Frank, who is a Jew with a Jewish heart, and who does good for us."

La Guardia struck back with a handbill printed in Yiddish; it challenged Frank to debate him on the subject: Who Is Best Qualified to Represent All the People of the Twentieth Congressional District? The debate, La Guardia stipulated, was to be conducted ENTIRELY IN THE YIDDISH LANGUAGE. La Guardia knew that Frank, though "a Jew with a Jewish heart, and who does good for us," did not speak a word of Yiddish. He also knew that Jews were prone to ask a devastating rhetorical question when made aware of a Jew who did not speak Yiddish: What kind of a Jew is that?

La Guardia's handbill caused Frank and his underlings to panic. They had to give an appealing, acceptable, untruthful reason why Frank could not accept La Guardia's challenge to debate him—IN YIDDISH. Frank was sick. Of course. Men running for high office became sick just like anyone else. That was it. Frank was too sick to debate.

La Guardia gave three speeches—each in Yiddish, each presenting his unflattering view of Frank for not accepting his challenge. His Jewish audiences ate it up. They could not have been more pleased, for he spoke their language—literally, figuratively.

Aware that he was losing the Jewish vote—and therefore the election—Frank made an irrational, desperate move. He wrote to La Guardia, explaining, with more bitterness than conviction, why he had refused to meet him in debate. As part of his conclusion, he said, "You are certainly not qualified to represent the people, and you will know it on the day when the people send you back, bag and baggage, to your little cottage and sun-parlor on University Avenue in the Bronx. . . ."

This enraged La Guardia. Nothing could ease the painful memories Frank had stirred up by that statement except to reveal, from every street corner, the depths to which his opponent had sunk. "For Frank to refer to the 'sun-parlor' in my home," he said, "is as low and unmanly an act as a man could resort to. He knows that I was compelled to move out of my district and purchase that house with the sun-parlor in order to try to save the life of my poor wife."

La Guardia also pointed out that Frank was appealing for votes on purely religious grounds, asking for their vote simply because he was a Jew. "After all," La Guardia said, "is he looking for a job as a *schamas* [*shammes*] or does he want to be elected Congressman?"

Shammes is the Yiddish word for a beadle in a synagogue, a glorified janitor. Not only had La Guardia, presumably a *goy,* an *Italianer,* used the word, but he had captured its pejorative tinge, the condescension with which it is frequently used, by placing it incongruously beside *Congressman* in a beautiful perfect ad hominem arrangement.

Still moved by desperation, Frank tried a final ploy on the night before the election. He appeared at a police station bearing a letter supposedly written by the Black Hand, a society, both lawless and secret, which ordered Frank to withdraw from the election.

But it was too late; La Guardia and his Yiddish and his passion were too far out front to be overtaken. What happened at the polls made it all official.

A final ironic twist to the comedy: Miller, whom the Republicans had been able to run for governor after La Guardia had been lured from the competition, lost to Al Smith, who for years had hated and fought Hearst. And selfless Hearst, who claimed he merely wanted a progressive in the governor's seat, didn't even make a try for the office.

CHAPTER TWELVE

WARREN G. HARDING'S FATHER—FEELING THE DE-
spair with which all fathers can identify—said to his son, "Warren, it's
a good thing you wasn't born a gal. . . . You'd be in a family way all
the time. You can't say No."

By the time the 68th Congress convened in December 1923, cerebral
apoplexy had already made Harding incapable of any speech. There
was some theorizing that he had committed suicide or been poisoned
by his wife; in any event, Calvin Coolidge reigned. (As governor,
before Coolidge could get around to doing anything about the Boston
Police Strike, it "fell to pieces." Thereupon Coolidge came out defiantly
against the strikers and appeared effective against lawlessness. This
phony effectiveness brought the "sour Vermont apple" to Washington,
and his fame as vice-president had consisted in "keeping silent in
sixteen different languages.") Sandy-haired, with eyes as clear, calm
and blue as a picture postcard lake, the new President had the expression of an individual "looking down his nose to locate that evil smell
which seemed forever to affront him." To him, *no* and *yes* had the
virtue of not being overly verbose; he used them invariably in answering questions. When he received his first paycheck as president, he was
moved to volubility and even a suggestion of humor. To the bearer of
the check, he said, "Call often."

Thomas L. Blanton of Texas, who won a seat in the House by
promising the taxpayer that he would fight for less expensive funerals
for deceased House members, was tied with La Guardia for the title of
most garrulous in Congress. Of all the words La Guardia used, he felt
that *lousy* was most called-for. Once when he put it in a telegram,
Western Union asked if he would take it out, and he shouted, "No,

damn it, it's the right word!" Understandably, there were those who regarded him as noisy. His landlady in the boardinghouse on G Street disagreed with that evaluation, describing him instead as "hearty." However, she—obviously a motherly sort—liked La Guardia.

His conservative colleagues disliked him thoroughly; he was far too hearty for their taste. Still, newspaper reporters viewed him with gratitude as a "splotch of color on a gray scene." La Guardia was forever springing from one of the long padded benches in the House Chamber—which was huge and oblong—and this alone could rouse dozing congressmen beside him, but he also waved his arms frantically in order to be seen and recognized by the Speaker. La Guardia, moreover, muttered his displeasures loudly enough for those in the gallery to hear, thus amusing and informing them.

But above all else, indolent congressmen could not forgive La Guardia for his fanatical diligence. One morning at the House restaurant, he was served so promptly that some women at the next table wondered aloud about it. "Oh, I work here," La Guardia told them. "They know I have to get to work." And he always did; it was a rare day on which he was not in his seat in the House. Lunchtime found him munching peanuts, instead of having a meal, for fear that if he were not on hand some enemy of the people would slip a bill through. At night, he occupied himself with material that he'd taken home, constantly on the alert "to detect flaws, skulduggery or good points in new legislation." And he never played hooky to go to a ball game; he waited instead until Sunday to see Ruth and Lazzeri, his favorites.

As it happened, the times—and how they were handled politically—were tailor-made for La Guardia's glandular makeup, the drives of his subconscious, and all the rest of his volatile nature. In 1920 the postwar boom began to deteriorate, though former munition workers might still have their gaudily striped silk shirts and Model T's. By the following year, five million were unemployed, and it rained bankruptcies and farm foreclosures. The line on the economic graph began a tentative, uncertain rise in 1922—suggesting President Harding's cure-all, normalcy. But this statistic did not bless every individual—far from it. Among the excluded was the part owner of a haberdashery in Kansas City, Harry S. Truman. When the hard times forced him out of business, he blamed the Republicans—specifically, President Harding and Secretary of the Treasury Andrew W. Mellon, who during his first four years in office had given himself a $404,000 tax refund. In fact, Truman felt that nobody in Washington with power "gave a good goddamn what happened to people. Except for the very rich." (Because Truman was understandably incensed, he overlooked the fact that the Democratic Party, at that time, just like the Republican Party, was conservative and attentive only to the biddings of big business. La Guardia damned both parties.)

The prosperity that appeared in 1922, and was to dip and rise a few times before it plunged off the graph in '29, had a grievous flaw: a disproportionate distribution of wealth. The experts of that day stated that $2,000 equalled a living wage. A third of the nation did not earn that amount; a fifth did not make even half that amount. But unemployment was low. Some salaries, unquestionably, were high. The sale of two novelties, automobiles and radios, increased year after year. And this singular prosperity had two stimulants: a brand-new gimmick called "installment buying" and stock speculation.

President Harding could certainly not be expected to assay the prosperity of the two-plus years he spent in office. Right from the start, in his inaugural address, he spoke sentences that teetered drunkenly on the brink of meaning. In office—incredibly, inexplicably—he believed that the United States should adopt a protective tariff "as will help the struggling industries of Europe get on their feet." And though he did stop drinking, because he felt that it wasn't quite right for the president of the United States to drink when drinking was against the law, he couldn't say no—or she, Nan Britton of Marion, Ohio, couldn't— and he and she made uncomfortable love in the White House coat closet. In addition to *The President's Daughter* by Miss Britton, a bestseller revealing "six and one-half years of intimacy" and dedicated to unwed mothers everywhere, the scandal of Teapot Dome tarnished Harding's administration beyond refurbishing.

The advent of Calvin Coolidge hardly ameliorated matters. He slept at night, during the day, and at any other time the opportunity presented itself. Thus when Dorothy Parker was told of Coolidge's death, she asked how they could tell. And Will Rogers told the whole story of President Calvin Coolidge's administration in a sentence: "He didn't do anything, but that's what people wanted done."

But that was not true of all the people, not of those in the 20th District, East Harlem, who were Italian, Jewish, virtually all white. Ethnically and economically, this slum district called for progressivism, La Guardia's progressivism. At the 1924 Convention of the Progressive Party in Cleveland, La Guardia said that he was there to let them "know there are other streets and other attitudes in New York besides Wall. I speak for Avenue A and 116th Street, instead of Broad and Wall." To his way of thinking, the Progressive movement could be explained quite simply: "Exploitation, the result of favored legislation; poverty, the result of the greed of monopolies; dissatisfaction, the result of privileged government—have resulted in the alliance between the farmers, industrial producers, the believers in democracy and the true lovers of America. That is all there is to it."

But, as events proved, there was more to it than that.

The movement had to have a leader, one capable of winning the presidential election in 1924. A few years earlier, Robert Marion La Follette, the stocky, dynamic progressive Republican senator from Wisconsin, had been dead politically. His resurrection had the speed of miracles, but a causal explanation: scandals in the departments of Justice, Navy and the Interior—and elsewhere.

La Follette's uncertain health made him reluctant to accept the arduous, thankless undertaking; besides, both his wife and his physician urged him not to. And he must have felt some of the eroding frustration of another seasoned campaigner, George Norris of Nebraska, who after twenty years lamented, "It is almost impossible to obtain effective legislation in the interest of the people." From the depths, he said, "There is no way of beating it."

Eventually, La Follette felt that he simply had to make one last try at grasping the brass ring, "restoring government to the people." Though the distinguished—and distinguishing—pompadour on his leonine head was as thick as ever, age and the rigors of thirty years of crusading had turned it gray. And notwithstanding that he had every reason, like Norris, to be disillusioned and cynical, his oratory still held the emotional heat of dedication. "Fighting Bob," as an appellation, continued to fit him.

And so the campaign got under way, as moralistic as the one in 1912, in which La Guardia's hero had used the stump as a "bully pulpit." Now "cleanliness in government had been projected as the immediately transcendent issue," and what they clearly had to do was "turn the rascals out." They also formed special committees to look into all aspects of the Republican administration. One committee, for example, was to report "on the hearing in the investigation of the price of gasoline and petroleum products."

The persistent, probing ways of the Progressives struck La Guardia as "right." He had to bolt his party, he said, because "if a man does that which he knows is not right, he loses his soul; but if by doing right, he becomes 'irregular' and loses a nomination, he really has not lost much. This is 1924. The world is progressing. Times are changing. What *is* 'party regularity'? It is never urged until a party asks an individual to do something which he believes is wrong. *I would rather be right than regular!"*

The Republicans therefore picked Isaac Siegel, instead of La Guardia, as their candidate for the 20th District. Siegel, whose son Seymour would one day be sworn in by La Guardia as assistant program manager of WNYC, had been a congressman and had also once served as La Guardia's campaign manager. Now La Guardia and Siegel, two old friends, stood on opposite New York street corners and threw verbal mud at each other. When they were done for the day, La Guardia would sneak up the back stairs of Siegel's home at 104 East 116th Street to have a delicacy which he loved—Siegel's mother's gefilte fish.

Meanwhile, the Republicans chanted "Coolidge or Chaos" and "A Vote for La Follette Is a Vote Thrown Away" and "Stay Cool with Coolidge." The Democrats ran John W. Davis—conservative to the marrow, a lawyer in the employ of ogre J. P. Morgan, but a charming and cultivated individual.

Coolidge won a landslide victory; for 1924, by an economic quirk, was riding the crest of a boom. And the Progressives, it turned out, had been blinded by the effulgence of a faulty premise: the needs of the People would direct the People to utopian reform. The Progressives' sacrosanct People were in reality a collection of all-too-human grasping groups. The A. F. of L., one such group, stood for the practical, nonidealistic goal of getting "more and more—and then more." Farmers also had their feet solidly on the ground; those in Iowa summed it all up neatly: "When corn is $1.00 a bushel, the farmer is a radical; when it's $1.50 a bushel, he's a progressive; and when it's $2.00 a bushel, he's a conservative." And a farmer in upstate New York expressed essentially the same philosophy when he interrupted a speaker with a shouted "What's all that got to do with the price of hogs?"

Because the inhabitants of New York's 20th District were Progressives rather than Republicans, La Guardia won. But he found trouble lying in wait for him in the House. He, after all, had bolted the Republican Party; this unconscionable act wouldn't be forgotten quickly. To the threat of being read out of the party, La Guardia declared, "No one is going to read anyone out of any party." But there were those who felt that he had no place in the party. One said, "He is no more a Republican than the representatives of Soviet Russia are republicans." He was also spoken of as an occasional Republican; more often as a socialist—though, unlike socialists, he wanted to abolish poverty, but not private property.

Conservative Republican congressmen felt that La Guardia had to be punished for what he had done, and they punished him by keeping him off of committees. This hurt, for La Guardia had his heart set on being on the Judiciary Committee. Still, he put on an air of being undaunted, pointing out that he couldn't be kept off the Committee of the Whole House. And his enemies found out that it was impossible to silence La Guardia by denying him the floor, for he possessed a bag of assorted parliamentary tricks: "questions of personal privilege," "parliamentary inquiries," "points of order." He also had the *chutzpah* and the capacity for delivering an entire speech "as part of his statement of a single point of order"!

While battling hostile Republicans, La Guardia's personal life was no less emotional and difficult. Without funds in 1924—owing to the debts he'd incurred because of the sickness and death of his wife and child—he started *Americola*, an Italian-American newspaper. No advertisers appeared. And there were not sufficient subscribers for the newspaper to exist on that basis, and so, in short order, the publishing venture collapsed. As an economy measure, and undoubtedly to escape concrete reminders of Thea and Fioretta, La Guardia moved from the University Avenue address in the Bronx to 109th Street and Madison Avenue. But there was never complete escape from his tragedy. He received a letter—an innocent enough letter, but one that was nonetheless painful—from Dr. Vincent A. Caso, publisher of the *Bensonhurst Progress*, informing him of the birth of a daughter who had been named Thea.

"My dear Vincent," La Guardia replied. "I was so happy to receive the happy tidings. Congratulations to you both. To little Thea I send all my love and may she grow to be as charming, intelligent and lovable as was her beautiful namesake. I do hope to see her real soon. . . ."

Needing to be a father, he became one vicariously by taking Vito Marcantonio, a dark, intense boy, in hand. They had met when La Guardia had spoken to the student body of De Witt Clinton High School, having been preceded by Marcantonio, who lectured on, of all things for a youngster, old age pensions and social security. The boy wanted to be a lawyer. La Guardia therefore advised him sternly "to cut out your evening appointments, your dances, your midnight philosophers for the next five years and devote yourself to serious hard study of the law. From 1907 to 1912 I did it. . . . Be careful in your personal appearance. Get a Gillette razor and keep yourself well groomed at all times. Be always respectful and courteous to all, the humble as well as the high and for goodness' sake keep your ears and eyes open and keep your mouth closed for at least the next twenty years. Now my dear boy take this letter in the fatherly spirit that I am writing it. Keep in touch with me. . . ."

Marcantonio was to do more than that. Slight and short, he proved to be a "volcano of energy." When the Republican machine moved into La Guardia's district after its 1924 victory, he organized a machine exclusively for La Guardia. He also helped take care of the endless, varied problems of La Guardia's constituents.

At no time did La Guardia show the remorse and accompanying humility expected of him by the Republican Party. When he gave his annual report to his constituency in the spring of 1925, he struck at Coolidge by way of "President Coolidge's bad angel," Secretary of the Treasury Mellon, "small, emaciated, shy, giving the impression of being timid." He charged Mellon with embracing the twenty-fifth verse of the fourth chapter of St. Mark: "For he that hath, to him shall be given; and he that hath not, from him shall be taken even that which he hath."

In other, nonbiblical words, La Guardia abhorred Mellon's proposed tax reduction plan. "Something is wrong with the economic system of a country," he said, "when the Chief Executive of that country in his Message, asks for charity for dependent widows and orphans; and his Secretary of the Treasury asks for a bill to repeal taxes on incomes of $5,000,000 a year. . . ."

The basic rules of practical politics dictated wariness, ambiguities, a subtle—if not blatant—wooing of the Republican Party, in order that La Guardia retain his congressional seat in 1926. Instead, he ridiculed "Coolidge prosperity" on the floor of the House, with a charade concerning the high price of meat. "Why, I have right here with me now—where is it? Oh, yes, here it is in my vest pocket." He pulled a meagre, pathetic chop out of that pocket and held it up. "30¢ worth of lamb. . . ." From another pocket he produced "$1.75 worth of steak." And from still another pocket he drew a minuscule roast valued at three dollars—a prohibitive price to the average wage earner. "Now, gentlemen, we simply have to eat. We have formed the habit. Whether it is a good or bad habit, I need not discuss. We want the people in the city to live up to the American standard. That standard is easily definable, and it includes good and sufficient nourishment. I remember when I was a kid, out in Arizona, we enjoyed an American breakfast; ham and eggs, bread and butter. These are luxuries in New York City today. We want to restore the American breakfast to the children of this age!"

With equal verve and creativity, La Guardia fought a long-drawn-out war against Prohibition. To bring beer back to the people, La Guardia dramatized the absurdity of the Volstead Act. He announced that he would appear at 9:00 A.M. on June 17, 1926, in Kaufman's Drugstore, 95 Lenox Avenue, and demonstrate that by mixing two legal drinks, malt extract and near-beer, one could produce an illegal beverage. He would then drink what he had made and wait to be arrested. Almost everything went as planned. Dressed in business suit and fedora, La Guardia created his illegal drink at Kaufman's soda fountain and—with a flourish—drank it, but no officer would contribute to his publicity act by arresting him. (The skyrocketing sales of malt tonic and malt extract were one tangible result of La Guardia's performance.)

All his anti-Prohibition tactics drew support to him from Wet members of Congress who two years earlier had ostracized him. As the leader of these Wets, he proclaimed, "I believe God Almighty when He made grapes intended that grapes should be enjoyed by all of the people. And I don't vote that He intended [that] grapes be made into jelly. Prohibition will be a success when Congress by an act or by a law will be able to stop fermentation, or to repeal the law of gravity."

The Drys, too, had an article of faith: effective enforcement, through severe laws that would serve as deterrents. This stand even had the backing of a Viennese biologist, who must actually have believed in the inheritance of acquired characteristics, because he maintained that "future generations of Americans will be born without any desire for liquor if Prohibition is continued and strictly enforced."

La Guardia had his opportunity to get revenge, just one year after his 1924 misbehavior, by turning down the requests of Republican candidates in New York City elections for his support. And when it was suggested that he run for mayor as an independent, he unhesitatingly said no and predicted—accurately, as it turned out—that

Tammany-backed James J. Walker would win and that Walker's administration would be of an "everybody-getting-his" sort. Obviously unrepentant for having bolted the party, La Guardia backed the Socialist candidate, Norman Thomas.

In continuing to fight Prohibition, he embarrassed the administration with his incessant help—reporting violations and lobbying for ludicrous additions to the enforcement budget. "In order to enforce Prohibition," he said, "it will require a police force of 250,000 men and a force of 250,000 to police the police."

And enforcement must be fair. He pointed this out when an agent was discharged, after seizing liquor in the home of Hugo Gilbert de Fritsch, a member of a socially prominent family. "I want to determine," he said on the floor of the House, "if there is to be one sort of enforcement for the rich and another for the poor. Whether it is necessary for an enforcement agent to carry a Social Register along with the Statutes of the United States in enforcing the law in New York City? I am informed that the liquor was returned with apologies. . . ."

The government, La Guardia found, was involved in an even more astounding way, was actually operating a speakeasy, the Bridge-Whist Club, at 14 East 44th Street in New York, and agents were also selling liquor in Norfolk, Virginia, and Elizabeth City, North Carolina. "Beer is flowing as fast," La Guardia said, "as the law of gravitation will permit."

Although in warring against Prohibition, La Guardia again gained power in Congress, he did not limit his battles to that arena. Censorship—of all kinds—raised his hackles. He regarded it as the "handmaid of oppression," as "an agency for the prevention of thought." Films should be free of it; this meant that kissing on the screen should go right on unabated. "If more husbands would learn from the stage and the pictures just how to kiss, and then go home and practice on their wives, there would be happier homes and fewer divorces."

The Ku Klux Klan, sanctifiers of chastity, viewed kissing as the first step to fornication, as un-American; and the Klan—which in 1921 had grown to a membership of over half a million—hated La Guardia with a tar-and-feather-party hate.

In declaring why Americans—white and Protestant—should not vote for him, the Klan said, "He is a member of the Sons of Italy, and boasts the friendship for the Jewish immigrant. He thinks more of keeping the bars down for the Jews and Italians to come in, than to keep America for Americans. He bolted the Republican Party and has cast his lot with the Socialists." But the Klan failed to mention—surely from ignorance and not oversight—that La Guardia's mother was Jewish, that La Guardia had said of congressmen who worked to unite immigrant families, "Whether St. Peter is a *goi* [goy] or a Roman Catholic, he'll let them into Heaven for that."

La Guardia opposed immigration legislation whose object was to cut off the flow of immigrants from southern and eastern Europe. To a congressman who took pride in having ancestors who came over on the *Mayflower*, La Guardia said, "I hope you can understand my pride when I say the distinguished navigator of the race of my ancestors came to this continent two hundred years before yours landed at Plymouth Rock." And he had a ready retort for one who maligned his ancestry: "For every year by which your ancestors preceded mine to this country, mine can boast an additional century of civilization."

With the advent of 1926, La Guardia sent a letter to Secretary of Labor James J. Davis concerning Countess Vera Cathcart, who was "attractive, dark-eyed, vivacious and twenty-eight," and also an alien in trouble. La Guardia came to Countess Cathcart's defense, for being "detained at Ellis Island and ordered excluded" because she had "committed adultery with one William George Bradley, 5th Earl of Craven, who arrived in the United States on the S.S. *Belgenland*, November 20, 1925, now living in New York City. Clearly, if the Countess Vera Cathcart is excluded as a person having committed an act involving moral turpitude, so must be the said William George Bradley, with whom she is charged with misconduct. . . ." After all, "we have but one standard of morals in this country. . . ."

While holding on to this single standard, La Guardia made quixotic forays on George W. English, a federal judge, who as a really big offender had been given special consideration and who had the audacity to resign. For some time, La Guardia had fought to have Judge English impeached because of "improper administrations in bankruptcy cases." He felt the judge had no business resigning, because he should be impeached and brought to trial, so that justice could be done.

And now that 1926 had arrived and had put La Guardia in a highly critical mood, he took a good look at the men in New York who called themselves Progressives and, as one might expect, he didn't like what he saw. "Just because a man cannot get a political job with one of the two old parties," he said, "does not necessarily make him a Progressive." Eventually, he announced that this time he would run for Congress as an independent.

Inasmuch as La Guardia had gone out of his way to harass Republican regulars by insult, condescension, radicalism—even going so far as to propose the nationalization of coal and oil—it would seem the Republican Party would have taken his announcement with a sigh of relief. Instead, they picked him as their nominee. And he, as unpredictable as ever, accepted. (Patently, the Republican leaders had made this seemingly inexplicable move "to increase the Republican vote in the Harlem section of Manhattan and to bring about the election of one more Republican representative from New York City.")

It was rumored—strenuously maintained by some—that in return for the nomination and victory, La Guardia was going to back Coolidge policies. His behavior denied this. On the floor of the House, he vowed, he would continue to "fight against special privilege."

Then on Coolidge's fourth anniversary as president, reticence and reason having momentarily forsaken him, he announced, "I do not choose to run for President in 1928." Thus Herbert Hoover became the candidate of the Republican Party, and La Guardia's new target. (La Guardia, in turn, was put on the blacklist of the D.A.R. and the Key Men of America, a list of those "considered so subversive that they were to be banned from speaking at meetings of the two organizations throughout the country." Forthwith, the *Nation* threw a blacklist party for all those on the blacklist, which included Rabbi Stephen S. Wise, Felix Frankfurter and Clarence Darrow. Many, certain of their eligibility, were disappointed that they hadn't made the blacklist and therefore couldn't go to the party. Heywood Broun, whose "It Seems To Me" column never pussyfooted, was "incensed" to have been omitted.)

Much psychological profundity might be extracted from the way Hoover's hat rested squarely on his head, without so much as a suggestion of frivolous tilt, and the precise positioning of the man's head on stiff, wide collar. But La Guardia's antipathy drew sustenance from substance rather than appearance, and from epic pronouncements such as the one "the Great Engineer, the Great Administrator, the Great Humanitarian, the Great Idealist" made on August 12, 1928, in accepting the Republican nomination: "We in America today are nearer to the final triumph over poverty than ever before in the history of any land."

CHAPTER THIRTEEN

FOUR MONTHS AFTER HERBERT HOOVER EXPRESSED
great hopes for the country's economic future, La Guardia experienced a lightning flash of realization that illumined his future with joy.

It happened during the course of working very late one wintry December evening with Marie Fischer, who had been his devoted and admiring secretary for twelve years. While routinely shouting at her for misplacing some figures, it occurred to him that it was almost midnight and she hadn't eaten dinner. Just as in the cliché, he noticed her for the first time *as a woman*—and not merely as a secretary. He told her to go home, that they would finish the work the next day. But no sooner had she left, than he found himself running after her, calling her name as he ran.

She wanted to know what was wrong, when he caught up with her, and he shouted, "Marie, you're fired!"

"Why, Major, you don't mean—"

"I mean it. How can I court a girl that works for me?"

They were married the morning of Thursday, February 28, in La Guardia's home, 1633 Q Street N.W., by Representative O. J. Kvale of Minnesota, a Lutheran minister who had defeated Andrew J. Volstead for Congress in 1920 with the slogan "Drier than Volstead." La Guardia's best man was John M. Morin of Pennsylvania, chairman of the House Committee on Military Affairs; Marie's maid of honor was Mrs. Ray Tucker, wife of the Washington correspondent of the *New York Telegram*.

Immediately after the ceremony—instead of rushing off on a honeymoon—forty-seven-year-old La Guardia and his thirty-three-year-old bride headed for the House.

At twelve noon, the business of the House started with a prayer by Rev. James Shera Montgomery, D.D., in which God was entreated to bless the motives of those present and "make them chaste and pure."

Remarks were read into the Record on the achievements of the Baptist Young People's Union of the Fifth Avenue Baptist Church of Huntington, West Virginia.

Mr. Norton of Nebraska spoke for fifteen minutes, all of his allotted time, on "the farm problem."

La Guardia broke into the proceedings occasionally—his mind clamped on the business at hand, in spite of his having just been married. During a conference report on a naval appropriation bill, he pointed out that "on every contract that has been given for a battleship or a cruiser to private yards the contractor has come in for an increased amount of money after the contract has been awarded." (Obviously, marriage had not—as yet—mellowed him.)

To mollify La Guardia, he was told that the increase in cost was due simply to a change in construction plans.

Always on the alert for shenanigans, La Guardia asked, "Is it not true that, as a matter of fact, when a private yard finds itself in difficulty on account of underestimating, changes are made so as to get around the estimate or bid?"

But this customary wariness did not explain his presence; being in the House on his wedding day required this more compelling reason: Senate Bill 2901, to amend the national prohibition act so that possession of intoxicating liquor made one subject to five years in prison and a $10,000 fine—a bill which came to be known, with possibly the affection of a diminutive, as the 5 and 10 Bill.

Though marriage may not have suddenly mellowed La Guardia, it had put him in high good spirits. He produced laughter when he said that if he were recognized in opposition to the bill, he would "send forth his best guns and his heaviest artillery."

His armament proved inadequate; the yeas had it over the nays, 284 to 90.

Just before adjournment, late, in the early evening, Representative Boylan of New York said, "Mr. Speaker, I desire to make a very important announcement to the House, and with the permission of the Speaker I will make it; and that is that our distinguished colleague from New York, Representative La Guardia, was married to-day."

Applause caused Boylan to pause.

"Our ministerial colleague, the gentleman from Minnesota, Mr.

Kvale, tied the knot, and I move you, sir, that the felicitations of the House be extended to the happy couple."

More applause. And through it, Speaker Nicholas Longworth said, "It is carried unanimously."

Seated in the private gallery, Mrs. La Guardia beamed as the House continued to applaud her husband and members crowded around him to congratulate him.

The announcement of the La Guardia wedding was followed by Mr. Abernethy's remarks on a contemplated historical pageant at New Bern, North Carolina.

Finally, Mr. Tilson moved that the House adjourn. It did at "6 o'clock and 39 minutes P.M."

As Mr. and Mrs. La Guardia left, girl secretaries surrounded them and offered their congratulations. La Guardia grinned and, with mock, exaggerated regret, said, "Sorry I can't marry all of you."

The newlyweds didn't go off on a honeymoon the next day; La Guardia was back in the House speaking in favor of a Nicaragua canal: "a real agency for bringing the people of the world closer together and, therefore, being a greater agency for peace." And on the following day, a Saturday, he rose in the House "to formally impeach Francis A. Winslow, a Federal judge of the southern district of New York . . . and here charge him with the commission of high crimes and misdemeanors as herein set forth." La Guardia then requested "immediate reference of this resolution to the Committee on the Judiciary of the House."

It wasn't until the session of Congress ended that Fiorello and Marie left for Panama and a honeymoon.

Always in La Guardia's thought was the tragic death of his wife and child—and in 1921, the year of that tragedy, he had also been cheated out of the mayoralty nomination. He was determined that 1929 would be different. He hadn't achieved New York City's highest office with Thea; he would with Marie.

One could serve too long in the House, he felt, reach a point when the "piddling little department errands and office chores" became more than just irritants. And your tiny little office in the House Office Building, made even smaller by files, desks, frenzied activity, eventually gave you the claustrophobic jitters. No wonder—all things considered —really good men quit the House in disgust or moved up to the Senate. In the Senate, at least, you were one of 96, instead of one in

435, and could accomplish more. But as mayor of New York City, you were it, *the one*. So he'd had the dubious record of offering more amendments than any other congressman. So he had seen some of his bills pass after long years of struggle. ("I tell you it's damned discouraging trying to be a reformer in the wealthiest land in the world.") So he might puff smugly on a two-for-a-nickel cigar and say, quite glibly, "The function of a progressive is to keep on protesting"—prohibition, child labor, power monopolies, and a national sales tax—"until things get so bad that a reactionary demands reform." Granted there was pleasure in battling on the floor of the House—for "old age pensions, national unemployment insurance, employer liability laws, government operation of Muscle Shoals"—but that joy in conflict wasn't enough . . . .

James "Jimmy" J. Walker had served a term as mayor; he, too, was dissatisfied. The thought of continuing in that capacity—even as "Jimmy the Jester," "Our Jazz Mayor," "Playboy of City Hall"—didn't appeal to him. The second-highest office in the land, he had learned from experience, kept one from being a thoroughgoing, unrestrained hedonist.

Just before running for mayor of New York City in 1925, the Gentleman Jimmy style of life had also been a problem. Al Smith, a mighty power in Tammany, wouldn't support a giddy, fun-loving Walker, and so Walker—to make Smith change his mind—stopped frequenting night spots and saw to it that when the press took his picture, his wife stood lovingly by his side. (All this would have been utterly impossible if it hadn't been for a penthouse on West 58th Street, donated by an understanding friend, in which Walker was able to whoop it up clandestinely.)

The day came when Smith asked Walker how he had been able to achieve such a complete transformation.

"We all grow up sometime," Walker answered, straight-faced.

"You've proved that you can rise to the occasion. I've checked up on you, Jim. I've decided to approve your candidacy."

As soon as Walker received this blessing from Smith, he raced to the penthouse—as to an oasis—told his friend that "virtue is its own reward," and opened a magnum of champagne to celebrate.

The apparent change in Walker, which had hoodwinked Al Smith, was also responsible for the apprehensive speculation that Jimmy, once in office, would become dignified and reserved, weighed down with the responsibility of guiding a city that spent almost a million and a half dollars a day. That Jimmy might, in horrendous fact, become a bore like Hylan, his predecessor.

This fear proved unfounded, for Walker managed with the greatest of ease to be mayor and have his fun, too. Almost every day a brass band blared in front of City Hall and Sartorially Splendid Jimmy—wearing spats, unusual light-gray spats—welcomed "a (more or less) distinguished visitor." And because he believed, as did President Calvin Coolidge, that the best government was one that governed least, he felt obliged not to drop in at City Hall until around noon and still leave early, making use of the slightest excuse for quitting work for the day.

When he was late for an appointment—and he usually was—he would pass his lateness off with a grin and a cheery "Well, late as usual." Those who had been fuming while waiting for him found the chilly reception they'd prepared melt rapidly in the warmth of his irresistible personality.

A big event in Walker's life happened at the opening of the musical *Oh, Kay!* on November 8, 1926. When he went backstage to see Gertrude Lawrence, who was in the show, he met Betty Compton —dimpled, with black bobbed hair and large brown eyes. In his midforties, he was twice her age. Since she didn't respond to his unfailingly effective charm, this intensified his interest.

Finally, to relieve his heartache, because he had made very little headway with the beautiful Miss Compton, he went off to Europe on the *Berengaria* with his unsuspecting wife and an extensive wardrobe: "forty-four suits of clothes, twenty white pique vests, twelve pairs of fancy striped white trousers, six topcoats, one hundred cravats, shirts by the dozens, and a basketful of shoes. . . ."

Unlike Miss Compton, Europe could not resist him or his obvious diplomatic flattery. He informed each city he visited that it was the greatest. In France, he observed, "It's not hard to understand the French people if you have an ear for music." He did not hesitate to use his favorite wisecracks more than once: "This meal is the best I have yet drunk." And he enjoyed telling the American tourists whom he met that they were "fellow refugees from the 18th Amendment."

Upon his return—it was as though he had needed the trip to come to a marital decision—he separated from his wife, moving his comprehensive wardrobe into the Ritz.

Walker made no pretense of concealing his attachment to Betty

Compton, appearing brazenly with her in public. The word reached Al Smith and, as a good Catholic and politician, he did not like it. After all, he had been responsible for Walker's nomination. But he didn't want to make a break with Walker, for in his coming race for the presidency, he wanted Walker to campaign for him. So in public, Smith acted as though Walker were the finest human being extant, and Walker proclaimed that Smith would definitely be the next president of the United States.

Jimmy feared that if Al won in '28, Tammany might ask him to be governor—and as a Tammany stalwart, he couldn't—wouldn't—refuse. So he might very well end up an inconvenient distance from New York City and its sensual pleasures. The Man with the Brown Derby, however, lost, receiving only 15,000,000 popular votes to Hoover's 21,500,000; not only was Smith a Catholic and a Wet, but voters had come to like the Republican prosperity-oriented philosophy.

The Happy Warrior—somewhat unhappy now and shorn of considerable power—told Walker why he shouldn't run for a second term, giving numerous reasons, but failing, noticeably, to mention Miss Compton.

Walker demanded to know why Smith was beating around the bush, why he didn't come right out with the real reason: Mayor Jimmy Walker had a girl—and, at the same time, a wife. Angered, Walker told Smith he hadn't intended to run—because he was fed up with living in a fishbowl—but now, by God, he would go for the office.

A man who prided himself on his impeccable taste, Walker knew he could not possibly announce he was running for reelection. Finesse dictated that he must be asked to continue in office. And so he and his police commissioner, Grover Whalen, cold-bloodedly—but in high good humor—arranged for over six hundred bipartisan notables to appear at City Hall and entreat their mayor to run again.

On July 18, as prearranged, the Citizens Committee packed the chamber of the Board of Estimate, and "voices and sound" were broadcast from 12:00 to 1:00 P.M. over WEAF and WOR. It was fervently desired, so the committee revealed, that Walker run so that he might "complete the unsurpassed constructive program of public improvements which is now under way." They also let it be known that Walker "had worked diligently for the happiness and welfare of the people." Perhaps what they had in mind was Walker's having restored boxing to New York City, and having given it Sunday baseball. (On that very day, however, William H. Allen, the director of the

Institute for Public Service, asked Governor Franklin Delano Roosevelt to remove Walker from office, charging Walker with prodigiously wasteful neglect, inefficiency, broken pledges, false official publicity, misspending, overtaxing, unfair assessing, encouraging of graft, etc., etc. Also on that very day, William Bullock, chairman of the city affairs bureau of the Republican County Committee, charged Walker with paying out $26,207,590 for contracts during his three and a half years in office without competitive bidding.)

While the petitioners in the Board of Estimate chamber were running out of fulsome praise for Walker, the object of their exuberance and his advisors were wrestling with a dilemma in his office. If Walker said yes to the Committee's entreaty that he run again, it would appear that he was ignoring Tammany, which had the final say. No wouldn't do either.

Walker's slim, boyish, 132-pound figure moved with nervous restlessness; under the pressure, his sharp blue eyes became even more intense, and his quizzical eyebrows urgently sought an answer.

He had been on a spot, too, in his very first political after-dinner speech, because he had been preceded by an extremely able and witty speaker. Nervous to the point of trembling, he told his audience that he would have been far better off if he had spoken first. "But we can't all be first," he continued. "Even the first President of this country wasn't first in everything. He was first in peace, first in war, and first in the hearts of his countrymen. But, gentlemen, he married a widow." This caused everyone present to burst out laughing, and Walker no longer had the problem of winning his audience.

Now Walker knew that he could no longer keep the crowd in the Board of Estimate chamber waiting. As he headed decisively for the door, one of his advisors told him plaintively, "But you can't go without knowing what you're going to say—"

An ovation greeted Walker. He started his talk by reviewing his four years in office, four years that he said had been a great adventure. He told his listeners a budget should not be figured in dollars and cents, but in what it provided for the people.

He talked on and on, but he did not give the committee the answer it wanted to hear. As a consequence, the committee became as apprehensive as Walker's advisors. They heard their Jimmy refer feelingly to his father, who, little more than sixty years ago, had arrived at Castle Garden as an immigrant from Castlecomer, Ireland, a penniless immigrant, and now his son was mayor of the greatest city in the world. But this also was not what they had come to hear.

Finally Walker said, "Ladies and gentlemen, you have come to me, six hundred of the most influential citizens in our city to ask me to run again for Mayor. And my answer is—'Who could say no?'"

On the same day that Walker was being petitioned to run, the New York Republican Club gave a dinner in La Guardia's honor at Town Hall. La Guardia used the occasion to point out, by easily-arrived-at inferences, that he was *the* man who could defeat Tammany's James J. Walker. Even before the dinner, he had said as much. He had just arrived in New York from Little Rock, Arkansas, where he—at his wife's insistence—had gone for a much-needed rest and where he had had his tonsils removed. "I feel in shape now for anything," he exclaimed. Anything was Walker. "And I'm even tempted to take on Max Schmeling." By Schmeling, he, of course, meant Tammany. (Schmeling, who resembled Dempsey, teutonically, had fought twice in the United States and was being groomed for the big money.)

Pushing metaphors aside, La Guardia told his audience in clear, simple prose that amateurs could not beat Tammany. He went on to explain that the person selected to run had to know his "city government," and also his "political onions." As for the cry that some candidates—by which he meant himself—would not do because they couldn't get enough campaign money, he said, "I know of no better recommendation for any candidate. Large contributions have been the curse of American politics. Any candidate who can be elected to office only by reason of large contributions given with expectation of returns cannot give the people of this city a fair, constructive, honest administration."

Then La Guardia tore into Walker's much-lauded civic improvements, revealing that it had taken Walker's administration three and a half years to find the plans of previous administrations in the files. Everything was still in the blueprint stage. He therefore observed that "you can't move families now crowded in unsanitary tenements into a blueprint and you can't cross rivers on an engineer's drawings." The only improvement Walker could point to with pride "is the funny-looking octagon caps forced upon the heads of the Police Department." But the Police Department itself was in bad shape—not because of the funny-looking caps, but because of "funny business at the top."

Unlike Walker, La Guardia faced extremely high hurdles between him and the nomination. The "rabidly dry and Nordic" detested the Wet Wop. Conservative, rich, influential Republicans viewed him with

119

discomfort, as a bit to the left. (La Guardia had them in mind when he said, "As long as a person talks about great American standards he is applauded; when he asks to put them into practice he is a radical.") And Republicans in New York City, of all persuasions, were greatly outnumbered by Democrats. However, La Guardia did have the allegiance of the rank and file, might "gain heavily in some normally strong Democratic districts" and—early in the game—appeared to have the Progressive vote.

In spite of these pluses, and with the August 1 convention just weeks away, the Republicans were completely at sea as to which of the five possible candidates they should pick. Finally the field narrowed to La Guardia and Congresswoman Ruth Pratt. Though Mrs. Pratt had supporters who felt she would make it difficult for Walker because of her knowledge of city affairs and the widespread attention her attacks on his regime would receive, her influential friends took the stand that the time wasn't yet right for a woman candidate to be successful in a mayoralty race.

Like La Guardia, Mrs. Pratt was a representative from a New York City District, but her district encompassed opulent Park Avenue. Her money, millions, had flowed from Pratt Standard Oil. Tall, subdued but expensively dressed, she had fire and wit—facets of her independence. These traits were in evidence when, two years earlier, she had been on the Board of Aldermen, a lone woman among sixty-four males. She evaluated these male colleagues as undeserving of their five-thousand-dollar salaries. If they had been, they would have done something about the million dollars of waste which was an integral part of the annual budget. She concluded that men—these men, at any rate—were simply poor housekeepers. And when they paid her the compliment of smoking and swearing in her presence, but in a restrained, gentlemanly manner, she confessed she was tempted to join them in these "sedatives for frayed nerves. But my fellow aldermen are not yet, it is to be feared, advanced enough to view any such action except with alarm."

The chance that this capable, personable woman might receive the nomination caused La Guardia to recall how he had been tricked in 1921. He therefore met with Republican leaders—with blood in his eye and a plot up his sleeve.

"I am refusing to be the goat," he told them. "You intend to nominate Mrs. Pratt. You expect that I will then split the Party and so provide you with an alibi for a defeat which you all know is certain.

You think that you will then blame it all on La Guardia. Well, you can't."

They wouldn't be able to, he explained, because he wouldn't bolt. Instead, he would wait until the following year, until they nominated a governor. Then he would tell the voters how they had "refused to give the nomination to the only man who has ever been successful in defeating Tammany on a straight ticket." This revelation would defeat their choice for governor.

Then La Guardia said, with ultimatum emphasis: "Now, choose."

The stratagem worked. And on the night of August 1, in New York's Byzantine, ornate Mecca Temple, Mrs. Ruth Pratt's name was withdrawn and "with fixed smiles and synthetic cheers the delegates told this maverick of the herd that he might go forth against Tammany Hall." They told him this though they thought him impossible, "a Socialist, a foe of Prohibition, a menace to Americanism, common, vulgar and undisciplined."

Unlike Walker, who responded to his virtual nomination with the convoluted "Who could say no?" La Guardia merely said, "I accept the nomination."

The next day, La Guardia went to work, setting up headquarters in the Hotel Cadillac at 42nd and Broadway—in an inadequate suite because of meager funds. He labored as though he were intent on undoing his recuperative stay in Little Rock. Wherever and whenever he could find an audience, he talked—in Yiddish to Jews; in Italian to Italians; in the King's English, and in his own brand of English—as the occasion required.

At first, he concentrated on matters close to those who lived in the slums: housing, parks, the high cost of food. At no time, however, did he overlook the corruption and crime of the Walker administration. He produced a check signed by the murdered Arnold Rothstein which indicated a tie-in between the gangster and Tammany; he also brought forth proof that Magistrate Vitale of the Bronx had "borrowed" $19,940 from Rothstein.

In late August, in a speech at the Italian-American Club, 235 First Avenue, La Guardia claimed that Police Commissioner Grover Whalen had juggled facts and figures to conceal the true state of crime in New York City, had kept as quiet as possible about various murder cases.

In the course of denying Whalen's assertion that organized gambling did not exist in the city, La Guardia paused and asked, "What street are we on?"

"Fourteenth Street," a voice replied.

"Why, I can take you to a crap game less than 200 feet from here. And the bosses of Tammany Hall know it. I'll give you details later in the campaign."

And he did give audiences all sorts of details. But though informing the public was important, he also needed the monetary support of his party and the verbal, day-in and day-out backing of the press—and he received neither. Wealthy Republicans gave La Guardia token, verbal support after his nomination, and only that, merely out of loyalty to the party. The Citizens Union couldn't see La Guardia as a reformer. The tremendous influence of Hearst went to Walker. And in spite of the fact that the *Nation*, which reached those intellectually superior to Hearst's journalism, had many good things to say about La Guardia— "independence, courage, true liberalism, and an honesty of utterance and purpose"—it concluded that he was "not of the same stature as Norman Thomas." Thus the *Nation* split the Progressive vote—neatly, irrevocably.

It appeared that these reversals failed to touch La Guardia's confidence. In seven campaigns, after all, he had come out gloriously on top. And he kept recalling, with narcissistic relish, that in 1919 he had won the presidency of the Board of Aldermen by 1,600 votes and that that had been the first citywide Republican victory since 1901.

As for the betting odds, they didn't bother him in the least. "There is a long shot winning in Saratoga every day," he reminded all who would listen. "There is one thing I know how to do and that is to beat Tammany Hall."

Taking their cue from him, La Guardia's followers bravely sang:

> Seven times he's won elections,
> Seven times he's reached the top.
> He is proud he's an American
> And he's proud he is a Wop!

But as election day loomed ever larger, La Guardia—aware of certain, inescapable facts—became overwrought, desperate. He fired an aide for echoing what must have been tormentingly in his own thoughts: that he couldn't win.

Because he feared defeat, he snapped at Walker's heels with extraneous personal matters, rather than continuing to express valid charges. Walker, he said, dressed like an "English fop," had an autographed picture of the Prince of Wales in his apartment—in short, was an anglophile.

Unruffled, campaigning in the most casual manner, Walker—who wore neither belt nor braces, but supported his trousers with special tabs sewn to his waistcoat because this arrangement ruled out creases —simply had to answer La Guardia on the subject of clothes. He told La Guardia, "If I thought I might serve the taxpayers better by appearing at City Hall clad in overalls"—that attire would have been torture, the supreme sacrifice of a public servant—"or even a snood, I should do so. But until we have an ordinance to the contrary, I shall bathe frequently, as is my custom; and change my linen often, as is perhaps my eccentric desire; and patronize the tailor of my choice."

La Guardia harped on corruption—graft was everywhere, involving pushcart peddlers, the Street Cleaning Department, Queens sewers . . .

Good-naturedly, Walker asked, "Can anyone expect me to keep my good-nature in this campaign? I refuse to go any further than the gutter. I will not go down in a sewer." (Judge Samuel Seabury would and did, the very next year, in following the trail of municipal corruption.)

La Guardia wanted to know what Walker had to say about Tammany's easing of tax assessments on Untermyer, Heckscher, Rockefeller, et al.

Always cool, Walker asked La Guardia why he had left Bridgeport, Connecticut, on June 1, 1929.

La Guardia answered, with a show of vast impatience, that he hadn't been in Bridgeport in fifteen years.

How cleverly, Walker pointed out, has he denied having been in Bridgeport last June.

"What does he say happened on the June first I am alleged to have been in Bridgeport?" La Guardia wanted to know.

Walker said he wasn't interested in questions, but in an answer. He felt that it was obvious that La Guardia "does not dare to tell the voters why he left Bridgeport."

After the election, La Guardia asked Walker what he had meant by that whole Bridgeport business.

Walker said, "Nothing, Fiorello, nothing at all. I don't know whether you've ever been in Bridgeport. But it worked, didn't it?"

It most certainly had—it and Walker's "charm, wit and handshaking" and the postwar period and all of its psychological ramifications;

for Walker was voted back into office with an overwhelming 865,000 votes to La Guardia's 368,000 and Thomas's 175,000.

Marie tried to comfort her husband. If she had had foreknowledge, she could have told him that just two weeks before the election—with the arrival of the Crash—and also a few weeks after the election—with the charges of corruption that La Guardia had made having been sustained—forces were set in motion that would give him a far better try at the mayoralty the next time around.

CHAPTER FOURTEEN

LA GUARDIA RETURNED TO THE HOUSE, WHERE—IN his opinion—you fought and seldom won, but curiously remained undefeated. You found yourself fighting for fighting's sake, when objectives were clearly unattainable. It was also the importance of a goal that kept you swinging, refusing to give up, drawing zest from a martyr's heroism.

The main battle now focused on poverty; even skirmishes with Prohibition were part of that battle, for the vast expenditures to achieve enforcement—in a land writhing from need—smacked of stupidity and sin. Poverty, of course, had always been a part of the hedonistic twenties; then, seven months after Hoover's inauguration, the Crash occurred.

But a preternatural optimism filled the air, and more than one optimist predicted recovery within sixty days. Being a humorist, Will Rogers noticed this euphoria and felt obliged to observe that optimism was more talked of and less practiced than at any time in history. Vaudeville theatres did their part by forbidding jokes on stage about either the Depression or President Hoover, because the humor tended to be black. (Tall man: "What? You say business is better?" Short man: "Sure is." Tall man: "You mean Hoover died?" And, of course, a "Hoover flag" couldn't be flown at half-mast. How fly an empty pocket turned inside out?) And while all this was going on, Mrs. Hoover, who called her husband "Daddy," prescribed that one be friendly and neighborly with those who had had bad luck, and her husband, perhaps because he had become an orphan at the age of eight, valued "a wealth of human sympathy" and "the precious warmth of a friendly hand." Though shy, quiet and programed for efficiency, her husband told crooner Rudy Vallee, "Well, if you can sing a song that would make people forget their troubles and the Depression, I'll give you a medal."

Surprisingly, Adolf A. Berle Jr.—a solid, no-nonsense lawyer with a considerable talent for economic analysis—saw a scientific, cause-and-effect sequence in all this manufactured good cheer. If people laughed, they could not at the same time be afraid of losing their jobs; and being unafraid, they would spend money which, in turn, would keep the factories going and employment up.

As it so happened, smiles-and-heads-held-high economics failed to produce the desired results. Therefore, instead of being "friendly and neighborly," some went so far as to speak ill of President Herbert Clark Hoover; they charged that the great mining engineer had, in short order, "drained, ditched and damned the United States." (When Hoover was in his eighties, Justice Earl Warren recalled this animosity and said, "But now, Mr. President, everyone loves you. How come?" Hoover answered, "I outlived the bastards.")

Such bitterness merely aggravated the petulance in Hoover's makeup. Before becoming president, the first from west of the Mississippi, Hoover had never held an elective office; this might explain why he didn't know that accommodation was an invaluable political tool. On the other hand, Franklin Delano Roosevelt—not shackled by one set of economic principles—would say in 1932, "It is common sense to take a method and try it. If it fails, admit it frankly and try another. But above all, try something." This objective stemmed from compassion, for on another occasion he pointed out, "Let's concentrate upon one thing—save the people and the nation and, if we have to change our minds twice every day to accomplish that end, we should do it." Come what may, Hoover maintained and believed with all his heart that a balanced budget should be held inviolate, that something as crass as federal aid would upset this delicate monetary equilibrium. To do his personal bit in keeping the budget balanced, he cut his $75,000 salary to $60,000.

For the President's benefit, Edward F. McGrady of the American Federation of Labor told a Senate committee, "There are another two B's beside balancing the Budget, and that is to provide bread and butter." And, as events proved, more than a buttered staff of life was at stake. "Viewed in retrospect," John Kenneth Galbraith observed, in commenting on a balanced budget, "it would be hard to imagine a better design for reducing both the private and the public demands for goods, aggravating deflation, increasing unemployment, and adding to the general suffering."

The President insisted intransigently that aid must be viewed as a private and local matter. With a forensic ring and personal passion, La Guardia declared that hunger crossed state lines and thus its alleviation was a federal, rather than a state, county, or municipal, duty. For the country to open its treasury and provide charity, Hoover argued, would be to damage the self-reliance and initiative of its citizens.

Such platitudes, presented as axioms; the verbose emptiness of sociology; and charts and graphs and columns of figures—the lifeblood of political scientists—could not obscure the specific, individual instances of poverty. In a Brooklyn clothing factory, fifteen-year-old girls were paid six cents an hour, $2.78 a week, for sponging pants. Farm laborers, in 1933, received $1.11 daily—as though to give the lie, by a mere eleven cents, to that old saw "a dollar a day is a white man's pay." But they worked, earned something. Obviously, worse off were those who did nothing and had no income. In a small Illinois town, population 1,350, only two men had a job. And when 750 were needed to do the hard, dirty, thoroughly unappetizing work of digging a canal by hand—for two dollars for a ten-hour day—12,000 eager individuals applied. (As always, the unemployed were accused of not wanting to work. One to two million of them, it was said, enjoyed roaming about the country in boxcars and getting handouts at kitchen doors from softhearted housewives. No wonder these transients sang a bitter song: ". . . You wonder why I'm a hobo and why I sleep in the ditch. / Well, it ain't because I'm lazy; no, I just don't want to be rich.")

Even industrialists suffered—in ways peculiar to their station. One of them not only had to cut his employees' wages, but wrote his two divorced wives, to whom he was paying alimony, "Owing to business conditions, I regret. . . ." Another made a drastic cut in the wages of his employees with heartless—and undoubtedly sardonic—encouragement: "They should be able to get along on 2¢ a meal." Among the more compassionate, a midwestern manufacturer went off to Europe on a big, opulent liner, explaining that he did this to get away from "answering phone calls from people in need of help which we couldn't render, of seeing our well-to-do friends go broke, of feeling our purse strings tighten."

La Guardia and Hoover had different approaches, different attitudes; Hoover thought of humanity as an abstract quality instead of a collection of highly differentiated personalities. The plight of helpless, innocent children especially saddened—and infuriated—La Guardia. In a small town in Illinois, two thousand hadn't tasted milk in a year. As malnutrition spread, so did sickness. Mental health problems of the young also increased, for idle fathers could not play the role of normal fathers; idleness and all its ramifications broke homes and scarred children for life. Men walked away from it all. (The father in Tennessee Williams's *The Glass Menagerie* "was a telephone man who fell in love with long distances.") Whatever diminished a home marred children, and all children were La Guardia's Fioretta Thea. For all these reasons, he was furious when the Brooklyn Edison Company discharged 1,600 employees. This monopoly, with it exorbitant profits, had the gall to "turn a man out of work in the morning and cut off his light at night!"

To find an answer to the Depression (by the fall of 1931 it had become the Great Depression), La Guardia pored over books. What had European countries done when struck by depressions? There was certainly no question that something was wrong with the whole economic setup and that it needed overhauling. And it would definitely not be sufficient to take care of the present dislocation and not do what was needed to prevent others from occurring. He saw public works— the construction of airports, highways, playgrounds—as part of the unemployment solution. Slum eradication would also put men back to work, give them purchasing power; this, in turn, would lead to production and this to more employment. To stave off personal economic tragedies in the future, La Guardia proposed many reforms that anticipated the New Deal: unemployment insurance, wages-and-hours legislation, old age pensions . . . Some went boldly beyond it.

His constituents mailed him all sorts of surefire methods of containing and uprooting the Depression. One sent a panacea in the guise of a mathematical formula. The nostrums kept coming ad infinitum. Their ingenuity must have rubbed off on La Guardia, for he proposed that every man who was employed should buy a suit of clothing for some unemployed individual who, when he found a job, should go and do likewise. This chain of philanthropy would create a need that would make the garment industry hum once again, and this would . . .

Meanwhile, Senator George W. Norris of Nebraska worked on legislation to alleviate the deprivation and anguish he had seen in the coal mines of Pennsylvania. In a cemetery, he had read a miner's epitaph: "For 40 years beneath the sod, with pick and spade I did my task, '

The coal king's slave, but now, thank God, I'm free at last." This moved him deeply. Not only had Norris experienced a childhood of poverty, but—like La Guardia—he also had a compassion for the underdog that had been intensified by the death of ones dear to him. When he was three, both his father and his older brother died. His wife died in childbirth. And his second wife almost died in giving birth to twins, who did die.

Norris was determined to make the yellow-dog contract illegal; it prevented a miner from joining a union, from complaining about intolerable conditions, or from obtaining another job. And he was as adamantly opposed to this contract's use of the injunction, which restrained unions and made just demands unattainable.

It wasn't surprising that La Guardia introduced and championed Norris's bill in the House, for it would "give the miner emancipation from the slavery that had prevailed for years in the coal mines of America," would make him "free at last." It appeared that President Hoover would veto the bill, for he had been vetoing all progressive labor legislation. Now, however, the sympathy of the American people for labor's demands had reached such a high point that the President, on March 23, 1932, signed the Norris-La Guardia Act.

The bill failed to impress Labor, because conditions were so bad that "the law was a lone bright star in an otherwise dark sky." It made more of an impact on reactionaries. Before its passage, one of them, James Beck, a Pennsylvania Republican, observed that what was happening constituted "a long march toward Moscow."

The accusation of being a radical and a communist was an old story to La Guardia, and therefore no longer disturbing. This time he retorted that the best way to take care of communism was "to give employment to the unemployed."

Instead of backing a sales tax, as a way to balance the budget, La Guardia fought—successfully—to "soak the rich," through income and inheritance taxes. To the charge that this ran counter to the Constitution, he said, "If the Constitution stands in the way, well the Constitution will simply have to get out of the way."

All such talk sounded precisely like socialism to Hoover, and Hoover feared socialism; he also spoke solemnly of communism, in his "plodding, somewhat mournful" voice. Such talk was on the same level as the attempt made by La Guardia and other radicals to take over power, specifically the federal administration of Muscle Shoals—and Hoover vetoed their Muscle Shoals Bill. (Its eventual passage, in just a matter of a few years, bore the signature of Franklin Delano Roosevelt.) But Hoover did not veto the Smoot-Hawley Bill, created by Reed Smoot of Utah and Willis C. Hawley of Oregon, for it protected American industry by an upward tariff revision.

Hoover also brought into being the RFC, the Reconstruction Finance Corporation, which gave monetary assistance, hundreds of millions, to banks, railroads, commerce, industry, and agricultural agencies, and maintained that in time benefits would trickle down to small businesses. This promised trickling-down process did not elate La Guardia. He called the RFC "the millionaire's dole." He wanted it to help individuals and small businesses directly—and in the present. From the floor of the House, he compared bankers, who were to blame for the Depression, to horse thieves of the old West, who were sometimes hung by those they victimized. A fellow congressman asked if he proposed hanging bankers. "What would you do?" La Guardia shot back. "Give them a medal? Yes, I would hang a banker who stole from the people."

All efforts to stem the rise of unemployment failed. Bread lines grew in length and breadth; those in them seemed to be without individuality. Women refused to stand in the lines. And Will Rogers, everlastingly chewing his cud, while fondling his lariat, drawled his assessment of bread lines and inadequate relief: "You eat just as much loafing as you do working. In fact, more; you got more time."

And you did more thinking. Some may have found sanctuary in the conclusion expressed by Rudy Vallee, whom Hoover had implored to lift the people out of the Depression on wings of song. In *George White's Scandals*, Vallee sang that life was merely a bowl of cherries and not to be taken too seriously. Other singers pointed out, consolingly, that a kiss was still a kiss and that plenty of nothing could be completely satisfying. Most of the country, however, was removed from such philosophical whimsy; its concern was with the immediate, pressing problem of survival. Thus World War I veterans hit upon a fairly obvious idea, one that made sense. In 1924, over Coolidge's veto, Congress had passed a Bonus Bill, said bonus to be paid to veterans in twenty years, in 1945, still thirteen years off in the future. Why not get that money now, in 1932, when it was desperately needed?

A group of veterans in Seattle, Washington, under the leadership of a tall, sunburned, unemployed cannery worker, headed east to let Congress know that they wanted their bonus, $500 per veteran, at once. Word of their mission spread. Veterans from all over the country, about twenty-five thousand, moved on Washington. They constructed shacks on the Anacostia Flats, across the Potomac, prepared to stay there until 1945, if they had to in order to get their bonus.

Such makeshift, unsanitary housekeeping in the seat of government of the United States proved an embarrassment—as did the encampment of some veterans right on Pennsylvania Avenue, between the Capitol and the White House. President Hoover spoke out with indignation against the whole unseemly project. These so-called veterans were—for the most part—communists and ex-convicts, bent on stirring up trouble.

The Chief of Staff, General Douglas MacArthur who was finally called upon, on a sweltering July 28, to clear the lot of them out, expressed serious concern over their threat to the nation and its government: "That mob . . . was a bad looking mob. It was animated by the essence of revolution. . . ." (His aide, Dwight D. Eisenhower, regarded it all as "a street corner brawl," in which the General should not get involved. One of the General's officers, George S. Patton, Jr., led a cavalry charge on the ragged, pathetic bonus marchers.)

To give the bonus to the veterans bothered La Guardia; it smacked of special privilege. After all, nonveterans were also struggling to free themselves from the Depression's grip. So he voted against the immediate payment of a bonus—even though he would soon be up for election and such a vote was unadvisable politically. But he did everything he could to provide the veterans with lodging and food while they were in Washington, and he was the first to suggest that fare home be provided for those veterans who wished to return home—the amount, however, to be deducted from their bonus in 1945. And when President Hoover finally called out the army, who clanked down Pennsylvania Avenue in monstrous tanks and went on to tear gas the veterans, their wives and children and then burn up their ramshackle, pitiful homes, La Guardia scribbled a telegram and slammed it down on the desk of one of his law clerks. "What do you think of *that?*" he asked.

The clerk read what La Guardia had written: "Beans is better than bullets and soup is better than gas—F. La Guardia." Then—almost reflexively—he said, "You've got to say 'Beans are better than bullets' or 'A bean is better than a bullet.' You see, you can't have a plural subject with a verb in the singular—"

"A wise guy!" La Guardia screamed. "The Capitol in flames and *you* talk *grammar*. Wise guy!"

Franklin Delano Roosevelt, running for the presidency for the first

131

time, regarded Douglas MacArthur as pure ego, as dangerous. (In burning out the veterans, he had disobeyed the President's order not to cross the bridge to the Anacostia Camp.) Roosevelt noted that when MacArthur routed the Bonus Marchers, the general had strutted about like a dictator—chest out, hands on hips. If conditions worsened—and that seemed most likely—Roosevelt felt that MacArthur was the sort who might try to take over the government in order to run it the way it should be run—his way.

And the people as a whole didn't at all like Hoover's refusal to meet with the veterans or his calling out troops to get rid of them, for these veterans epitomized their own downtrodden state.

Since this was an election year, there was speculation as to who would possibly vote for Hoover, grayer now, with a stoop to his shoulders that suggested discouragement, and with resignation—rather than querulousness—characterizing his speech. Everyone knew whose vote Roosevelt would get: "all the defeated, all the disgruntled, and all the underprivileged," and their vote resulted in a solid majority of seven million—22,829,501 to 15,760,684.

In great measure, Roosevelt's impressive victory led to La Guardia's defeat.

CHAPTER FIFTEEN

AFTER THE INAUGURATION, AFTER THE UNBELIEV-
able burden of the Depression had been passed ungraciously by
Hoover to Roosevelt, Will Rogers observed, "The whole country is
with him, just so he does something. If he burned down the capitol
we would cheer and say 'well we at least got a fire started anyhow.'"
And this pep talk went up on the walls of the Thomas Edison company
in New Jersey:

President Roosevelt has done his part: now you do something.

Buy something—buy anything, anywhere; paint your kitchen, send a telegram, give a party, get a car, pay a bill, rent a flat, fix your roof, get a hair-
cut, see a show, build a house, take a trip, sing a song, get married.

It does not matter what you do—but get going and keep going. This old
world is starting to move.

The country did indeed need overt action, some movement to dispel
its stagnant apprehension and uncertainty. Hoover had failed and
President-elect Roosevelt was an unknown quantity—whose patrician,
didactic confidence might be no more substantial, in actuality, than a
stage set. The faith of the people in leadership, after all, was gone, and
mistrust in all areas had taken its place. (A man entered a bank and
said, "If my money's here, I don't want it. If it's not here, I want it.")

This need for action had been in Roosevelt's thoughts even before
the election; he even feared, though he later maintained only fear was
to be feared, that his victory might be too overwhelming, possibly a
ten-million majority, indicative of a desire for immediate, impossible
results. Adolf A. Berle, Jr., a member of his Brains Trust, recruited
from the Columbia Law School by Raymond Moley, conjectured with
alarm that the majority might go to over twice that amount. There was

133

even talk, after the election, that pressure would force Hoover to resign, so that Roosevelt could take over at once and get to work immediately.

Understandably, therefore, President-elect Roosevelt did not simply
wait out the months of the interregnum. He wanted to have vital bills
drafted and referred to appropriate committees so that they would be
ready to be passed as soon as possible after his inauguration in March.
To do this chore he called on Berle who, though he had overestimated
FDR's landslide victory, had a personality which combined drive and
brilliance in the field of economics and government. (He had entered
Harvard at thirteen, graduated at seventeen and finished his study of
law at Harvard at twenty-one.)

For advice, Berle went to John "Cactus Jack" Nance Garner, the vice-
president-elect; he saw blue eyes set in a red complexion and a nose
like a hawk's beak. Garner had just served two years as Speaker of the
House. He was an ancestral blend of English, Welsh and Scotch, born
in Blossom Prairie, Texas; his education had been limited to a rural
Texas high school; he invariably had lunch in his office, cooked on an
electric grill by his wife, Elizabeth, who also served as his secretary.

"We want to put some legislation in," Berle told this plain man, the
possessor of a "complacent, country sagacity." "Is there any way to find
somebody to hammer that Congress together?"

Garner shook his head. "No, unless it's Fiorello La Guardia. Nobody
else can make sense out of this Congress. The power machinery has
broken down. The various cliques are working together. Nobody trusts
anything and until Roosevelt gets his government organized, this is
going to be a madhouse. But if anybody can make any sense out of it,
it would be Fiorello. He has a combined group of urban liberals and
agricultural liberals—the grassroots group—and he can come nearer to
making sense than anyone else." Then, with condescension and affection, Garner summed up La Guardia as "a good little wop."

Berle could understand Garner's endorsement of La Guardia, serving out his last few months in Congress, for he had been impressed
when he had met La Guardia for the first time. Paul Kern, one of
Berle's corporation law students, who worked for La Guardia in the
drawing up of bills, told Berle that La Guardia thought highly of his
new book, *The Modern Corporation and Private Property,* and wanted
to meet him. (The book criticized the system, and "in financial circles
and circles of great wealth . . . was very unpopular.") Berle invited
both to his 142 East 19th Street home for dinner.

FIORELLO LA GUARDIA

In a note to Raymond Moley, dated November 28, 1932, Berle wrote, "I have a couple of matters on my mind . . . if names come up for jobs, I should be glad if you would have in mind, (1) Fiorello La Guardia. You know all about him. He is going to be important in the short session. I am having him to dinner tomorrow. His career is not over by a long shot and I think he might be annexed. . . ."

The dinner went better than could be expected. And, at first thought, this was surprising, for Berle was the first intellectual La Guardia had met close up. Physically, they were opposites, for Berle suggested both a jockey and a "nervous, thin-lipped, slender pedagogue." That they were both long-range reformers made them kin, and they hit it off right from the start. The meeting, in fact, sparked a friendship which lasted until La Guardia's death. (Mrs. Berle recalled the steadying influence her husband had on La Guardia: "When Fiorello was really getting up a head of steam, Adolf took him out and talked to him and calmed him down. And there was no question that Fiorello appreciated this. Poor Fiorello, when Adolf went off to Washington and Fiorello had all sorts of trouble as mayor, he would fly off the handle very much more often than he had before.")

Of the first meeting with La Guardia, Berle said in retrospect, "The thing that struck me was that here was a man who had unbounded energy, unquestioned honesty, but had not had the continuous contact with the kind of intellectual machinery that every other politician in New York was taking for granted. He didn't have any group of university men to work out his problems for him."

Moley, in response to Berle's November 28 note, agreed that La Guardia ought to be a part of the Roosevelt administration—"ought to be on our team somehow or other."

As prelude to this objective, Berle began a campaign of introducing La Guardia to some of the people "he should know." They included Alice and Nicholas Longworth.

At one of numerous parties after the election of 1932, Berle spoke to Alice Longworth about La Guardia. She agreed with Berle on La Guardia's qualities: honesty, inexhaustible energy, the capacity to do a great many things. She also felt that he didn't have "as much contact with and support of the more sophisticated community as he was really entitled to." (Alice Longworth enjoyed teasing this diminutive Italian-Jewish politician from New York who, she felt, was "one of a kind, so to speak." Both she and her husband "liked him enormously" and had fun calling him a communist.)

Berle also reported to FDR, in a memo, on his meeting with La Guardia: "Congressman Fiorello La Guardia came to see me on Monday. He has a bloc said to be twenty-six in number, mainly western Progressives, which he claims to control in the next House. I gave him the guy-ropes of the Farm Relief program; likewise some of the legislation we talked about in the campaign, which he expressed himself as very anxious to support. . . . La Guardia insists that with the Democratic contingent they will be able to pass a Farm Relief bill even over a veto."

Farm relief was desperately needed. Farmers, who had lost foreign markets after the war, had been hit harder by the Depression than city workers. Foreclosures proliferated. Farmers fought for their homes and land, threatening, in some instances, to kill those who attempted to evict them. ("Outside of Pleasanton, Kansas, someone found the murdered body of a man who had just foreclosed on a five-hundred-acre farm.") It was obvious that the National Bankruptcy Act, which originated in remote 1898, required renovation: the act did not cover corporations; its main concern was to establish a uniformity in liquidation procedures—and in 1932 the main concern was not liquidation, but keeping as many businesses going as possible.

Though technically the farmer's plight was outside La Guardia's jurisdiction, it fell within the bounds of his interest and compassion. He therefore introduced a bill which permitted courts to stay the hand of creditors, to put off liquidations; another established a Farm and Credit Home Bank to refinance mortgages at a three-percent interest rate. While involving himself in such legislation—wide in scope and far-reaching in significance—he busied himself during the lame duck period with a congressman's innumerable routine chores.

The President-elect spent December and January of that interval in the little White House in Warm Springs, for it had therapeutic "warm waters heavy with mineral salts." It also had a flood of visitors, giving him advice on "economy, beer [which would bring in considerable revenue], and farm relief."

As for the La Guardia-introduced bills, FDR was primarily concerned that they pass—even though Hoover would veto them—merely to give the impression to the troubled country that he was doing something. (And in spite of what Will Rogers had said, Roosevelt had to do something more constructive than burn down the Capitol.) Just getting the bills passed would be quite a trick, for they had to be approved by a Republican Senate and a barely Democratic House. The trick required a getting together, somehow, of the Democrats and those progressive Republicans who had supported Roosevelt during the campaign.

La Guardia viewed the 72nd Congress with disquietude—the docile way its members marched behind Speaker Garner. He said, "This isn't a session of Congress; this is a kissing bee." The state of the Congress was made all the more reprehensible by a hunger march on Washington by three thousand unemployed shortly after the start of the Congress's first session.

The state of the nation—and the nature of its legislators when faced with crisis—was dramatized one day in December 1932 when a twenty-five-year-old man, employed in a Sears, Roebuck sporting goods department, rose in the House gallery, waved a .38 menacingly and yelled, "I demand twenty minutes to address the House. Whoever tries to stop me will die. Is that understood? I want to be heard."

The reaction of the legislators to this request was virtually unanimous. One, more original than the rest, ducked under a table, and in the process his head acquired a cuspidor. Most lunged for the door.

La Guardia, however, dashed for the gallery. While he was on his way to overpower the gunman, Melvin Joseph Maas of Minnesota, a stocky ex-marine, walked to a spot under the gunman and, looking up, said, "All right, son, you can have the floor and make your speech. But you can't do it with that gun in your hand. Come on, drop it down to me."

The young man merely looked down, as in a daze.

"Throw me your gun. That's a good fellow."

Just as the revolver dropped into Representative Maas's hand, La Guardia arrived behind the citizen who wanted to be heard and grabbed him.

Other drama—more subdued, more significant—occurred before the lame duck Congress came to an end. The finish of La Guardia's long fight with Prohibition drew near, for in December 1932 both the Senate and the House approved the Twenty-first Amendment, which repealed the Eighteenth Amendment. That same month, La Guardia attempted to relieve victims of the Depression by lowering interest rates to three percent—even lower, if possible. He presented his resolution in simple language, he said, to make sure "the bankers of the country can understand it." The following month another one of his battles brought the result he desired: the adoption of the Twentieth Amendment, which eliminated lame duck sessions and enabled a newly elected president to get on with his program without delay.

And this Congress approved New Deal–inspired bills which La

Guardia introduced. Still, his time as a congressman had run out, and he was despondent. On the day of Roosevelt's inauguration, he met a few old friends in his apartment. His belongings were all packed, and the empty rooms deepened the sadness. "That's politics," La Guardia said, as though continuing the line of his thought. "Here I am on my last day without food or drinks for my friends."

That day, he and his wife left for New York.

Four months earlier, because La Guardia was a casualty of the FDR landslide, he had momentarily lost all zest for anything political. Usually not one to surrender without a stubborn fight, he could not, this time, resist the histrionics inherent in self-pity.

He lamented that his political career had been wrecked, that he was too old to start all over again. Facing up to these facts, he accepted a sensible conclusion: "I'm going to get a little place in the country and settle down and raise chickens." In short, he was going to enjoy life.

Drama also required that he turn aside all of Marie's attempts to comfort him. Told that in two years he could get back in Congress, he knifed this optimism with: "You know the power of a Representative depends upon the amount of seniority he has acquired. I have forfeited all mine. I would have to begin all over to try to work myself up to a chairmanship. It would take too many years. . . ."

He spoke of practicing law once again; of perhaps, eventually, becoming an instructor in a law school. (Teaching law was a recurrent daydream, the recurrence sharing arcane significance with the dream itself. And how explain his desire to participate in the creation of lawyers who, in his view, were manipulators of semicolors and on a par with tinhorns and millionaires?) Though he made these plans, he could not help but wonder how it had come to pass that he was now winding up his many years in the House. Surely, he had been as effective as a congressman could be. The flood of letters after his defeat, from all manner of citizens, said as much; these letters expressed sincere regret that he would no longer be in Congress.

It was also natural that he would recapitulate the elements of his defeat. He had had no campaign money. Things were so bad financially that he was about to be evicted from his headquarters. It was all like a melodramatic movie serial; in the nick of time, one of his men appeared with a check for $25,000 from the president of a New York utility. La Guardia took a look at the check and, without hesitating, in the tradition of a silent movie hero, tore it in half. He then handed the pieces back to the man who had brought the check, saying, "Tell him I'd rather have my headquarters in the back of a Mack truck."

In spite of this lack of money, La Guardia carried on his usual vigorous campaign. He delivered innumerable street corner talks. Greater crowds could be reached, too, for he had the help—as did his Tammany opponent, James J. Lanzetta—of a new amplifying device, the loudspeaker. Violence erupted. Bricks were thrown from rooftops. One had to be constantly on the watch for them—and for fraud.

The night before the election, La Guardia took Ernest Cuneo, his loyal, dedicated law clerk, aside and asked, "Ernest, what are you going to do if they try to steal the election tomorrow?"

"I'll arrest them, or get killed trying to."

La Guardia shook his head. "No! We don't want arrests; we want votes. If they rush the machine, knock them away from it. Then cast as many votes for me as they stole. You hear? Vote until they knock you out . . . !"

But fraud, like FDR's landslide victory, wasn't the total explanation for his defeat. There had been President Hoover's determination to see La Guardia eliminated, for having opposed practically every measure of his administration. No wonder that only once during that administration had La Guardia been a guest at the White House—the occasion, a visit by a minister of the Italian government. Cordiality did not mark the reception of La Guardia and his wife. Their departure, however, bordered on the sensational. As limousines were called up for ambassadors, senators and sundry dignitaries, a doorman asked La Guardia if he could get his car. "He nearly fainted," La Guardia recalled, "when I answered: 'We haven't a car. We'll have to walk.' There was a kind of hush as he repeated it aloud, and then Marie and I hoofed it away from the White House toward our apartment, while the big limousines rolled by. They acted like it was the first time anybody ever had *walked* out of there."

The Republicans in general could not forget that it had been La Guardia who had virtually single-handedly defeated the sales tax, even though Garner had most of the House's members lined up behind the tax. (One newspaperman described La Guardia in action in the course of this battle: "He does not rise to speak. He bounces. He puts tremendous energy into his oratory, bouncing around, crouching, rising on his toes and swinging his arms. . . .") The Republicans wanted to end the Depression by means of the sales tax; La Guardia roared that the sales tax put the burden solely on the consumer; instead, the rich should be soaked, the rich should contribute more towards balancing the budget through income and estate taxes. Obviously, La Guardia didn't act or think like a Republican. He didn't even regard himself as a Republican. Once when asked if his party favored subsidies for corporations, La Guardia said, "Which party?" Why, the man couldn't even afford a car. As a consequence of all these blatant flaws, La Guardia received no support from the party machinery—national, state, or local.

La Guardia therefore tried to get Democratic backing, by stressing his role as a Progressive. Powerful Tammanyite Jimmy Hines, who was to end up in a cell in Sing Sing, reacted with a flat refusal. But La Guardia had somewhat better luck with John McCooey, a Tammany power in Brooklyn, who declared with feeling, "Mr. La Guardia, I'd like to see you made Ambassador to Australia; but, failing that, I'll try to send you back to Washington. Anywhere, so long as you're kept out of New York City."

Could it be that McCooey was a boss with prescience? For La Guardia's melancholia, which had turned his thoughts to a bliss of chickens and law, faded away in a matter of days and was supplanted by an old desire—to be mayor of New York City.

The nature of his innermost thoughts could be detected in a letter he wrote to Oswald Garrison Villard about two weeks after his defeat:

While everybody is talking about the necessity of a change in our City government, there is nothing really practical, concrete and definite being done. Public opinion must not only by crystallized, but must be translated into action through the medium of an actual fighting organization of determined men and women. The election machinery cannot be overlooked. The best of intentions and good will even of a minority of the people cannot, unless properly prepared, overcome the crookedness, corruption and violence of an entrenched political machine.

Also, after acquiring Town Hall for the night of November 28, he invited those opposed to Tammany to attend a rally. Only four hundred showed up. This didn't dampen the fire of his oratory. He brought the small, dedicated audience to its feet with: "You can't start a few weeks before election and beat professional politicians who have been crooked for a hundred years."

These moves may have been oblique, but in the late spring of 1933, he told Berle quite plainly what he had in mind. Berle could not have been more pleased with the idea. And he went to work in La Guardia's behalf—in part, to repay La Guardia for what he had done for FDR during the lame duck session.

His earlier defeat by Walker did not deter La Guardia, for much that was vital had occurred between 1929 and 1933. Walker's corruption—at which La Guardia had pointed the finger—had been exposed by Samuel Seabury, and Gentleman Jimmy had left New York in the fall of 1932, left a city distraught, near financial ruin and—to use a figure that he might have used—gasping on the ropes. The five-cent fare was threatened. The licensing of new teachers and the construction of badly needed schools had stopped. Decent housing was needed; tax relief was needed.

Brazenly, Tammany went on as before, refusing to clean its house. There was therefore an excellent chance that it would go down in defeat before a reform mayor on a Fusion ticket. But Tammany's strength lay not in numbers, but in the disorganization and bickering of its opponents.

On arriving in New York City, La Guardia found that he had not only to eliminate a host of possible candidates, but also to survive political intrigue of a most involved and deadly variety.

CHAPTER SIXTEEN

L A GUARDIA JOINED IN THIS POLITICAL BATTLE—
which would build in viciousness and acrimony for five months—with
a hope that was more than wishful thinking. He observed that something most surprising had occurred in the New York City special
mayoralty election of November 1932; this gave him a buoyancy and
confidence in striking contrast to the despairing mood brought on by
his defeat at that time.

Tammany, for numerous reasons, had not wanted the deposed
Walker to be renominated. They therefore informed him by wire:
"True to our promise, we offer you the nomination as Mayor. Be sure
that you decline." For as many reasons, Tammany's choice was not
Mayor McKee, though McKee achieved the spotlight when, as acting
mayor, he slashed a few parasites' salaries and eliminated a few automobiles used at the taxpayers' expense by Tammany officials, and he
had been praised for riding to City Hall on the subway and upon his
arrival, unlike Walker, working diligently. (Tammany didn't call the
Acting Mayor Holy Joe out of love; in its eyes, he bore the taint of
reformer and of anti-Tammany Democrat.) The man Tammany
picked, Surrogate John P. O'Brien, loomed a giant physically, with
heavy jaws and brows and a brush mustache that ineffectively shel-
tered a protruding lip. But he was not a mental giant. When a reporter
asked him who his police commissioner would be, he said—without
hesitation or thought—"I don't know. I haven't got the word yet." A
Catholic lay leader, he had a predilection for urging higher moral
standards, an urge never experienced by fun-loving James J. And for
decades he had toiled loyally in Tammany's vineyards.

So O'Brien was selected, and he won. However, Holy Joe McKee, who was not on the ballot, received an incredible 241,899 write-in votes, which said quite plainly to a suddenly elated La Guardia that there were numerous Independents and that they were zealous enough to go to the inordinate trouble of writing Joseph V. McKee on their ballots.

La Guardia realized that Fusion had a chance for a simple, irrefutable, arithmetical reason: the total of McKee's votes and Republican and Socialist votes was more than the votes cast for Tammany—which received less than one half of the city's vote.

Just a few weeks after this election that made the ponderous O'Brien mayor of New York City, McKee—forty-four, handsome, a blend in appearance of upright executive and arrow collar man—delivered a speech before the State Chamber of Commerce that came out forcefully against Tammany and as vehemently for revolt. Overnight, as a consequence, he became the idol of Fusion forces. They looked to him as their leader in a Fusion crusade. Curiously enough, even La Guardia, on April 3, a few days after he himself was reported to be a candidate, solemnly proclaimed, "I will support Joseph McKee as a candidate for Mayor if he will run on an anti-Tammany ticket with a platform pledging the removal of all incompetent, unfit office holders, with a constructive platform rehabilitating the finances and morale of our city. . . ." As stiffly, he asked that McKee make his intentions known by May 1. (A sizable fraction of the press was ecstatic about McKee. However, the New Republic observed, long-facedly, that McKee broke with Tammany not out of moral indignation—as his oratorical outburst "sick and tired of the inefficiency and corruption of Tammany" would have one believe—but because he realized Tammany was tossing him on the junk heap.)

But time, to some extent, eroded the spell of McKee's oratory; besides, other, newer, fresher messiahs popped up that winter and spring —La Guardia among them. Some may have wanted to run for mayor in 1933 on a Fusion ticket. Some may have implied as much. But none came out, as La Guardia did, as unequivocally, as persistently, as raucously, in demanding that he be the candidate. To Maurice P. Davidson, chairman of the City Fusion Party, he would on occasion say: "Well, who's the latest Mayor?" And when Davidson told him, La Guardia would jump around, shaking his fist, saying, "Well, there's only one man going to be the candidate, and I'm the man. I'm going to run. I want to be mayor." He also issued an or-else ultimatum: if he were not nominated, he would run in the Republican primary. This was a disturbing threat to those running the Fusion campaign, because the Republican nomination for the Fusion candidate was highly important if not essential, and to defeat a determined street fighter like La Guardia would not be easy.

Berle had no objection to La Guardia's spectacular behavior; after all, though thoughtful, introspective, some said Berle had a cocksure brashness. Out of friendship, he introduced La Guardia to Seabury, whose prestige as an indefatigable, veteran hunter of the Tiger made him the deciding factor in picking the Fusion candidate. Seabury was a thoroughly patrician figure of English stock whose family motto, emblazoned on their crest, was Hold to the Most High. Something of the Anglican ecclesiastic was in Seabury; something of the Briton was in his "suave voice and manner." His personality included pince-nez, a glacial, omnipotent poise, and the stern visage of Old Testament prophets.

The day came when Berle went to see Seabury in his office in order to sell him on La Guardia. He started off by saying, "Judge Seabury, you said that you don't want the nomination for Mayor of New York. If you do want it, just say so, and we're all on board. I'm taking your statement that you don't want it at face, but if I'm wrong about that, just let me know. . . ."

"No, I think you can take it at face," Seabury said. "I've even taken one or two steps, such as having my residence out in Long Island instead of in New York City, which perhaps demonstrates that I'm not looking for this nomination."

"Well," Berle said, "everybody knows you deserve it. . . . If you are not disposed to take it yourself, I'd like to have you consider Fiorello La Guardia. I've been having some experience with him during the last two or three months in the Congress of the interregnum, and I'm impressed with the man's ability and his devotion and intricate knowledge of the City of New York."

"I haven't foreclosed my decision on anyone yet," Seabury said. "I'm still open and I will give very careful consideration to Fiorello La Guardia. As you know, there are several other people who are looking for it. That's the way I feel."

When Seabury met La Guardia, he was cordial; La Guardia, in turn, exhibited sufficient "sincerity and zeal" to impress Seabury. In spite of their being utterly dissimilar in personality and lineage, they were joined by a bond stronger than blood: an implacable, lifelong hatred of Tammany. But at this early stage of the game, the spring of 1933, Seabury was not ready to commit himself.

The May 1 deadline that La Guardia had given McKee came and went, without a decision from McKee. But two days later McKee made a most unexpected announcement. He would not be a Fusion candidate, would have nothing more to do with politics. He was moving on, as of May 15, from his seven years as president of the Board of Aldermen to the presidency of the Title Guarantee and Trust Company, one of the oldest and finest firms of its kind in the country, at a salary reported to be in excess of $50,000 a year. When he was asked if his resignation meant he was disgusted with politics, he snapped, "You're telling me!" He had, he elaborated, felt "hemmed in by party limitations." In his new position, he believed he could be of service to the "masses of small mortgage holders" set adrift in a turbulent economic depression.

McKee's departure struck Fusion a blow. The general sentiment: it would be hard to find another man of McKee's type.

La Guardia put on a crotchety act. "This is no time for experienced, competent and honest men to leave the public service. Mr. McKee's action is a loss to the city and must be a disappointment to his friends." Might there be the implication here that *he* was not among those friends?

On May 8, a Monday, La Guardia made a public statement: "This is not the time for pussyfooting, timidity or hesitancy. . . . The hopes of 6,000,000 people surely cannot be deflated because one individual has voluntarily removed himself from the fight. . . . We should not be preparing for a front parlor reception when there is a dirty backyard to be cleaned."

He also let it be known that on Thursday, the eleventh, he would make a definite statement—presumably about his candidacy. On that Thursday, he proposed the fantastic—and therefore attention-getting —ticket of Al Smith, Mayor; Norman Thomas, Aldermanic President; Robert Moses, Comptroller; John F. Hylan, Borough President of Queens; and on and on, in that newsworthy vein. (He admitted that he had drawn up his ticket without the knowledge or consent of any of the proposed candidates; but, after all, the city was in need, and it was therefore their duty to serve.)

In the interview in which he made public his ticket, La Guardia nominated O'Brien for surrogate with a characteristic wave of the hand, saying, "Oh, we'll let him be Surrogate again." As flippantly, he stipulated that if this ticket of his were not possible, its equivalent should be substituted. And if Smith did not want to run—finally, La Guardia departed from make-believe—he would.

145

Earlier in the day, in a serious vein, he had taken part in a rally of 100,000 at Battery Park, protesting the treatment of Jews in Germany. He said that the peace of the world was being threatened by the Nazis. And he concluded, "America must not permit this to happen."

On the same day, he spoke out against spoiling Central Park with playgrounds; a playground should be a playground and a park a park. "It is ridiculous," he said, "to think of putting all this hodge-podge in Central Park."

And on that same day, as though he were determined to establish a record for versatility in public service, he appealed on WEAF for funds for the Salvation Army, an organization "that for seven days a week does all that the preachers preach about on Sunday."

Unlike La Guardia, some Fusionists were focusing their energies on a single activity, plotting on how Holy Joe McKee might be brought back into the fold. Others hounded Seabury, hoping that he would change his mind about being their candidate. They reasoned that he had exposed Tammany's corruption and therefore he should run the city and give it a pure government. This struck Seabury as a non sequitur. More importantly, he feared that should he run, it might appear that all his municipal reform had been a means to this personal end. (Whispers hinted at a less lofty motivation: Seabury had his sights set, not on City Hall, but on the White House.)

La Guardia, always predictably unpredictable, also picked Seabury. It proved to be on an occasion which grew out of Berle's having introduced him to Newbold Morris, another of the Republican gentry, who, like Seabury, came from fine, blonde, blue-eyed stock, was a lawyer in a dignified old firm and had been a schoolmate of Berle's wife.

Berle brought La Guardia and Morris together by inviting them to dinner in his home. Side by side, they made an incongruous pair—La Guardia five two, Morris six five. Berle recalled that "Fiorello's weakness was that he had no organized Republican support. The Republican Party had about as much interest in Fiorello as a Mohammedan might have in St. Peter. They just weren't in the same league." During dinner, Morris, cooperating with Berle's desire to have La Guardia win over Republicans, asked La Guardia to speak before the Republican Club of his district, of which he had just become president. Morris's 15th Assembly District Club at 122 East 83rd Street was extremely conservative, opulent and antagonistic to *radical La Guardia*. After a day's hesitation, La Guardia accepted Morris's invitation—and its challenge.

The members of this silk-stocking Republican club exploded with anger that "that filthy radical" had been invited to address them. Nonetheless, the press, whose sustenance is drama, gave the event a great deal of space; and when La Guardia appeared, the clubhouse was packed with Republicans who had come "to see the 'fireworks.'"

That La Guardia arrived ten minutes late added to the tension. At last he stood before them, heavy at the waist, "his mouth, with its heavy underlip, set and determined." When he started to speak, everyone expected a piercing verbal onslaught, but instead the man spoke so softly it was difficult to hear him.

"I apologize for being late," he said. "Marie, my wife, sent the only tuxedo I own out to be pressed, and it didn't come back until a few minutes ago. I couldn't leave the house until it was returned." The surprised audience—"the men resplendent in their boiled shirts, the women in their low-cut gowns and jewelry"—roared with laughter. "I'm very proud to be here tonight," La Guardia continued. "But I don't know whether you ladies and gentlemen have decided to admit me to the social register, or whether you just wanted to go slumming with me."

This cinched his hold on the audience, even though he went on to say, "But I can tell you that whoever is the next mayor of New York will be in both at once whether he likes it or not. As things are running here, there won't be any more distinction between the right people and the wrong people because New York City is going to be in so bad a jam that we will be lucky if all of us come out of it with a whole skin."

He then pointed out that the leadership of the Republican Party in the city and state was ineffective and that it would be fatal to have the Fusion candidate for mayor picked by them. He next presented an eight-part program, the first part of which urged that the Fusion committee be enlarged to include representatives of all groups, factions and organizations opposed to Tammany, as well as representative women, now conspicuously absent from the committee. He also ignored the smug conservatives present by tactlessly speaking of the number of unemployed, the percent of unemployed, the length of their unemployment and the fact that federal aid was needed to alleviate wide-scale misery. In conclusion, he declared his choice for the nomination—Seabury. This declaration must have been the antidote for the radical things he'd said that evening, for one of the most conservative members of the club actually rose and proposed that the former congressman be thanked for his speech.

Berle thought the evening had been a great success: "These people had thought of him merely as a kind of wild man. Suddenly, they found a quite different picture of the man. He was not their type. But I think that had a great deal to do with breaking down the resistance in the conservative Republican side."

With the coming of summer, the field of possible candidates narrowed to Robert Moses, John F. O'Ryan—who had the distinction of having been the youngest divisional commander in the A.E.F.—and La Guardia. And by this time Berle had sold Seabury on La Guardia—his honesty, his effectiveness as a politician, his ethnic appeal. Seabury bided his time in making known his selection, for patrician poise and impulsive behavior do not mix. Finally, he went all out for La Guardia.

At the end of July, when Moses was seriously proposed, Seabury lost his composure and his temper. Why, Moses had worked as Al Smith's secretary of state, and as far as Seabury was concerned, this linked Moses for eternity with Tammany. (His antipathy for Tammany went back to 1916, when Tammany had nominated him for governor and then failed to support him.) His negative reaction to O'Ryan approached in virulence his opposition to Moses. O'Ryan was bland, weak, a traction interests puppet. (He didn't stress—or mention, really —that Charles S. Whitman backed O'Ryan, and that Whitman had defeated him for the governorship in 1916.)

Because Moses knew he didn't have a chance without Seabury's backing, he removed himself from the running with a simple, disdainful statement.

La Guardia at this time proclaimed, "My coat is off and I am set to go. I am not fighting for a nomination. I am fighting Tammany Hall and to redeem New York City. . . . Seabury's work must not be permitted to be lost in a mesh of selfishness, personal ambition, petty politics or Tammany intrigue. The Seabury program must be translated into action. To the people of the City of New York I report for duty."

La Guardia's dynamic offer was not accepted; as always, he grated on the gentry's sensibilities. Having nowhere to turn, the Fusion Conference Committee made another attempt to somehow circumvent Seabury and bestow the nomination on Moses.

On the very day, July 27, that Seabury had gone to lunch at the Bankers Club with Davidson to say that he had decided on La Guardia as the Fusion nominee, Davidson had to tell this god of reform that the committee had picked Moses. Seabury rose to the full height of his grandeur, struck the table with his fist so hard that the dishes rattled. Then in the suddenly tensely silent dining room, he shouted, "You sold out to Tammany Hall . . . !"

Before Seabury's anger had cooled, the Fusion Committee met on August 1 and turned to O'Ryan as their candidate. Seabury blasted this as treachery, "a complete and disgraceful sellout to Tammany." Seabury's accusation astonished O'Ryan—military in bearing, hair sheared to the scalp, an independent Democrat, and presumably independent of Tammany.

This failure by high-minded reformers to employ their assumed store of goodwill, humility, selflessness and thoughts of a better life in an imperfect world tossed a foundering reform movement on the rocks. (A *New York Times* editorial said that there was a great opportunity to overthrow Tammany. "To permit it to be lost through needless divisions of opinion and working at cross purposes, and indulging in personal and party squabbles would be a civic crime.") Whitman's Fusion group and Seabury's Fusion group had to be reconciled, if Fusion was to have a chance in the coming election.

La Guardia feared a dark horse would appear as a unifying force and be victorious. Frustrated, discouraged, he asked Berle, "Why is it that every time you get to a point where you can do some good the nice people move in and block you? That's what drives a man like me to be a demagogue, smacking into things."

Then resilience, another of reform's virtues, came into play. Fusion leaders met on August 3 and once again considered General O'Ryan and La Guardia—with a bit more heat than reason, though harmony was the meeting's objective. Harmony required that La Guardia be the candidate—to satisfy Seabury; at the same time, it also required an impossibility: that Whitman's O'Ryan be picked.

Charles C. Burlingham was chairman. A sage of reform in 1913, he was now, at eighty-two, a revered sage—sufficiently revered to be able not only to call Seabury by his first name, but to tell him to sit down when he misbehaved. Still, six hours of assorted wrangling occurred. Finally, miraculously, a majority of the committee selected La Guardia as Fusion's candidate.

When La Guardia heard the news, he told Seabury, "I promise you faithfully you will never regret this." And before leaving to join his wife in their rented summer cottage in Westport, Connecticut, La Guardia said the campaign would not be "merely a political contest but a citizens' movement for the salvation of the city."

The campaign proved to be even more noteworthy than that serious, dedicated objective implied. To excel it in sheer excitement, one would have to go back, at least, to Mitchel's fight for City Hall in 1913; some maintained there hadn't been anything like it since 1886, when labor-socialist Henry George went forth against Tammany armed only with Single Tax and the other lances of his idealism. Newspapers—here and abroad, filled with the political battle—took sides, too. After all, this was the drama of the tabloids, but with social significance: the wily Franklin Delano Roosevelt stealthily weaving a web in which to snare the Republican Party. And the greatest city in the world in revolt, enacting the most ancient of morality plays: Good versus Evil.

When La Guardia received the nomination, the wise pols, with a solemn nodding of heads, predicted Tammany (Evil) would win. They also knew that a few days in political time, in terms of what can happen, equalled a much longer period of normal time. In just a few of those days, Mayor O'Brien was in special disfavor—and for good reason. He slashed the budget. Per the machine's orders, he slashed allocations for education, hospitals, relief, and blithely retained unnecessary political jobs for the Tammany faithful. It appeared that he was unaware of a simple political axiom: to gain the favor of the common man (voter), consider his needs with compassion and come to his aid with money.

In addition, the press could not restrain itself from quoting the Mayor, for the sake of objectivity and the reader's right to be amused. When O'Brien spoke to the Ladies of the Theatre Assembly, he actually said:

During the week I have momentous matters to attend to. I meet great people and I must go here and there to make up the addenda that goes with being Mayor of the City. Therefore, when I come here to this great forum and see before me flowers and buds, ladies, girls and widows, emotion is running just riot with me.

La Guardia had a different style, more controlled syntax. In the course of an interview, he employed a distaff analogy to make a mayor's job more understandable—and possibly to catch the eye of female voters.

Running a city resembles running a house. If the servants are honest, if the cook and chambermaid and the butler are not receiving graft, if they are devoted to the people they are serving, then the house can be managed well

The Honorable Fiorello La Guardia

The Little Flower receives the 1933 nomination for the office of Mayor and pledges to fight on the side of the angels.

Mrs. La Guardia, Jean, the Mayor, and Eric enjoy an early breakfast together.

Mayor La Guardia,
with a trick cigar
in his mouth,
umpires a baseball game
between City Hall reporters
and Aldermen.

Mayor La Guardia and Fire Commissioner Patrick Walsh
at the scene of a fire.

La Guardia and Kenneth Dayton, Acting Budget Director, chop away at figures in an effort to reduce the proposed 1938 New York City budget.

The Little Flower conducts the Rochester Philharmonic Orchestra during the Cavalcade of Music program at the World's Fair.

La Guardia
in a pensive moment
at the Municipal Building.

Mayor La Guardia, Class of '10, on his way to New York University's commencement in 1939, at which he received an honorary doctoral degree.

Mayor La Guardia arrives at the scene of a racial disturbance in Harlem.

In the dead of winter,
1942, Mayor La Guardia
appears at a
43rd Street pier fire,
where he was treated
at the scene
—for frost-bitten cheeks.

President and Mrs. Roosevelt and Mayor La Guardia en route to review the fleet.

Mayor La Guardia and Eleanor Roosevelt chat on the occasion of Mrs. Roosevelt's being sworn in as La Guardia's assistant in the Office of Civilian Defense.

and economically run. If the morals of the head of the house are good, this goodness will permeate all the way down.

When a tenant moves into an apartment or house which has been occupied previously, the first thing to do is give it a thorough house cleaning. That is exactly what the city needs. Its walls must be scraped; whitewash will not do the trick.

On the other hand, to ingratiate himself with a black audience, Mayor O'Brien spoke of Harlem as "the garden spot of New York." And to the very men who knew no pity in quoting him word for ill-chosen word, he gushed, "Oh, I would love to be a newspaperman, because I love the classics and I love good literature."

Obviously, on rhetoric alone, La Guardia had O'Brien licked hands down. Voters were arriving, without difficulty, at a disturbing conclusion: they had "the stupidest Mayor New York has ever had." Voters in the Bronx also came to this conclusion; a poll in that borough showed that Democrats—in alarming, unbelievable numbers—were going to vote for La Guardia. In part, this may have been because O'Brien "talked funny" and had the grace of an oaf. More significantly, the people—including Democrats, urban Democrats—wanted reform.

Boss Ed Flynn, "a tall, red faced, white haired, blue eyed Irishman," pondered all this. An urbane, successful lawyer, he had learned his political lessons from the late Charles Francis Murphy, at whose burial Walker had said, "The brains of Tammany Hall lie in Calvary Cemetery." Flynn once remarked that to reveal what he had learned from Murphy "would be like trying to tell what you learned from your childhood nurse." In any event, he realized that you had to give the people what they wanted; and if they now wanted reform, that, by God, was what he'd give them. And in the person of Holy Joe McKee.

Flynn conferred with James A. Farley, FDR's astute political manager, and they agreed that by means of McKee they had an unparalleled opportunity to gain control of New York's Democratic machine.

In the meantime, President Roosevelt had also been pondering the New York situation. He invited Flynn to come down to Washington and have dinner with him on September 21. As friends, they had met socially—chatting, drinking—at Roosevelt's home and at the White House. At their September get-together, they decided that McKee should run for mayor—the decision stemming from their separate individual motivations. (Flynn: If McKee, a resident of the Bronx became mayor, then Flynn, the boss of the Bronx, would have a firm grip on the entire city's politics. Roosevelt: Tammany must lose. Besides being moribund, it had opposed Roosevelt's nomination in Chicago in '32.

And it was equally important that the Republicans be defeated. If they won, they would threaten Lehman's run for governor of New York and Roosevelt's bid for reelection.)

The President suggested that various committees be formed of individuals representing a variety of professions and that they come out for McKee and "demand that he run." By the time dessert had been served, the President let Flynn know that he would not openly back McKee. Then not to mar the bonhomie of their meal, he said he would invite McKee to the White House "just to show the way the wind was blowing." And for further reassurance, Flynn was given to understand that individuals prominent in the administration would come out in bright daylight, so to speak, for McKee.

A jubilant Flynn headed back to the Bronx. On the surface, it appeared that he would have a difficult time convincing McKee—who just a few months earlier had left politics because he'd had enough of it—to run for mayor of a demoralized, virtually bankrupt New York City. McKee's vanity proved a mitigating factor. After the other nominations, he received over 2,000 telegrams asking him to run. How could he possibly not be moved by this sudden abundance of attention, entreaty, flattery? In spite of his belief that he'd had his fill of public office, he now said, "I suppose subconsciously, I did like public office." When a survey which he conducted showed 52 percent of the public were in favor of him, he admitted, "I am only human and I was naturally pleased." And when a citizens' committee asked him to run, he was torn "between a desire to do so and the realization of what I was giving up and what I was in for." Even Samuel Untermyer, eminent lawyer and Democrat, joined in. And Roy Howard and his *World Telegram.* And a poll by the *Literary Digest*—scientific, objective—revealed with irrefutable numbers that in a three-cornered race for mayor of New York City, McKee would emerge the winner.

Still, McKee—his Scottish ancestry at work—wanted to be sure that he was indeed being offered a sure thing. This was evidenced by a wire that Berle sent to Roosevelt on September 24.

Joe McKee is telephoning you tonight to confirm your part in following arrangement: Joe has been promised by Ed Flynn that if he will run for mayor of New York you will furnish Flynn enough patronage to assure election. . . . All of us feel strongly you ought to stop this unauthorized use of your name and prestige in a situation which can result in nothing but harm to you. . . . Better adhere to your principle of keeping clear of local fights and especially steer clear of being in position of rehabilitating Tammany.

Though everything indicated that the President paid heed to Berle's admonition, five days later McKee publicly declared he would be in the mayoralty race.

The Fusion forces felt a sudden, heart-stopping panic. They had taken victory for granted—a state of affairs too good to be true in the world of politics.

Tammany rallies were a study in despair. The *boom-bah* band on hand, as in the good old days, blared forth, but with rhythmic noises that now failed to express gaiety and optimism. And what had happened to the red fires and their festive glow? Now, the red fires appeared pale. And now there were empty seats, formerly occupied by regulars. Even when the band pounded out the Tammany anthem, the audience responded out of duty, without verve.

Undoubtedly, some of the blame for this malaise was due to the candidate, John Patrick O'Brien. He had the physical dimensions of a commanding figure, but none of the subtler, essential attributes. Though he might arrive at a political meeting with fanfare—policemen on motorcycles paving the way with screaming sirens—he preferred judicial calm and quiet. For twenty-one years, after joining Tammany, he worked in the corporation counsel's office on tax matters. For ten years, after being elected surrogate, he settled family feuds, solicitous in his care of widows and orphans. Now his police guard virtually had to push him—a reluctant, perspiring charge—onto the speaker's platform. After that, he perspired even more noticeably, as he fumbled about, painfully ill at ease. He was not above proclaiming, "These are times that try men's souls," or declaring that Curry's "word is as good as his bond." (Curry was Boss John F. Curry, who pulled the strings to which O'Brien, his puppet, was attached.) O'Brien would also speak of Tammany's activities among the poor; how the district leaders took care of their constituents. (Obviously the Mayor didn't realize that Fusion was "an extraordinary conglomeration of incompatibles," united by a common hatred of just such Tammany activities.) And O'Brien defended Curry, explaining that before Curry became a Tammany leader he had had a prosperous insurance business, "and yet," O'Brien said, "people say he made his money out of politics." Why, Curry didn't swear, tell an off-color story, drink—and as for smoking—he just smoked a little. "All I ask is fair play," O'Brien said most pitifully, "and no distortion of facts."

This was the man who had been passing as an opponent worthy of Fusion. Now the main thrust of battle had to be directed at McKee—a much smoother, much more articulate proposition, and one with connections in Washington. Born in Newark, New Jersey, Irish Catholic, McKee had taught Latin and Greek at Fordham, his alma mater, and English at De Witt Clinton High School. From academe, with nothing of the pedagogue clinging to him, he moved frictionlessly into Tammany. For seven years in the State Assembly and seven years on New York City's Board of Estimate, he sat quietly and did nothing—when far too much was being done all about him. Before his defection to Reform, while serving as acting mayor, he had declared, "I am an organization Democrat, always have been, and always will be."

Unlike O'Brien, McKee appeared eternally unperturbed. At his campaign quarters, he was a rock in the turbulent stream of people that flowed in and out of his office. Blue eyes and a broad forehead enhanced his arrow-collar-man handsomeness; with this appearance went well-cut clothes, "snappy clothes," compared to O'Brien's or La Guardia's. When McKee spoke, he habitually turned down the corners of his thin-lipped mouth, but the McKee smile had an appealing, boyish quality. It helped win over those who came to hear him. As O'Brien, in classic cliché, might have put it, "He constantly has his fingers on the pulse of the audience." Shrewdly, the backers of McKee's candidacy linked his fight with the President's social efforts by calling McKee's party the Recovery Party. Economic recovery, due to FDR's work, had started—a small upward trend. In the Depression, the very word *recovery* had a magical pull.

La Guardia continued to be a forceful, passionate campaigner. His campaign song: "Who's Afraid of the Big Bad Wolf?" His short arms pumped; his fists pounded the rostrum. (McKee's gestures had a short range, were controlled.) William Chadbourne, La Guardia's campaign manager, tried to calm the fighting candidate when he became explosive; invariably, he prefaced his entreaty with a plaintive "Now, Fiorello. . . ." Nothing could withstand La Guardia's skill in starting off slowly, informally, and then building to a storm of invective. He shouted that it was a vicious system—not the Democratic or Republican Party—that he was fighting.

In this system, men who enter politics for what they can get out of it are the real rulers. In New York City, the majority of them are district leaders who have risen to power by the dispensing of patronage. By favors the machine grows.

After such a shouted statement, his voice broke.

There is not one department in the city in which there are not hundreds holding down useless jobs because they are friends or relatives of politicians. Such jobs are a burden on the taxpayer and must go.

This kind of vow lifted the crowd to an emotional high point. (His meetings were marked by wilder demonstrations than those of the other candidates.)

And La Guardia pointed out that New York City not only had to beg for money, but it had to pay high interest rates. When he was an alderman, twelve years ago,

I warned the city of the danger of bankruptcy. A city no more than an individual can borrow itself out of debt. City accounts should be public so that an average business man can see exactly what is happening. Would you say these ideas are radical? You know I have been pronounced dangerous.

(He did speak out for "low-rental housing, slum clearance, social security.")

I suppose I really am dangerous, but not dangerous to honest men, whether they be poor or rich. I have been dangerous to crooks, no matter how high their position. Perhaps I have been radical, too, in advocating policies which have been adopted several years after I proposed them and I have been radical in fighting against existing evils. . . .

On and on his high-pitched voice squealed for support. As October arrived, O'Brien appeared out of the running. The poll in the *Literary Digest* of October 14 showed that La Guardia had three times as many supporters as O'Brien—and McKee had a long way to go.

Boss Flynn waited stoically for the White House's invitation to McKee. It did not come as promised; neither did members of the administration declare themselves for McKee. As for Roosevelt, he remained silent. Circuitously, his silence now spoke in La Guardia's behalf. (FDR, after all, hadn't forgotten that Congressman La Guardia had been of help in getting New Deal legislation under way, and he also realized that should La Guardia become mayor, they could work together.)

As it turned out, it was Seabury's lack of silence that caused trouble for La Guardia. The judge spoke out injudiciously against Governor Herbert H. Lehman, charging him—and the Democrats—with improper handling of relief funds.

Governor Lehman was a little man, stocky, nervous in manner, dignified, respected, colorless—and a Jew. He was a member of Temple Emanu-El, the opulent, Fifth Avenue synagogue, and associated with the Hebrew Sheltering Guardian Society and the Bureau of Jewish Social Research, and Jews voted for him dutifully, as a bloc. McKee pounced on Seabury's attack on Lehman as a clear, unconscionable case of anti-Semitism. He knew—and so did Boss Flynn and all the other Recovery Party powers—that Jews made up one third of the voting population of New York City. They also knew these Jewish voters had been made uneasy—an understatement—by what Hitler was up to. In short, tainting a candidate with anti-Semitism meant destroying him.

On a fall Saturday afternoon, while attending a rodeo with some children and having a boisterous good time, La Guardia received a wire from McKee, denouncing Seabury for his attack on Lehman—and thus on the Jewish people.

La Guardia paid a hurried call on Seabury. "My God, Judge," he said, "you're ruining me! Stop attacking Governor Lehman!"

In desperation, La Guardia also wrote an answer to McKee in which he disassociated himself from what Seabury may have said concerning Lehman. La Guardia's advisors strongly urged him not to send it, for this would give the public the fatal impression that a rift had developed between the Fusion candidate and Seabury. La Guardia found himself writhing with pain, uncertain of what to do.

Dilemmas of one sort or another had always been part of political campaigns, but this campaign differed in its increased use of radio and automobile. In 1933, political meetings—without the discomforts of crowds, but with the annoyance of static—came right into the home; and automobiles, unbelievably, "carry candidates to widely separated sections of the city in a single evening." Still, democracy remained unchanged; this was true of dirty tactics, too.

McKee used an ancient, brutal one—the smear. To retaliate, Fusion considered using it. In the remote past of 1915, McKee had written an article in the *Catholic World* that could be construed as anti-Semitic. This article and its significance had surfaced during the preceding year in the *Brooklyn Eagle,* and had been stored in the Fusion arsenal, a quiescent item with explosive potential. Now it was brought forth, hurled.

McKee knew it would be futile to plead that a prejudice of his youth had been eradicated by maturity, especially since Hitler was then in his ascendancy and the Jews, with reason, had become suspicious of such self-serving excuses from those after their votes. "Are you trying to draw a red herring," La Guardia wired McKee, "across the cowardly, contemptible and unjust attack that you have made and published against a great race gloriously represented by our Governor? Answer that, Mr. McKee, and think twice before you send me another telegram. . . ."

The disclosure of McKee's slight case of anti-Semitism spelled ruin for him. At once, Untermyer withdrew his support, and this symbolized the reaction of New York City's Jewish population. McKee might have followed up his first smear with a second—a devastating technique, one worthy of Clausewitz. Perhaps McKee didn't know that La Guardia's mother was Jewish. If he had known—in view of the despair that darkened his camp—wouldn't he, at least, have considered revealing this fact? There were difficult, embarrassing questions that he might have posed. Why hadn't La Guardia mentioned being a member of God's chosen people? An oversight? Hardly. Was shame involved? If so, hadn't *he* been guilty of anti-Semitism? (La Guardia was all politician, but only a half Jew. He had the Italian vote and the Jewish vote, and his private thoughts, very likely, decided that he leave well enough alone and be silent about his ancestry.)

At this point, the only option Flynn had was to go running to the President of the United States and prod, cajole, entreat and, above all, remind him of his promise to come out in the open for McKee when the time was ripe—and point out that now the time was overripe. FDR had undeniably felt a half commitment to McKee. Now he had a way out—not wanting to get involved in the anti-Semitism brouhaha. Berle was absolutely right about neutrality, especially in this instance, being a virtue.

After returning to New York, a disheartened Flynn acted as if Roosevelt's silence didn't exist. A huge sign in Times Square said, without qualification, "A Vote for McKee is a Vote for Roosevelt." Larger-than-life pictures of Roosevelt were displayed at McKee rallies. Speakers stated flatly that McKee was the one who would bring a New Deal to New York City. In short, everything conceivable was done to mislead the voter into thinking that McKee and Roosevelt were as one in political thought and action.

In October, as the candidates put forth their utmost efforts, Berle attempted to negate the McKee deception. At Cooper Union, he said, "No one without the direct authority of President Roosevelt has the right to steal his name and prestige and particularly no one, especially a raiding crew, has the right to embarrass him by misusing his name as a part of a political boarding party."

In the middle of the month, another *Literary Digest* poll—in which two and a quarter million voters had been mailed ballots—indicated La Guardia was in the lead, but with McKee's breath hot on his neck. (That La Guardia led in this poll was an additional reason for FDR not to come out for McKee. At a press conference, the President stated that he was not taking any part in the election, brushing it off as a local election, of which there were many in the United States. Nonetheless, Berle in an October 21 wire urged, "I feel that another statement of neutrality might be in order. . . . It will head off the cry that a La Guardia victory is a reverse for you. . . .") And Flynn, clutching for a surer grip on victory, emulated a tactic of the Hearst papers: in headlines or in eight-point type, La Guardia was "the little red flower of Communism." Tammany, too, exercised its considerable skill with ad hominem argument, issuing a pamphet entitled "No Red, No Clown, Shall Rule This Town."

A few weeks before November 7, La Guardia's chances to lead New York down new paths brightened considerably, for Moses came out for La Guardia—after some urging, for he was far from fond of La Guardia's liberalism. Moses's backing proved invaluable; it merited front-page press coverage and, more importantly, it gave the impression that Moses was also speaking for Al Smith—always the derby-wearing cigar-chomping darling of New York—who had remained out of the campaign.

The fight continued even on election day, to the very moment the polls closed.

It was a day of violence, of Keystone Kops action, and especially a day of vindication.

Determinedly, Tammany set out to steal the election, in order to be sure of winning. From Dutch Schultz down to the lowly pickpocket, Tammany had willing helpers. Tammany, after all, protected criminals, and it was therefore to their best interests to see to it that Tammany stayed in power. Why, Dutch Schultz—notorious beer runner and racketeer—paid Tammany off, to the tune of between twelve and fifteen thousand dollars, for the election of his candidate for district attorney. Even civil service employees backed Tammany, for Tammany made it possible for them to get their jobs without benefit of an examination.

Fusion set out early in the morning to prevent grand larceny at the polls. Those who stood alertly watching for irregularities were called "fusioneers," and they ranged from prizefighter Tony Canzoneri to Park Avenue blue blood Clendenin Ryan.

Also on sentry duty, La Guardia came across a polling place in his neighborhood where twenty Tammany men had taken charge. Tearing the red Tammany badge off of one of them, he screamed, "You're thugs! Get out!" And when policemen, probably on Tammany's payroll, stopped him from hitting one of the "thugs," he vowed with blistering blue words to kick these hoods in uniform off the force as soon as he got into office.

Watching the returns in the den of Seabury's East 63rd Street home was like watching them in another world, a world of elegance, a world without thugs. The returns had a utopian air, too; La Guardia was clearly winning.

An urgent phone call from a reporter at the Hotel Astor, where the Fusion victory celebration was to be, sent La Guardia racing across town. The celebrants at the Astor joyously mobbed La Guardia. Finally, he learned from the reporter who had called him and from W. Arthur Cunningham—a Catholic banker from Queens who was running for comptroller and expected, as a Catholic, to capture the Catholic vote—that Cunningham's enormous lead of 50,000 had dropped to 4,000, and the returns from four hundred precincts were being held up.

"Come on, Arthur," La Guardia said. "I'll go get those four hundred precincts for you."

The men sped to Police Headquarters, in downtown Manhattan, and rushed to its top floor, where the Tammany-controlled Board of Elections were up to their nefarious work. Upon La Guardia's entrance, those in the vast room went into a shocked silence; then the police began to overwhelm the Mayor-elect with obviously fawning, servile attention.

La Guardia thrust them aside, bolted into the room; though technically, until he was sworn in, he had no right to give orders, he shouted, "I want 400 patrolmen mobilized behind headquarters just as fast as they can get here."

"Yes—Mr. Mayor," a captain said, and started for a phone.

La Guardia turned to an inspector. "Get me 400 patrol wagons. Roll 'em into the alley behind headquarters as fast as God will let you."

"Yes, Mr. Mayor."

"As fast as each patrolman gets here, send 'em to one of the 400 precincts in which the count for Comptroller is being held up. Tell 'em to mount guard over that voting machine with drawn gun."

"Yes, Mr. Mayor."

"As fast as the patrol wagons get here, send one of them to each precinct. In every case the cops are to load the voting machine into the patrol wagon and bring it here at once."

"Yes, Mr. Mayor."

"By God, I'm going to count those votes for Comptroller myself."

And La Guardia would have, but word of what he was up to spread fast and effectively, and the returns that had been held up from 400 precincts started coming in. And they elected Cunningham to the office of comptroller.

"There you are, Arthur," La Guardia said, "you're elected. Let's all get a drink."

Back at the Astor Hotel, La Guardia climbed up on a table in the packed grand ballroom and said, after managing to silence the cheering in his honor, "My first qualification for this great office is my monumental personal ingratitude. I want you to remember that a cause, not a man, has succeeded. It will not be easy for our administration to say to you, after this successful campaign, 'Sorry, there is nothing in this for you who made the success possible.' But that is the way it must be. I will hire the best men for every job, even if they happened to vote against me."

He made many other statements not usually expressed by a victorious candidate. "They didn't elect me for my looks," he said. "They wanted things done [a bankrupt New York City had to be made solvent] and they knew damn well I'd do them."

La Guardia also told his campaign workers, after both his opponents had conceded: "We licked both wings of Tammany, but I have only the votes of a plurality." (The final tally: La Guardia 868,522, McKee 609,053 and O'Brien 586,672.) "I am determined to give this city the kind of administration that will provide me with a thumping majority four years from now."

Finally, La Guardia, his wife, and a friend escaped the crush at the Astor and made it to the La Guardia apartment, small, far from luxurious. In the midst of their private little victory celebration, Mrs. La Guardia said to her husband, "Now we can afford to get a new rug for the living room. You know how long I've wanted it."

CHAPTER SEVENTEEN

LA GUARDIA CAME INTO OFFICE LIKE A LION AND would go out—eventually, twelve years later—still roaring and clawing, though a bit subdued.

The times called for belligerence, for belligerence usually went with action. The Major even had a chip on his shoulder concerning his inauguration; there would definitely, he said, be none of the customary flowers, speeches and "hail to the Chief." And he brought up the Depression in explaining why: "I never heard of a receiver taking possession of a business with a brass band. Ordinarily one looks forward to inauguration day, but in this case there seems to be little left to enjoy, and what little is left is rapidly being taken away." After the inauguration, just as lugubriously, he told the press, "The first few months will be taken up clearing away the debris and repairing the ruins."

His hostility, aside from being an expression of his personality, stemmed from the realization that the odds were heavily loaded against him. For the past sixteen years, graft and corruption had gnawed away the city's financial underpinnings; to make sure it didn't topple, thirty million dollars would be needed. The city's credit had been shattered, however, and loans or grants from the federal government could therefore not be obtained, though cities all over the country were receiving them. As one consequence, eighteen miles of the city's subway system—which had cost the city $152 million—lay idle, and the system could not be completed because this would require $23,160,000, an unobtainable sum.

La Guardia knew that he had to somehow balance the budget; until he did, he could not get to work on his utopian dreams: beer gardens

161

on the Harlem River; music and art that would make New York City an equal culturally with the capitals of Europe; the ripping out of the slums; the creation of parks, playgrounds, low-cost housing, health stations . . . But he had to balance the budget, first of all, and he had to do it in two ways certain to be very unpopular: drastic cuts—in jobs, in salaries—and additional taxes.

La Guardia also had to keep his eye on the Tammany Tiger, wounded and therefore desperation-dangerous. It had veto power in both the Board of Aldermen and the State Senate. It opposed the elimination of jobs, for without jobs to be handed out, Tammany could not exist.

La Guardia blustered to scare the Tiger. In various quotable ways, he let it be known that his administration would not be shaped or confined by partisanship: "I'm retiring from politics for the four years of my term"; "there is no Democratic or Republican way of cleaning the streets"; "to the victor belongs the responsibility of good government."

When a politician started to criticize some of his appointments, La Guardia shot back, "Didn't I say I'd appoint men competent for the job?"

"Yes," grumbled the politician, "but that was during the campaign."

The Mayor-elect's dark eyes flashed. "Ah, but I wasn't fooling."

From a traditional, conventional standpoint, La Guardia's appointees were most unusual. As his fire commissioner, La Guardia picked, of all people, a fireman, a man who fought fires and thoroughly understood the prevention and extinguishing of fires. It obviously didn't bother La Guardia that his selection for commissioner of accounts, Paul Blanshard, had been—or might still be—a Socialist, one who had teamed up with another Socialist, Norman Thomas, to write a book about what was wrong with New York. (It most certainly bothered Tammany that Blanshard, in addition to being a Socialist, was a member of the Anti-Tammany City Affairs Committee, and that he would as commissioner have access to the books of any office financed by city funds, and the power of subpoena over any official on the payroll.) Never before had out-of-towners—simply because of their competence—been selected for office, as was the case with John L. Rice and Austin H. MacCormick. And Robert Moses, hated though he was by Seabury and—unbeknown to La Guardia—also hated by President Roosevelt, was named park commissioner. He was picked for a variety of political reasons and because he was an expert who produced in astounding volume. (When Moses reprimanded the sanitation commissioner for putting garbage cans near a park, the commissioner asked how garbage men were to know that, when they put down a garbage can, a new park would spring up beside it the next day.) Through Langdon W. Post, the tenement house commissioner appointee, La Guardia voiced again his determination to provide housing at a cost of "somewhere between $6 and $8 a room." There seemed to be no end to the newsworthy aspects of La Guardia's selections. Of Berle, La Guardia said, "There isn't a job in city government I wouldn't give him. He's an economist with vision. He stimulates me." Stimulated, La Guardia, in need of Berle's expert financial advice, made Berle city chamberlain, a sinecure, which Berle vowed to abolish —and would accept only on the condition that he receive less than its $15,000-a-year salary. (James J. Walker had raised his own salary to $40,000. And he joked about how much he would have been worth if he had worked full time. In his first two years in office he had seven vacations, 143 days away from the duties of City Hall.)

Now—as one of those assembled in the library of Judge Seabury's home for the midnight swearing-in of the new Mayor—Berle's thoughts were troubled; he was worrying that it might snow.

That Sunday, December 31, 1933, was an unusually warm day, the kind with clouds—a gray overcast—and a threat of rain rather than snow. That threat didn't keep a crowd of 300,000 from jamming Times Square. On this night, the revelers had something special to celebrate; for this was the first nondry New Year's Eve in fourteen years. The Times Square crowd and all the other New York City crowds were therefore "aglow with legal spirits." It was as though they had only one solitary problem: legal whiskey just hadn't had enough time to age.

A gallant attempt—on a number of fronts—was made to negate a very real, ever-present problem, the Depression. That, at least, it was on the way out was deduced, not too scientifically, from the size of the crowds. One *New York Times* headline joyously declared: "New Year's Revels Gayest in 14 Years." Wealth, it seemed, had once again displaced poverty. What evidence of this? Why, Park Avenue florists checked the barometer of their trade and made a happy announcement. The previous year, roses, plebeian roses, had been purchased; it was a "rose crowd," but this year's crowd was an "orchid crowd," and orchids sold from $1.50 to $5.00.

Evidence of the demise of both the Depression and Prohibition could also be noted at the Waldorf-Astoria. Tradition, of course, required the playing of "Auld Lang Syne"—and eight orchestras did their level best to keep together in playing it. Significantly, they then left the maudlin tempo, picking up the snappy "Happy Days Are Here Again." And could something optimistic be deduced from the dancing? There were very few waltzes; people still wanted, needed, jazz, but now, it seemed, instead of expressing a what-the-hell attitude, jazz was the exhilaration of welcoming those happy days that were back once again.

Economist and financial wizard Berle felt none of this keyed-up, alcohol-inspired faith. As he moved among those assembled in the well-appointed Seabury library, prior to the swearing-in, part of his thought kept returning—insistently and worriedly—to the possibility that the threat of rain might turn into actual, devastating snowfall.

Should snow fall, for every inch that fell 1,360,000 cubic yards would have fallen on the streets of New York City—streets which if put end to end, for the sake of a familiar graphic illustration, would reach from New York City to Los Angeles, a street 3,500 miles in length.

Berle may not have known this specific gee-whiz statistic, but he did know that New York City was "busted," and that he did not want it mortgaged to the banks. At the chamberlain's office, assisted by a few men, he found that the city was 250 million dollars more in debt than the books showed; bills hadn't been vouchered, and they'd piled up—ever higher and higher.

When the snow began to fall that night, just as Berle had feared, it pleased only children and the unemployed who had signed up ahead of time for snow removal jobs. "We had to clear it up," Berle recalled decades later, "and I didn't know where the money was coming from to pay the bill. So I spent all that night finding a way to steal some money—it came pretty close to that, I'm afraid—to just pay the current bills. The method we finally discovered was to sell short term notes of the city to the Teachers' Retirement Funds, which had a great deal of cash piled up in them. And since you sell six months notes, I figured within the next six months we'd find some way of getting in some more money. And we did."

As the snow fell New Year's night, Berle, of course, didn't know the skies that winter would dump 31.5 inches of snow on New York City's streets—or 1,360,000 cubic yards multiplied by 31.5. (A critic of the administration said 52 inches fell.) And he also didn't know there would be approximately six weeks during which those streets would be covered by snow-turned-to-ice. Ashes to prevent slipping made this ice as hard as cement. Snow removal equipment couldn't remove ice; when this was attempted, it ruined the equipment. Finally, men attacked the piles of ice with air-pressure drills. And all this was but one of the city's operational expenses that winter.

While the snow was falling, La Guardia—a few minutes after midnight—stood before a friend of his, Justice Philip J. McCook—"Puddin-head" to La Guardia—solemn and official now in a black robe. The male guests present wore tuxedos. La Guardia appeared to have made one sartorial concession; his business suit was freshly pressed. La Guardia's right hand was up; Justice McCook recited the oath; La Guardia said, "I do so solemnly swear"; and as his first unofficial act upon becoming New York City's ninety-ninth mayor, he turned to Marie and kissed her. But he turned back to business fast; no more than a minute later he ordered the arrest of Lucky Luciano, a Mr. Real Big of crime.

Before the newsreel cameras, he had this to say: "I have just assumed the office of the Mayor of the City of New York. The Fusion administration is now in charge of our city. Our theory of municipal government is an experiment to try to show that a nonpartisan, nonpolitical local government is possible." (La Guardia might have mentioned Seth Low and John Purroy Mitchel, for they had been fusion mayors and had attempted municipal reform, but that would have diminished the fantasy that New York City was his and that, by God, he was going to mold it into an ideal municipality.)

Immediately after the swearing-in, Berle rushed downtown to his chamberlain's office; there was something of paranoia in his headlong rush. Though he said he "went out of instinct," he also added that the first thing one did upon being appointed to an office was "take possession pronto." Had this been expressed by a cartoon, the shadows about him would have been labeled "Tammany" and "Financial Battles."

La Guardia and his wife merely went home, to their "modest" apartment, so everyone described it, at the unfashionable, unaristocratic end of Fifth Avenue. Now that he was Mayor, the apartment house in which he lived would be distinguished from the others in the block by a solitary policeman standing guard at the door. The elevator that took the Mayor and his wife to the sixth floor was ancient, creaky, a slow-moving cage which in a cartoon might be labeled, à la the Berle office shadows, "The Office That Our New Mayor Has Inherited," the implication being that La Guardia's methods would be modern, his pace fast.

The apartment was indeed "modest." One glance at its furnishings, and you knew that an interior decorator hadn't been consulted. A bedroom had been converted into a study, with a desk under a window from which one had a view of the northern end of Central Park. On the bookshelves lining a wall, not a single novel; instead, biographies of Washington and Lincoln and collections of their writings, Farmers Bulletins, Congressional Records, single volumes on economics and government. A puritanical, all-business library. The living room certainly did need the rug about which Marie had exclaimed on the night her husband had become mayor.

La Guardia went to sleep early. He believed in being well rested for the next day's work, in being prepared in every way for the four-year-war that lay ahead.

For years and years, La Guardia had his heart set on being mayor of New York; and, finally, victorious, he had been able to say of himself: "To the victor belongs the responsibility of good government."

To handle this inconceivably difficult job, a wide streak of masochism in one's makeup would help. The pressures are without end, as are the complaints and the work to be done. One's greatest accomplishments are certain not to be appreciated by someone or some group or some faction. By comparison, a governor's job is a lark; principally, because it does not touch people as directly. If an apartment is cold in New York City, or a subway car overcrowded, or garbage uncollected, the complaint can be placed on City Hall's doorstep. The Mayor's constituents expect him to take care of all such problems, and he has no place to hide, no one on whom he can shift the blame.

This state of affairs is not limited to the present, the immediate past or to the New York City mayoralty. Early in the twentieth century, Tom Johnson, the outstanding reform mayor of Cleveland, Ohio, said with a plaintiveness peculiar to his office, "If the cars were too cold it was my fault, if they were too hot it was my fault. If the cars were late, if they stopped on the wrong corners, if they were held up at railway crossings, if a conductor couldn't change a twenty-dollar bill, it was my fault. It is even said that a man who fell off a car one night exclaimed as he went sprawling on the pavement, 'Damn Tom Johnson.'" (Urban complexity, of course, has increased since Johnson's day, and the problems that any city's mayor might have would be magnified and intensified many fold—and especially in New York City because of its monstrous size.)

The people feel justified in blaming the mayor. They, after all, elected him to do a job, and—with at least one important qualification—he has the power to do it. Ergo, if he falls short of their expectations—in performance, in behavior, in style—they have the right, are even duty-bound, to blame him.

And they have access to him—by phone, by letter, even in person, and he must respond. A few weeks after he became mayor, La Guardia received a letter concerning the pronunciation of his name. He answered:

I have your letter of recent date. The name La Guardia is distinctly Italian and therefore should be pronounced La Gwardia. The pronunciation La Gardia seems to be taking much better. Perhaps it is like La Folletté now being universally pronounced La Foll'ette.

I think what is most important is not how people will be calling me, but what people will be calling me.

As the city's host, he is a welcomer, a hander-out of keys to the city. A guest of honor, a principal speaker at breakfasts, lunches, dinners, festivals—music, strawberry, et cetera. A layer of cornerstones, a snipper of ribbons, a puller of switches. All such events consume an enormous amount of time and energy, but they are a public relations contact with people and a source of power. (La Guardia emphatically vowed upon taking office, "I shall cut out all public dinners, and even smokers. Occasionally when there is a meeting of people from other parts of the country, I shall attend it. This, I feel, is part of a Mayor's duty. . . ." In a matter of weeks, however, La Guardia had delivered scores of speeches, engaged politicians at lunches and had even sat for Jo Davidson, industriously sculpting Mayor La Guardia's head.)

With a mayor's power comes the price tag of responsibility. For one thing, he must exercise good judgment in making appointments, appointing capable individuals who can deliver that which has been ordered and who are able to manage a heavy load. (Commissioner of Investigation Blanshard had an office a block from City Hall. Every few hours, La Guardia had Blanshard on the wire, commanding him to come right over to see him, for he had a scandal he wanted him to run down.)

167

Being omnipotent and omniscient, the mayor, of course, can handle effectively each and every crisis coming off the conveyor belt. His solutions for strikes, threatened race riots, blocked transportation must *be* solutions, and if they're not, he must answer to the people. (Before being in office two months, La Guardia had a taxi strike, had a laundry strike, had a waiters' strike.)

To add another straw to his unbearable burden, the mayor's power is limited by the State of New York. In order for a theoretically all-powerful mayor to handle his problems, he must obtain the legislation these problems require from an intransigent state, jealous of its own powers and secure, far up the Hudson, in a remote Albany fortress. (La Guardia had brawls immediately with Governor Lehman over New York City's right to cut municipal salaries and institute taxes.)

Among the city's innumerable other worrisome matters, it has an unending lack of money. This penury makes it difficult for the mayor to choose between this, that or the other. Eventually, something must be chosen; this means something, of necessity, isn't chosen, and that enemies of the undying sort are made.

When faced by impossible choices, the mayor must still make a choice. A leader, he must, naturally, appear decisive. To take but one case, involving a law which required that an apartment in a tenement have its own toilet. Compliance—that is, installing toilets—necessitated raising rents. When tenants were not able to meet such rent hikes, landlords had no choice but to evict and close up their tenements. La Guardia couldn't tell landlords to break the law and not install the toilets; but if he didn't do that, he couldn't insist that tenants pay a higher rent if they didn't have the wherewithal. Now, how could one appear a decisive leader in such a situation?

After fifteen years of impatient waiting, this was the far from idyllic office that La Guardia finally attained. But it was perfect for him; he went at its incredible challenges with the gusto of a reformer, the energy of a dynamo running at full speed.

The gusto and energy that La Guardia brought to the office—his view of it, his goals, his style of operation—determined what he accomplished. And his first day at the big walnut desk, with its half-dozen buzzers that brayed for assistants, presented, in miniature, the singular character of his twelve-year tenure.

La Guardia woke early on New Year's Day. That his first hours as mayor of New York City had been spent in sleep symbolized the sort of administration he would not countenance; better, therefore, that those hours be over and done with.

Dressed in an old blue serge suit, an old gray overcoat and the wide-brimmed black fedora that declared his individuality, vividly, visually, immediately, he descended in the ancient elevator. He left his home at 1274 Fifth Avenue, reporters noted, at 8:28. (As mayor of the City of New York, he now rated the precise recording of insignificant detail.) The Mayor then crossed the snowy sidewalk to the big Chrysler Imperial that had 30,000 miles on it, a hand-me-down from former Acting Mayor McKee. This city limousine didn't conform to a license-plate tradition: Walker's plate had been "W 1," O'Brien's "O B 1." City Hall witty talk held that "L A G 1" might, for obvious reasons, not be quite appropriate. So McKee's license number remained on the car.

In the future, the Mayor would head for City Hall by one of a variety of routes. This made it possible for him to see more of what was going on in his city, to stop and talk with street cleaners or policemen. Caught off guard by his unexpected appearance, they were, as a consequence, more revealing. On this day, special in many aspects, he was first of all driven to Police Headquarters to swear in Major General John F. O'Ryan as police commissioner. Wholesale swearing-ins would characterize this day.

The days ahead would demand a basic routine, subject to innumerable variations. (Crises, after all, cannot be scheduled.) Upon his arrival at City Hall, he would usually command his secretary to "Send in two stenographers!" Without breaking stride, off would come his coat as he made for the combination washroom and clothes closet adjoining his office. The clothes closet had many hangers, which had been used during other administrations, but would not be in La Guardia's. He simply ignored the empty hangers and hung his coat on a hook—a clear statement that he tolerated clothes but had not a moment's time for finery. At his desk, horn-rimmed glasses in place, he plunged into the heaped mail. To one of the stenographers, he dictated short, to-the-point answers. To get joy out of his mail, he employed sarcasm, a tongue-in-cheek approach, the punch line. Some letters he could dismiss with one of a three-word code: "nuts," "regrets," "thanks," and a form letter, expressing the sentiment of the code word, would then go forth. Almost simultaneously, the other stenographer would be told things La Guardia wanted done: matters to be investigated, people to be called.

After the mail, La Guardia made a few long distance calls and conferred—sometimes at length—with the heads of different departments, switching effortlessly from a problem related to parks, to one of education, to one of the budget. During all this, there were constant entrances and exits of individuals and committees; because a number of doors were involved, the activity appeared especially urgent, frenetic. For all, invariably, he had immediate answers, incisive criticism. (When the director of the budget read him a report that went into detailed figures and that was to be presented to the Board of Estimate, La Guardia said, "Cut those figures out. They're unnecessary. Don't you think the members of the Board of Estimate can subtract?")

The montage of varied activities seemed, at times, to pick up even more speed: a couple arrives and requests that La Guardia marry them and he does, with nonromantic dispatch and with—at his insistence—no photographs or publicity. A Board of Estimate meeting. Then visitors—and more visitors. Late lunch—a sandwich, at a restaurant on 14th Street. La Guardia's back at three; his overcoat's hung on its hook. He unbuttons his vest as he sits down at his desk. Upon the arrival of the Armory Board, men of serious mien, he rises and buttons his vest and, in short order, straightens them out on a technical matter in connection with the Building Code. A few new appointees are sworn in. More meetings, more visitors, more decisive solutions to problems . . .

Today, January 1, 1934, his first day in office, La Guardia charged out of the old limousine, before the chauffeur could go through the motions of assisting his passenger, and bounded up the stone steps of City Hall. In spite of the central hall's size, welcomers packed it, and he shouldered his way through them. After passing the office of the aldermanic president, which he had occupied twelve years earlier, he turned to the left and headed for the mayoralty suite at the west end of the building. There, O'Brien waited—his jowls flowing over his wing collar—to turn over the office of mayor to him, with cliché ritual and choice malapropisms.

On that New Year's day, he swore in the various members of his Cabinet, and in the process he told them—in hard-hitting terms—that he was giving them a free hand and he wanted efficiency and economy and complete absence of political partisanship. He also had a few specific words for each of them. To Corporation Counsel Paul Windels: "I don't care whether the Law Department is the biggest in the world. I want it to be the best." To Commissioner of Taxes Dominick Trotta: "There's something wrong in the tax department, but I don't know just what it is. See if you can find out." And so he went, from one to another, bulldozing his way verbally.

At Police Headquarters, in addressing two hundred ranking officers, he showed neither the charm of which he was capable nor the mercy. He informed them: "I have been told that Fulton Street has been considered the deadline for crooks. That deadline is now removed. It is replaced by the Hudson River on the west, the Atlantic Ocean on the south, the Westchester County line on the north and the Nassau County boundary line on the east." In addition to geography, his lesson for that day included dismissable offences: intoxication, being the recipient of a gift—even if the gift were no more than a nickel cigar.

That first day in office, La Guardia made it clear that he meant what he said. He also set the pace of his administration, expecting all to keep up with it. (L A G 1 was definitely not appropriate for La Guardia's license plate.) Because he attended to details of hundreds of departments and bureaus, he worked incessantly, especially in his first months in office. Because he didn't delegate authority, critics charged him with being a poor administrator; because he struck hard verbal blows, preferred the direct to the circumspect, shouted and ranted and screamed, the wounded charged him, with justification, of being a dictator, a bully. When city employees affected by La Guardia's economy measures complained, he let fly a nautical metaphor: "I found a shipwreck and I'm trying to get the city employees into a lifeboat until I can put them on a sound ship."

In recalling this difficult period, Berle came to the defense of his close friend. Those who accused La Guardia of unpleasant tactics weren't taking into account that "one fourth of New York didn't know where its next meal was coming from on the night of January 1, 1934. And we hadn't any money for relief, either." At such a time, Berle pointed out, "the last thing you're likely to argue about is matters of style. . . ." La Guardia had a job to do, and he was going to get it done *his* way, which very well may have been the only way. To clinch his defense of La Guardia, Berle said, "I personally don't think anyone else could have done that job at that time. . . ."

CHAPTER EIGHTEEN

T O BERLE, THE SNOW OF THAT WINTER DID NOT mean the delicacy, the geometric precision of its crystals—or the nostalgic emotion of Christmas scenes. The unemployed viewed the same snow as heaven-sent; its removal meant temporary employment. But a February of below-zero cold set in, and the homeless and dispossessed had to find more substantial shelter than that afforded by an entryway or a completely alfresco park bench.

For five years there had been talk of opening up the empty, little-used armories in the winter, for the poor. But when La Guardia became mayor and spoke, action resulted. He issued an order that the armory at 26th and Lexington, for a starter, open its doors at once, for the simple reason that men shouldn't be allowed to freeze.

Adequate relief required money—an interminable flow of it; and as mayor you had to be thoroughly pragmatic to keep it flowing. But relief also called for compassion, an emotion which has appeared tentatively throughout history and at an evolutionary crawl. Centuries earlier in London, the indigent—no matter what their age, sex or ailment—were thrown into the workhouse. In New York City's remote past, there were comparable brutalities. The pauper, in addition to the anguish of his situation, bore his stigma for all to see: a brightly colored badge on his sleeve inscribed with a large *P*. His scarlet letter —as odious as Hester Prynne's.

The poor continued to be regarded as being solely responsible for their plight, in spite of periodic economic upheavals, the regularity of which, at the very least, might have suggested inevitability: 1873–1879, 1893–1897, 1907, pre- and post–World War I. And what followed the crash of 1929 surpassed all previous troubled years in the relief that was required; still, the victims, as communicants of hallowed Free Enterprise, felt guilt and inferiority.

Eventually, Hoover's doctrine of private charity, and of each community taking care of its own, collapsed under the weight of inadequacy. The relief load of municipalities was given a helping hand by the state, in accordance with the Wicks Act of September 1931. Then the federal government came to the rescue, and its aid made it possible for state and local governments to have balanced budgets. (Right from the start, La Guardia had not only attempted to understand the causes of periodic economic disasters, but had realized that in addition to immediate help the individual had to be provided with future security. And if the system needed changing—radical though that thought might be—it should be changed. He thus anticipated the New Deal, and knew that he had, for he spoke of Franklin Delano Roosevelt as being "a distinguished faculty member of my school of thought.")

Haunted by the problems of relief, La Guardia spent more time with William Hodson, his commissioner of welfare, than with any of his other nineteen commissioners. He needed a man like Hodson, a professional social worker. He needed expertise, believed that the heads of all departments should be competent and effective. In welfare, he had inherited a mess from Tammany which lent itself to Ripley's "Believe It or Not": the biggest piece of social work any city had ever undertaken—its monthly cost, $20,000,000; the number on relief equalled the population of Detroit and exceeded that of Los Angeles; on relief, one could find a former $40,000-a-year man from Wall Street, a former member of Harvard's faculty; New York City had 164 bread lines; the relief rolls rose from the time La Guardia entered office until it reached its peak in March 1936, when one out of five depended on work relief or home relief.

Such statistics might evoke wonder, but they were separated by objectivity from even a single breathing, striving, dreaming individual. So La Guardia, in addition to spending an inordinate amount of time with Hodson, dropped into municipal lodging houses unannounced, incognito. He would stand in line, like the other unfortunates; but he had come to receive more than shelter: a truthful, unrehearsed view of how those in line were going to be treated. In addition, he could not help but feel the obvious hopelessness of the men—whose individuality had been lost, who had no present and, in all likelihood, no future.

Ineligible for relief, single men came here. And here they slept fitfully in vast fields of beds, tiered and as uniform as crosses in a military cemetery.

La Guardia preferred seeing for himself to second-hand reports. In addition to learning more, there was the promise of conflict—even of hand-to-hand combat. (Had he copied this dropping-in technique from Theodore Roosevelt, whom he greatly admired and who had used the technique like a big stick during his police commissioner days in New York? More likely, they were sufficiently alike in temperament —and objectives—for them to have arrived at this technique independently.)

One May morning during his first term, La Guardia appeared at a relief office on the Lower East Side because of an anonymous complaint. As he stood in line, he was shocked to find only one employee interviewing applicants, while many others lolled about.

Having seen enough, La Guardia charged through the line of relief applicants for the office of the director. A man tried to stop him, but La Guardia hurled him to one side, and gave another the same treatment. Then a third man—a cigar in his mouth, a derby on his head— tried to block him. With two swings, La Guardia knocked the cigar from his mouth and the derby from his head. "Take off your hat when you speak to a citizen!" La Guardia shouted. By the time La Guardia had reached the director's office and found that the director wasn't there, the employees had finally realized the awful truth: this little whirlwind was the Mayor of the City of New York.

La Guardia ordered a secretary to call Commissioner Hodson and tell him that he wanted to see him at once. By the time Hodson, who was a bald man with round spectacles and a mustache, arrived, La Guardia had seen to it that all the applicants had been taken care of; and, en masse, they gave him a cheer for what he had done.

"You wait here, Bill," La Guardia told Commissioner Hodson, "until your director gets here. If he doesn't have a good excuse for his absence, he's fired, and by good excuse I mean a doctor's certificate that he was ill this morning."

As La Guardia headed for the door, he paused long enough to point at the cigar-smoking derby-wearer and say, "Oh, yes, Bill. There's another S. of a B. that has no job."

At City Hall, La Guardia took complaints—including those concerned with relief—as they came. He didn't always resort to sending derbies and cigars flying. During his second term, three representatives of the Workers' Alliance, a liberal labor organization, called on him.

One of the delegation told La Guardia, "A family of three cannot make it, cannot live, on forty-five dollars a month."

"Boys, don't forget I am not a sovereign state." La Guardia squirmed as though his swivel chair suddenly didn't conform to his breadth. "It's hell the way you pound in on me. You crush me, because I'm decent." (In three declarative sentences, he belittled his power, complained of mistreatment, pointed out that he was Virtue Being Trampled in the Dust. After that, surely, it should be harder for this delegation to make demands.)

"We know it, Mr. Mayor," another of the three said. "That's why we ride you more than we do other mayors. You must excuse us. We have been crushed some, too. Over a thousand of us have been arrested in other cities and a lot of us have been badly beaten up."

"Boys, I don't altogether blame you. I will help as I can. But look at this desk." As always it was cluttered with work to be done, suggesting the extent of his daily labors. Who had time to look at the clock, or light a cigar as much as it needed lighting, or go to the toilet when one should? "What breaks my heart is that I am more interested in your cases than anybody else, and you ride me." (He was so good to them, how could they mistreat him so? He intended that his tactic should make them attempt to prove that his charge was unjustified by a sudden reduction of their demands.)

Before they could react—make other requests, possibly—La Guardia called a secretary and dictated orders that would ameliorate some of the conditions about which they had complained. And as they left, undoubtedly convinced that he had been "decent," he called for them to come and see him in a month if what he had ordered hadn't been taken care of.

Though La Guardia may have done some playacting with these representatives of Labor, he was, nonetheless, on Labor's side. But he made it quite plain that this was not the case with his Board of Aldermen, virtually a Board of Tammanymen and "dedicated to his undoing." Their feud zeroed in on relief. When La Guardia spoke up at a meeting for a relief budget of vast proportions, an alderman objected on the grounds that relief money was going where it shouldn't and that he had proof that some even went to prostitutes.

"I thought that question was settled two thousand years ago," La Guardia shouted, "but I see I was wrong!" He twisted about, as if trying to locate someone. "Mr. Sergeant at Arms, clear the room! Clear the room—so this big bum can throw the first stone!"

The aldermen fought back by starting an official inquiry into work and home relief, fought as though their backs were to the wall. The very concept of relief offended them; it was an un-American answer to the problem of unemployment. (Actually, what Tammany had against relief was that relief wrought havoc with patronage—the sine qua non of Tammany district leaders. How reward the faithful, when the faithful, in order to get relief, had to prove need? The only need experienced by most of the faithful was the need for special privilege.)

As a consequence, prior to La Guardia's coming into office, Tammany did not have its heart in the dispensing of relief. It doled out relief orders instead of money—and only to families. These orders could be exchanged for rent and food—nothing else—and thus branded an individual as dependent on charity, as incapable of handling money. Under Tammany, relief funds ran out, so relief orders couldn't be depended on to come regularly every two weeks.

Tammany had its pride, and it was hurt by the changes La Guardia made: relief in the form of money, instead of relief orders; the eligibility for relief of single men; regular monthly relief checks; an increase in relief with the increase of prices; no favoritism for political reasons.

Understandably, the Tammany men who conducted the "Aldermen Inquiry" did not employ tactics worthy of a bishop. "What's a boondoggle?" they asked a teacher of handicrafts, one of many unemployed teachers who had been given employment in a special subject, a subject foreign to the conventional curriculum. The question stemmed from a determination to show that federal money was being spent in an utterly irresponsible, nonsensical way. In 1925, a scoutmaster had coined the word *boondoggle* as a name for utilitarian articles made of leather or wicker. Now, laughter and ridicule gave the funny-sounding term a pejorative connotation. The government of the United States of America had gone in for boondoggling—making boondoggles. The investigators also badgered witnesses of the Relief Administration, insulted them and didn't permit them to reply to insinuations. In the same spirit, they branded twenty relief employees with having "criminal records," which turned out to be, in the case of nineteen, mere tickets for speeding or inappropriate parking. And the constant cry: relief was wasteful, riddled with corruption, boondoggly. Since this made good copy, the press headlined it, and more often than not, the published stories didn't jibe or live up to the headlines.

A reporter for an anti-La Guardia newspaper told a relief official, "We haven't anything against you fellows, but we are out to get the Mayor, and I guess you'll have to stand the gaff."

In getting the Mayor, they complained eternally that he gave handouts to the so-called poor. La Guardia had a comeback for that. He said he could buy a parrot for two dollars and, in a day, teach it to say "dole, dole, dole." "But that parrot," he added, "would never understand an economic problem."

Also bombarded by aldermen concerning the unworthiness of relief recipients, La Guardia struck back with Mayor La Guardia's Committee on Unemployment Relief. Its objective—unlike the destructive aldermanic inquiry—was to make the administration of relief more equitable, effective, humane. As evidence of the integrity of the Mayor's Committee, it not only found fault with relief, but it also found assistance inadequate; it found that people in poverty areas frequently had to pay higher rents than those with more money; and it discovered a blacklist for those unemployed who tried to join a union of some kind. Finally, it made recommendations as to what the city should do.

As a result of the investigation by his committee, La Guardia decided on a reorganization of welfare. He therefore brought in Charlotte Carr, very able, formerly commissioner of labor in Pennsylvania. He also called upon Justine Wise Polier, then Mrs. Justine Wise Tulin, who had served on his investigative committee as secretary and counsel and who was the daughter of Rabbi Stephen S. Wise. (Rabbi Wise, as vice-chairman of the City Affairs Committee, a reform group organized in 1930, had fought for the removal of James J. Walker.)

Mrs. Polier—a reformer like her famous father and possessed of his commanding presence—became quite unpopular because she would go down each month before the budget hearing to point out the inadequacy of fiscal support in the welfare field.

One day, Mrs. Polier learned from someone that La Guardia was planning on appointing her to a court, though up to that time, 1935, no woman had ever received such an appointment. (She later recalled that she did not regard his appointing a woman as a political move or an indication he was ahead of his time. "I sometimes think," she observed, "I was kicked upstairs because I was troubling him too much about welfare.")

When La Guardia did offer her an appointment, it was to the Children's Court; and she told him that she preferred the Magistrates' Court, which was dealing, at that time, with injunctions against workers who tried to organize.

"That's just like you," La Guardia complained. "I offer you a judgeship and you want a magistracy; when I offer a magistracy to anybody else he wants a judgeship, because there's more money in a judgeship—and more kudos." (He ended up giving her a sixty day appointment, after which she would be sworn in for a full term.)

During those sixty days, La Guardia asked her if she would meet with General Hugh Johnson, a former head of the NRA, who had just come to New York with a million dollars to spend as WPA administrator for New York City. He began auspiciously by accusing the city of not exerting enough effort to move people from welfare to work relief.

Mrs. Polier and Mrs. Carr met with General Johnson, who projected a first impression, and succeeding ones, of the tough, military man. Johnson spoke like a sergeant barking orders and had facial features that singly and in combination appeared those of a rock-hard personality. Though a heart of gold might have beaten beneath his brass exterior, a perceptive person would tend to doubt it. Now, surrounded by army engineer officers, his assistants, he angrily denounced the failure of people to apply for work and demanded of Mrs. Polier and Mrs. Carr that everybody, *everybody*, be taken off welfare until they were screened through the Works Progress Administration. Mrs. Carr, in her wisdom, calmly suggested that she put all her staff to work and thus provide two thousand applications a day so that all the people on welfare could be absorbed in that way.

A shambles resulted. The poor, forever charged with not wanting to work, showed up at the armories, eager, clutching at this unexpected hope. They stood in lines around the armories, through the night and all day, but there were not sufficient jobs to go around. They stood in line, though to many of them WPA was as odious as the pauper's P of New York's Middle Ages.

The lucky ones who were transferred from welfare to WPA found it took so long to get checks that eventually they didn't even have money for food. Mrs. Polier tried to see the Mayor about this state of affairs.

In the meantime, General Johnson—living up to his exterior, and, undoubtedly, his interior as well—continued to attack "these bums who are on Welfare and don't want to work." (He was also battling with City Parks Commissioner Robert Moses, who claimed WPA consistently sent him "bums" instead of skilled workers and foremen, who were needed to supervise and keep the men working.) And Mrs. Polier continued to call the Mayor's office, saying that she wanted to answer Johnson's completely unjust charges. She was told that the Mayor didn't have time to see her. La Guardia knew Mrs. Polier was intelligent enough to realize that he was dependent on getting federal funds through WPA; and as a consequence, he could not possibly cross swords with Johnson and the federal administration.

Since such plots never remain simple, Mrs. Polier received a call from the Mayor's office telling her to come to City Hall to be sworn in. She answered that she would not come until the Mayor saw her about the welfare crisis. The Mayor's office replied with a haughty no.

Priding herself on her independence and on doing what she thought was right, Mrs. Polier wrote an open letter to General Johnson which, in substance, said that it was unfair to indict poor people on welfare in order to cover up administrative errors. She also, for the first time in her life, called a press conference, releasing her letter at the same time that it reached the Mayor's office.

Now, finally, La Guardia phoned. Angrily, he demanded that Mrs. Polier withdraw the letter. He also informed her that he had told General Johnson not to open it.

Mrs. Polier said, "I can't withdraw it."

"I'm Mayor of the City of New York," La Guardia told her. "And I order you to."

"There're some things concerning which one can't take orders, when it's a matter of conscience."

La Guardia lost his temper in earnest; he shouted that he would ruin Mrs. Polier in the city, that he would have Charlotte Carr say that she had lied.

"That's up to her," Mrs. Polier said.

"I'll have you removed from office by Judge Hill, who's the presiding judge."

"That's up to him."

"I'm Mayor of New York, and I order you."

"I'm sorry. There are some things I don't take orders on."

Mrs. Polier then went to the country, for a few weeks, to visit her son. During this time, she half expected that she might hear from La Guardia, but not a word did she hear. So she returned to New York and inquired about a job with an old law firm; her husband had died, and she wanted to be independent.

As soon as she arrived home, she received a telephone call from Charles C. Burlingham, the Sage of Reform. He asked, "What's the trouble between you and La Guardia?"

She told him what had happened.

"Oh, La Guardia came up to see me, and he asked me for one or two names for your court. And I said, 'What are you trying to do, pay political debts?' And then it dawned on me what was happening, and I said, 'What about Justine?' And he told me, 'I've got to have discipline of judges.' I hit the ceiling. 'What do you mean, discipline of the judiciary?'"

Burlingham then told Mrs. Polier that he and Felix Frankfurter, who was visiting, talked turkey to La Guardia.

"You know," Burlingham continued, "I think he came to see me because he knew he'd lost his head and done something wrong, but he didn't know how to reverse himself. And I think if you call, this can all be straightened out. How do you feel about continuing?"

"I want to continue," Mrs. Polier said, "but I can't. I had to make a decision. The next decision is up to him."

"Will you call him?"

"No, I can't call him. This is his decision."

Burlingham talked on and on in the role of peacemaker.

Finally Mrs. Polier said, "The only thing I can do in good conscience is to write him, say that you called me and asked me to talk to him. And if he wishes to talk to me, I'll be very glad to talk to him."

As soon as La Guardia received her letter, he called her. "Justine," he said. "I got your note. I want to talk to you. Can I send my car for you and see you at the house? Because I'm going to have my hair cut."

When Mrs. Polier arrived, he opened the door himself, escorted her to a room with glass doors, slammed them shut and said, "I might have expected this of Bob Moses, but not of you."

"Look, I tried to see you three times. You refused to see me, and I could not stand by and have the poor in New York unjustly accused without answering on their behalf. And I had to do what I felt was right."

"That's the trouble with you Wises," La Guardia said, with an impatient wave of his hand. "You always do whatever you think is right."

Mrs. Polier said, "Yes. And the difference between you and my father is this. When I do something that I think is right, he never criticizes me."

La Guardia came up to her. "All right," he said, suddenly concilia-tory, putting his arm around her, "you want a reappointment?"

"Yes. I've got to have my independence."

"All right. Come up for breakfast tomorrow. You don't want a crowd." (The press had been needling him as to what had happened to his woman judge.) "And you don't want any publicity or big show."

The next morning, La Guardia swore her in over scrambled eggs, and there was no longer a breach between them.

Decades later, Mrs. Polier said of La Guardia, "He was really a fabulous human being. Brilliant, hardworking, caring and wanting the city to be decent—and wanting to help human beings, in a very real sense. At the same time, he was being hit at from all sides. Terrible financial and fiscal problems so that he frequently didn't do what I would have liked to see him do, but I also realized the extent of his responsibilities. . . . You got mad at him, but you kept on loving him."

The Polier-La Guardia incident was scarcely a squall compared to the storm stirred up by the La Guardia-Moses-Roosevelt-Ickes im-broglio. Both had one vital factor in common: La Guardia's depen-dence on federal funds. Both also showed the means to which La Guardia would stoop, when cornered by strong egos and intolerable circumstances, to gain an indispensable end—money.

When La Guardia took office he had shaken incompetents out of the Triborough Authority. In a statement to the press, he said, "We are going to build a bridge instead of patronage. We are going to pile up stone and steel instead of expenses. We are going to build a bridge of steel—and spell steel s-t-e-e-l instead of s-t-e-a-l. . . ." He then ap-pointed Moses to direct the Authority.

And it was Moses who constituted the core of the drama that fol-lowed. In writing to FDR, Berle said of Moses, "He is often impulsive, incautious, and difficult to get on with." On another occasion, Berle said that Moses "would be a hard man to get along with if you were trying to be St. James the Beloved." Tough General Johnson found Moses so difficult, losing battle after battle to him, that he retreated from his post as WPA administrator of New York City. FDR, who never even thought of emulating St. James the Beloved, hated Moses; and Moses hated FDR. When FDR became governor of New York, he refused to keep Moses on as secretary of state, the position Moses held under Smith, because, he said, in obvious understatement, Moses rubbed him the wrong way. In turn, Moses said, "He'll make a good campaigner, but a lousy Governor."

Many incidents caused the flame of their deep distaste to flare up. When FDR, who had been appointed by Governor Al Smith to the Taconic Park Commission asked Moses, in charge of state parks, that his close friend and mentor Louis Howe be made secretary of the commission, Moses turned FDR down. He also added injury to this insult: Howe, he said, had no interest in parks, only in furthering FDR's interest.

Surprisingly, La Guardia didn't know about the Roosevelt-Moses feud when he had appointed Moses head of the Triborough Authority. Ironically, in his blissful ignorance, he believed Moses would be able via his various public works to draw federal money to New York City.

Then, just a matter of weeks after La Guardia took office, he called his corporation counsel, Paul Windels, for he had to have someone on whose shoulder he could cry and lament, "Jesus Christ, of all the people in the City of New York I had to pick the one man who Roosevelt won't stand for and he won't give me any more money unless I get rid of him. Jesus Christ, I had to pick the one that he hated. . . ."

Harold L. Ickes, PWA head, became a tender of communication lines between FDR and La Guardia. Deafness in his left ear aggravated a cantankerousness of which he was proud. His stocky body, square face, heavy nose and gold-rimmed spectacles were props for his role as Compleat Curmudgeon. After telling La Guardia that Moses had to be fired, he wrote in his secret diary:

La Guardia regretted the situation and said that if he had known it existed he wouldn't have thought for a minute of putting Moses on the board. He expressed the highest possible regard for the President and asked me to give him a few days to see what he might work out. I told him he could lay the responsibility on my shoulders. . . .

But La Guardia knew that blaming Ickes wouldn't pacify a pacing, roaring Moses; and he'd also been told by Berle and others that he, as mayor, simply couldn't yield to federal pressure. The horns of this dilemma were painfully sharp, had impaled him irretrievably.

To ask Moses to resign was like asking God to cease being the ruler of the universe. Reflexively, Moses employed his kind of subterfuge. Sure he would resign, Moses said, but—in addition to resigning from the Authority—he would resign as park commissioner and tell the public that though he had unquestionably been doing a good job, Mayor La Guardia, yielding to outside pressures, was forcing him out.

La Guardia stalled; this was a decision of sorts, better than any other he might make. He made promises to Ickes, promises that he broke. Ickes kept on La Guardia's back, because FDR was on his. (In La Guardia's report, after two years in office, he pointed out that the New York City experiment was noteworthy because "it seeks out and applies the most scientific, rather than the most politically expedient, methods of municipal administration." In a formal report of this kind, mentioning such tactics as evasion, deception and promise-breaking would, of course, be unseemly, and thus inappropriate.)

At this point, Ickes confided to his diary, "I served notice that I would honor no more requisitions for funds for PWA projects in New York until the Moses case had been disposed of."

La Guardia was torn; on the one hand, he wanted to appear to be his own man; on the other, he had to have public works—which would provide vitally needed employment—but he could have them only if he received federal money.

Ickes wrote, "I suggested to Mayor La Guardia that I would be satisfied to go along if he would write me a letter that upon the expiration of Moses' term the latter part of June he would not reappoint him."

La Guardia led Ickes to believe that he would do this. (More stalling for time, in the hope, undoubtedly, that something unforeseen would eventually arise that would do away with the problem.) But then La Guardia informed Ickes that he would reappoint Moses.

For an established curmudgeon, Ickes reacted almost genially—in that his next move gave La Guardia the best possible excuse for dismissing Moses. Ickes and FDR issued an order, supposedly a general order, that no more requisitions would be honored "for a project where the supervising authority also held a state or local office," which, of course, covered Moses.

To make things still easier for La Guardia, Ickes, as he recounted in his diary,

advised him that if he would write me a letter that he would not reappoint Moses, I would be satisfied with that and it would not be necessary to force Moses out at this time. He said he would write such a letter. I asked him to mail it to me. This was over the long distance telephone some time ago. He said he was coming to Washington and he would bring it to me. He came in last Saturday and I again asked him for the letter. He said he would write it when he got back to New York and mail it to me. It has not come, nor will it.

That "nor will it" indicated that Ickes realized, at long last, that La Guardia was giving him a runaround. But there was still more to come. La Guardia showed the order to Moses, as proof of his innocence and to make clear that it was all the President's doing. Whereupon Moses leaked the order to the press, with an accompanying statement, as long as a diatribe, that explained that he was being shoved out of office, not for incompetence, but because he hadn't been friendly with the Roosevelt administration.

La Guardia, in the meantime, had held off sending the letter which he had promised Ickes—and which Ickes felt would never be forthcoming. (Burlingham talked turkey to La Guardia, as in the Polier incident, advising him not to "submit to an unreasonable and tyrannical order from Washington.") Ickes took to the phone again, and to his diary:

I told him very clearly and distinctly just how accomplished a double-crosser he in fact is. He equivocated and evaded, but I know that I had him dead to rights. This was a great disappointment to me. I had felt that La Guardia was a man of real courage and substance, but in this matter, he has acted like the cheapest kind of a double-crossing politician.

Because the public clamor in defense of Moses continued without letup, Ickes and the President decided that they had to bring the Moses matter to a close. How to do it and yet save face? La Guardia provided the answer. Negate the order that had caused so much trouble; negate it by saying that it did not apply retroactively, which meant that it did not apply to Moses.

The plot included a subtlety as transparent as clear glass. La Guardia wrote Ickes a letter about Langdon Post, chairman of the Housing Commission, who was in the same situation as Moses. The order, so the letter said, would not apply to Post. "Then, as a postscript," Ickes wrote in his diary, "the Mayor called attention to the fact that the issue also involved Moses."

Thus Ickes and the President backed down in the Moses cause célèbre and La Guardia—by lying, stalling, breaking promises, doing everything that was right pragmatically—would receive the usual grant given on PWA projects for the Triborough Authority: 30 percent of the money spent in constructing the bridge, which amounted to $9.2 million. Unemployed men found employment because of this project. And on Sunday, July 11, 1936—twenty years after it was first proposed—the Triborough Bridge's opening ceremony took place. Ironically, as the ribbon was cut and people marched across the bridge, Tony Bennett sang "Marching Along Together." Present were Moses, President Roosevelt, Ickes . . .

On that particular day—of strained courtesies, ceremonial amenities —not one of the three would have gone so far as to say of La Guardia, as Judge Polier did, that though he made you mad, "you kept on loving him."

CHAPTER NINETEEN

IN THE THIRTIES, GROUCHO MARX OBSERVED THAT THE state of the economy in New York must really be bad, for the pigeons in Central Park had started feeding the people. As significant as that bit of black humor was the increased value of a dime; "buddy, can you spare a dime?"—a popular song's question—sprang straight from life. This deflationary fact proved to be true of the entire country. When a hustler in Houston solicited a man with desperate insistence, and he finally claimed that he had no money, she argued plaintively that what she was offering him only cost a dime.

La Guardia hated gambling. He especially hated policy—an anglicized form of the Italian *polizza*, meaning a lottery number—and the slot machine, for policy and the slot machine robbed the poor. To those living from dime to dime, however, gambling offered hope, the joys of anticipation and of fantasy. Coin in hand, one stood before a machine, placed the coin in its slot, pulled a lever and the machine came alive: a whirring sound, the spinning of three wheels on whose wide visible edge were likenesses of fruits—a lemon, significantly, among the plums, pears, cherries. The excitement focused on the stopping of those three wheels, for if the same fruit lined up when the wheels stopped, there'd be a click, then a pause—as though to heighten the tension—and then coins would come pouring out, a fortune in coins.

The naive victims thought that was all there was to it; it was your lucky day or it wasn't. But some machines had been manufactured, with premeditation, so that the same fruit could not possibly line up. And at best, given a fairer machine, you had, mathematically calculated, one chance in a thousand of making a "hit." If you continued to

186

play obsessively on and on and on, you could be certain of only one monetary fact, that twenty-five percent of your money would be retained by the machines—governed not by chance alone, but by organized crime.

Policy, or numbers, offered odds that were not much better. With a dime, you could purchase three loaves of stale bread. But what would they do for your spirit? On the other hand a dime, if your number turned up, and after a percentage went to the various individuals involved in the transaction, would be transformed by 600-to-1 odds into fifty dollars—a veritable inheritance.

Even as a child, La Guardia would not be taken in by the ineffable daydreams inherent in gambling, and he had scolded his mother, who weekly dropped her dime into policy's insatiable craw, and told her that she could not win. And now, as mayor, he set out quixotically to rid his city of gambling—rid it of all crime: gambling, prostitution and narcotics. The odds were overwhelmingly against him, but, curiously, he thought he could win.

Shortly after La Guardia was elected, Lewis J. Valentine, captain of the 68th Precinct, received a call from La Guardia via Corporation Counsel Windels.

"La Guardia wants to see you," Windels told Valentine. "He would like you to have breakfast with him at his home tomorrow morning."

The next day, Valentine went to 1274 Fifth Avenue. His blue eyes mirrored indefatigability; he had a chin that was rock and a manner described, understatedly, as gruff. Withal a modest man, he towered over La Guardia.

Before pouring their breakfast coffee, the Mayor said, "Tell me what's wrong with the Police Department."

Valentine had a great deal to say on that subject, without even going into the way he had been unjustly treated. Once upon a time, Valentine had been a patrolman, a beat pounder, earning $3,000 annually. Then under Walker, Lieutenant Valentine became Inspector Valentine; among his duties, the raiding of political clubhouses suspected of gambling. Valentine did too thorough a job. (This especially irritated clubhouses that were paying Jimmy Hines, the Tammany district leader par excellence, for protection.) Thus when Walker appointed Grover Aloysius Whalen police commissioner, Whalen demoted Valentine to a precinct captain on the other side of the East River, where Valentine remained in exile for six years. Certainly, Valentine had ideas about the Police Department and what was wrong with it. The department's goal was the protection of the lives and property of seven million residents of New York City and millions of visitors, and to accomplish this goal the most advanced scientific methods should be used. (Valentine expressed himself like a true Fusion partisan. *Science* was the key word, displacing *expedient*—politically expedient.)

La Guardia and Valentine had a number of heart-to-heart talks. One, which occurred in December 1933, differed from the others. Valentine had his hand on the doorknob, in the act of leaving, when La Guardia said quite matter-of-factly, "I'm going to see to it that O'Ryan makes you Chief Inspector and gives you a free hand."

La Guardia had liked the way Valentine, without counting personal cost, had smashed Tammany gambling houses, had served as a star witness in the Seabury Investigation. Why, the man—though his voice was far from falsetto—actually sounded like La Guardia. An hour after becoming chief inspector, he told his men, "This Department has no room for crooks . . . I'll stand up for my men, but I'll crucify a thief. And I'll be more quick to punish a thief in a police uniform than any ordinary thief. The thief in uniform is ten times more dangerous. . . ." (La Guardia's statements on this subject might have been slightly different, but not in emotional tone. "If I find a policeman," he said, "taking as much as a Cremo cigar, from a communist or anybody else, I'll fire him.")

Right from the start, however, La Guardia did not hit it off with his police commissioner as he had with Valentine. O'Ryan—conservative, a military man—regarded La Guardia's views on labor as radical. He charged the Mayor with being soft on pickets; he couldn't bear La Guardia's giving orders directly to Valentine, thus ignoring the seemly paths of protocol. La Guardia actually had more respect for Valentine, who had been a cop on the beat; he therefore preferred going to him rather than to O'Ryan for advice. Because O'Ryan and La Guardia were constantly at odds, even a picayune matter gave them an excuse for quarreling. Common sense, La Guardia felt, proclaimed that cops should not have to wear their uniform coats in the heat of summer, but O'Ryan, always the military man, disagreed.

Finally, no longer able to stand La Guardia's meddling, O'Ryan blasted the Mayor, with a summation of accusations, and quit.

Then the honest cop, Valentine, stepped up the last rung on the promotional ladder; it was the first time in New York City that this had happened to a mere member of the police force. Commissioner Valentine went to work in "the Building" on Centre Street at a salary of $12,500 per annum. Reporters closed in on him with an all-important question: might not La Guardia go over his head as he had gone over O'Ryan's? Valentine fought clear of them with, "Any information on that subject will have to come from the Mayor."

Valentine not only looked tough, but demanded the same impossible discipline of his 19,000 cops that he required of himself. This led to his eliminating cops who wouldn't comply—244 of them in four and a half years. Eighty-three—for various reasons, all Valentine-induced—committed suicide. One reason for suicide: a no-graft regimen kept them from paying accumulated debts. And Valentine rid himself of "popes" and "rabbis," that is, meddling politicians. As for the crooks and racketeers, he ordered his men to "muss 'em up." (It may have been that La Guardia gave this order first and Valentine dutifully repeated it.) To the outraged cry of liberals that this kind of behavior on the part of the police violated basic American principles, Valentine let it be known that gangsters, as it so happened, were violating those very principles. And he added, "I want the gangster to tip his hat to the cop."

La Guardia gave no evidence that he viewed his ramrod commissioner, whose temper was becoming well known, with the least timidity. In fact, he chided him with lofty condescension; in La Guardia's celebrated reading on the radio of a Dick Tracy comic, he asked Valentine why his detectives weren't slim like Dick Tracy. Often his criticism lacked the gentleness of oblique prods. In connection with locating Dutch Schultz, he told Valentine, "Get your men off their butts!" And La Guardia concluded one memo to his police commissioner: "Let us have some intelligent action and less routine stuff. Of course, I am not mad about this, but I am damn sore." And he was sore enough not to cancel what he'd written—with a return of reason—by scrawling in the margin "not to be sent." (Valentine wasn't the only one singled out for pure vituperation. In the margin of a letter from Paul Blanshard, commissioner of accounts, concerning an offer of graft in a case in Brooklyn, La Guardia wrote in pencil: "Unsatisfactory. Only a naive moron would believe such an alibi. Do you or do you not know New York? Investigate further and if you do not know how—say so. When it comes to certain kinds of graft, tend to the business the law imposes on you, please. F.H.L." A secretary's penciled words in the margin read: "At Mayor's request *not sent*.")

And complaints would often go directly to La Guardia—as though he, rather than Valentine, were the commissioner—and La Guardia would take care of them in his singular way. One asked the Mayor to remove the detective posted at Powell Street and Lott Avenue for having made anti-Semitic remarks, among them "All Jews are on relief." La Guardia sent the complaint to Valentine, who reported that the detective under question was a superior officer and that he said the accusation was unfounded. But La Guardia had the last sardonic word: "I note that the detective says he did not do it. Please tell him not to do it again."

Even during his third term, complaints still came directly to La Guardia. On March 6, 1944, James Henle, the president of Vanguard Press, wrote, "Vanguard Press has been visited on three occasions by members of the Police Dept., in connection with the single complaint lodged by some anonymous person against *Studs Lonigan* by James T. Farrell." The visiting officers, on all three occasions, repeated questions that had already been answered. "Incidentally," Henle wrote, "the attitude of Sgt. Sullivan can best be judged from the fact that when he came in he seemed convinced there was some connection between *Studs Lonigan* and the present Lonergan Murder Case. I tried to disabuse him of this, but if you will have the kindness to question him yourself, I am afraid you will discover that I have not quite succeeded."

La Guardia made short shrift of the matter. He said that he had spoken to Commissioner Valentine, and "he knew nothing about any complaint. I am sorry to say I didn't know anything about the book. Perhaps I should, but I don't. I guess somebody got their "Studs" mixed or is it a Stud? I wouldn't worry any more about it if I were you."

Sometimes La Guardia acted as though *he* were the police commissioner. William J. Walsh, a campaign manager for La Guardia, recalled such an occasion:

He called me in and he said, "I want you to go down to Long Branch."
I said, "Okay. What am I going to do in Long Branch?"
He said, "I've got a couple of detectives down there, watching some racketeers, and I want you to watch the detectives."
I said, "When do I go?"
He said, "Now."
I said, "Who's going to watch me?"
He said, "Aw, go on."
So I went down and just looked around.

Sometimes, as in the case of Mr. Newmyer of the Hearst news-papers, La Guardia found that handling a trivial matter himself was pure joy. Mr. Newmyer told La Guardia, "My chauffeur (new to New York as we are) frequently has difficulty in parking when taking Mrs. Newmyer around. Is there such a thing here (as in Washington) as a police Courtesy Card that would facilitate things a bit, and, if so, could I impose upon your good nature?" Good nature wasn't even remotely related to the Mayor's response: "Mrs. La Guardia, Mrs. Vanderbilt and Mrs. O'Flaherty are treated all alike and get the same privileges. The only Courtesy Card we have for parking is that for parking baby carriages in our beautiful and well-kept playgrounds. How many such cards can I send you?"

Such activity was on a par with that required in minor infractions: not curbing a dog, or smoking on the subway, or making noise by using a horn instead of brakes, or blissfully driving the wrong way on a one-way street. But gambling offered a situation with potential, one in which you could sink your teeth, one capable of dramatization. And if you were going to get your message across, as La Guardia reiterated, you had to dramatize.

Slot machines struck him as evil incarnate, "mechanical larceny," "the world's meanest racket," the meanest, because—for one thing—when a kid went into a candy store, this racket took his lunch nickels away from him. For La Guardia's purpose, dramatization, slot machines were far superior to policy, though it, too, victimized the poor. They also ranked above floating crap games—floating because, to evade the law, they were never played twice in the same place. "Steerers"—bellhops and men hanging around such gambling locales as 49th and Broadway—directed strangers to the clandestine location of a game. And the stakes weren't the pitifully puny stakes of slot machines; they ran into the thousands. In the main, the victims of these floating games could afford their losses which, if sufficiently large, repaid the loser, in a sense, with status.

So La Guardia—not his commissioner—set out to dramatize the sinister, unfeeling slot machine. (He set out in spite of Will Rogers' manufactured-for-the-press comment: "We don't give our criminals much punishment, but we sure give 'em plenty of publicity.") One day, suddenly, unexpectedly, the Mayor appeared in the West 100th Street Police Station and sat as magistrate on a case involving a woman who had one of the between 25,000 and 30,000 slot machines of New York City in her small restaurant.

La Guardia said, "People's exhibit Number 1 is clearly a slot machine. The machine speaks for itself. It is not a vending machine and not even a Federal judge can make it a vending machine. It is a gambling machine. A slot machine."

La Guardia's vitriolic repetition and phrasing struck at a federal court decision which said the police had to prove a slot machine was used for gambling. An ambiguity was purposely built into machines in the form of a knob which, if noticed by the customer and if pulled, released a cheap, unpalatable candy bar, not meant to be eaten, meant merely to prove the machine was a vending machine.

La Guardia then had evidence introduced to show that a gangster had forced the woman to maintain the machine. Then, regularly, every week or so, this gangster collected receipts and gave the woman a small percentage of the take.

As La Guardia bustled off to some other duty, reporters asked him if this was the first time a mayor had sat as a magistrate. "I really don't know," La Guardia called over his shoulder, "but we create precedents."

Then the passage of the Esquirol-Robinson bill made it possible for La Guardia to play the part of a slot-machine smasher. Knob or no candy-producing knob, the bill described slot machines as gambling devices. Moreover, they could be seized on sight, whether or not they were in use. They were also not to be considered as personal property, but in the same category as unlawfully held firearms, and were to be summarily dumped into the vast, deep Atlantic.

A photographer snapped Valentine, sporting a straw hat and, what was more appropriate for the occasion, a grim, slack-jawed expression, at the point of tossing a gangster's weapon from boat to water. But it was La Guardia who put on a real show for the cameras. His props consisted of one twenty-pound sledge and a junk heap of slot machines. Intently, and with amusement, an audience watched. Without an audience, La Guardia demolishing slot machines with a sledge might have led one to believe that he had, finally, really, become unhinged. The center of interest, of course, was La Guardia, not in a knight's armor or overalls, but in a business suit, hair wet-combed and neatly side-parted. Sledgehammer held aloft for the cameras, expression stern, the hero of this morality play was about to blast from the face of the earth the machines, the racket they represented, and all the evils that stemmed from them. The machine became a voodoo doll pocked with the dents of the sledge.

This black magic, judging from Valentine's report after two years as commissioner, had been completely effective. But, like the sledge picture, the report—stressing successes—had a public relations ring. It claimed that criminals had started a general exodus from the city upon getting just a taste of the new administration, and that those who didn't leave were either watched constantly or arrested. As for the loathsome slot machine, it "has been eradicated." The report didn't go so far as to say policy had been eradicated, but maintained there were "marked inroads" into its deep-rooted organization. And the report's author must have really strained in announcing, "Political influence has been banished."

All claims notwithstanding, the immense 323 square miles of New York City had not become an oasis of morality. Arithmetically, it remained forever short of achieving that: a serious crime was committed punctually every seven minutes; arrests, however, were tardy, occurring every eleven minutes. Valentine's *eradicated* had been far too strong a word.

Fancy parlor houses were closed up—to all appearances, "eradicated": Mae Scheibles' place on Park Avenue, the midtown places of Polly Adler and Peggy Wilde. But their business surfaced in dozens of Manhattan call flats—by definition, a residence run by a madam who calls protitutes in for an evening's work. Many of these girls also free-lanced, strolling down Fifth, Madison, looking for a customer. "Pick 'em up!" La Guardia cried. But plainclothesmen had a problem in obeying this order. Though distinct as individuals, the detectives were as one physically, having the height and breadth prescribed by Civil Service. This made it possible for the girls to outwit them. All they had to do was solicit only those potential customers who were medium-sized or small—obviously not the regulation size of a cop. They had to be clever, had to keep making money, for most of them were drug addicts. Thus narcotics and prostitution were linked, and gangsters often dealt in both—as well as in other profitable illegal enterprises.

Another formal report—and therefore presumably objective—showed how La Guardia's first administration had outdistanced Tammany in the fight on crime: 19 percent fewer major crimes; only 4 bank robberies, as against 15 in the last Tammany administration; 30 percent fewer payroll robberies; half as many cases of grand larceny; 19,958 automobiles stolen, but during Tammany's rule 40,785 had disappeared.

This report—and others—had a grievous shortcoming. They ignored an inescapable fact: Seabury's investigation had resulted in Fusion, but Fusion's strength was limited to New York County; Tammany officials in the other counties continued to rule in prereform fashion. For looking the other way, police officers received much, much more than a free meal or a Cremo cigar. The payoff, bribe and shakedown flourished. And bootleggers, now that Prohibition was dead and buried, had to find some other illicit, profitable endeavor.

Conveniently, the racket arose; its genesis, curiously, had been in innocence. When an organization held a "ball," shopkeepers bought tickets to acquire or keep the trade of the ball's sponsors. Criminals, creatively inspired, saw big money in this setup. Why not hold balls? And if a shopkeeper wouldn't buy tickets, force him to, smash his windows, pour kerosene on his produce . . . From this simple seed, a variety of noxious plants grew. Their poison was intimidation; their fruit, extorted money, regularly harvested.

To battle racketeering, Governor Lehman appointed Thomas E. Dewey as a special prosecutor. Dewey defined racketeering "as the business of successful intimidation for the purpose of regularly extorting money," and he looked like the prototype of the groom figurine on a wedding cake. And he was short—as short as La Guardia—and compact and neat. In a size-of-ego contest, he was certain of making a good showing. Dewey's vanity was reliable, too; it never failed to be disagreeable. A reporter pointed out, "You have to know Dewey to dislike him." FDR "regarded him as a despicable character altogether, hardly to be tolerated in decent society, an opinion that came from watching Dewey's political behavior."

Though this thirty-three-year-old lawyer from Owosso, Michigan, in Shiawassee County, had a successful practice and a virtuosity in the courtroom, the *Baltimore Sun* was skeptical of what he might accomplish in his new appointment.

But Dewey marched forward (or set sail, for he was related to Admiral Dewey) with the greatest of confidence; soon, racketeers also found him unpalatable, for his indictments rarely failed to bring convictions. It certainly made sense to go after the big boys, the ones at the top who controlled the rackets, but it must also be said that Dewey felt the small fry were not worthy of Dewey. (He scoffed at the idea that *he, Dewey,* should be engaged in rounding up mere prostitutes.)

To cover the special prosecutor's expenses, the Board of Estimate appropriated up to $280,000 annually—though Tammany, to protect its criminal own, fought the appropriations. La Guardia also ordered

Valentine to give Dewey his pick of the Police Department. And a special squad of sixty-three officers and men was established to assist Dewey.

By creating an anticrime climate, La Guardia made it possible for Dewey to carry on his war. As always, the Mayor talked tough to tinhorns, small-time punks, clubhouse loafers, and even to Arthur Flegenheimer, better known as Dutch Schultz, who had moved, in adjusting to changed conditions, from Beer Baron to King of Policy. In a scolding, you-better-mind-me tone, La Guardia told Schultz, head-quartered in Malone, New York, to keep out of New York City.

Dewey did more than talk threateningly to Schultz; indirectly, he disposed of him completely. Schultz hated Dewey with such a passion that nothing short of murder would satisfy him. But the idea of mur-dering Dewey struck Schultz's colleagues as decidedly impractical. In effect, they felt that such an act would lower them still further in the public's esteem. When reasoning with Schultz wouldn't break the hold of his bloody obsession, they pumped bullets into him as he stood before a urinal in the back room of the Palace Bar and Chop House in Newark, New Jersey.

Charles "Lucky" Luciano was one of those who had voted for the immediate departure of Schultz, and it wasn't by mere coincidence that he became Schultz's successor.

Dewey went to work in his methodical, imperturbable way to snare Luciano, the power behind many illicit operations. Luciano deserved the nickname "Lucky," so his associates thought, because he had sur-vived a gangland ride to Staten Island, where he had been left for dead. Luck, coupled with Luciano's belief that it was a good idea to pay your federal income taxes, appeared to be on his side once again. Dewey could not manacle him with an income tax evasion charge, and his investigators could find no tie between Luciano and his various "businesses." So cleverly removed was Luciano from the sordid and the seamy, that the highly respectable Waldorf-Astoria thought noth-ing of his occupying one of their residential suites. (Luciano com-plained about La Guardia. "Why the hell did he have to say, 'Lucky Luciano is nothin' but a cheap bum?' That little bastard knew there was nothin' cheap about me: a guy who lives in the Waldorf Towers ain't no bum.")

Dewey's break came with the discovery that prostitution was not operated like a corner grocery store, but by one syndicate, and on the pattern of the chain store. To learn more, he had madams and their girls rounded up, but not treated like cattle in a corral—far from it. Dewey ordered that they were to be addressed, by police and lawyers, as *Miss,* and that the word *please* be used whenever possible. This uncustomary, courteous treatment threw these potential witnesses off balance, and liquor—which went with the softening treatment— removed their fears and inhibitions. It was thus that Dewey found out that Luciano was the invisible monarch of prostitution, and finally nailed him down with a 30-to-50-years sentence.

La Guardia welcomed what Dewey had accomplished, but he couldn't bear Dewey's having received nationwide publicity. La Guardia simply had to get into the act, and he managed to get onstage by making a recommendation. When Judge McCook sentenced Luciano, La Guardia said that Luciano "could never have run his rackets without the knowledge, if not the connivance, of some of the very people entrusted with law enforcement. I recommend that at least six public officials commit *hara-kiri.*"

Luciano out of the way, Dewey, as special prosecutor and then as district attorney, continued his drive against rackets. He broke many of them—poultry, industrial, electrical contracting, baking, restaurant—and sent the racketeers involved off to prison. But he did not obliterate the racket.

Undoubtedly, La Guardia would have readily agreed that Dewey's convictions had not given the coup de grace to crime; but when the July 1939 issue of *Fortune* did more than suggest that there was vice and gambling in his city, he was furious and wrote a complaining letter to publisher Henry Luce. Nonetheless, six years later, near the close of his last term in office, an exchange of letters with Secretary of the Treasury Henry Morgenthau indicated that gambling still flourished and that La Guardia had not given up the good fight.

In a letter dated February 3, 1945, La Guardia made a simple, reasonable request. Would the U.S. Treasury figures, published daily, be presented in round numbers—about $20,000,000,000, for example, instead of $19,823,490,069? This would foil the Numbers Racket; it used three figures of the Treasury Report as the winning number. La Guardia also asked Morgenthau that he "not just brush it aside as impractical and unimportant. Recently we raided a 'Bank' running a game and we estimated the 'take' to be about $30,000 a day and it only operated in one section of the City."

Morgenthau did indeed brush aside La Guardia's request. He reasoned that if he were to comply, the racket would merely go to some other set of published figures. And he was "anxious to report accurate figures on the financial condition of the Government."

In spite of this negative reply, the salutation of La Guardia's next letter was "My dear Henry." He mentioned that he was sorry Morgenthau would not comply, and that he had wired him that the Stock Exchange and the Curb Exchange had agreed not to publish their figures. He then went on to say:

I am personally pained and grieved, because only yesterday, following the announcement of the Curb and Stock Exchange, the dirty, filthy, nasty, thieving tinhorn gamblers were betting ten to one that "Henry would not do it." This is distressing because of some of the nasty implications which of course I know are not true.

Outside of this criminal element, I do not know really what difference the last six figures make to anyone in the whole United States. I could do no more than ask you.

I wish sometimes you could see the misery caused by these thieves.

While striving idealistically to stamp out crime, La Guardia required mundane applause. He also resented other officials' receiving it. In the case of Dewey, outright political clashes were to intensify his resentment.

La Guardia had set out—with adolescent exuberance and naivete—to rid his city of gambling, prostitution and narcotics. Edict and enforcement couldn't possibly accomplish that objective—even when buttressed by the determination of reform. La Guardia could do no more than temporarily contain a few of the evils of this world, and do that only until William O'Dwyer, a Democrat and former district attorney, succeeded him and loosed all manner of corruption.

CHAPTER TWENTY

A NEMESIS, BY DEFINITION, HARBORS SUCH NU-
ances as badgering, overshadowing, defeating, doggedly pursuing, in-
sinuating oneself nicely . . . In the summer of 1945, Governor Dewey
insinuated himself nicely in a New York City elevator strike.

La Guardia tried everything from blarney to bargaining to table
pounding in order to settle the strike; then, as a last resort, because
Dewey stood poised to step in and do what La Guardia appeared
unable to do, he contacted Lloyd K. Garrison, chairman of the National War Labor Board.

Garrison took the matter up with the board, but the board's immediate reaction was not "to get into it." The board had been quite successful, because the President of the United States backed it and could
seize plants and operate them in the name of the government if unions
couldn't come to an agreement. But the board realized it was both
bizarre and impractical to ask the President to take over a hundred
office buildings. Besides, there was a press of cases—far more worthy
ones, too; this strike, after all, was on the periphery of the war effort,
only tenuously related to it. The singular La Guardia had indeed made
a singular request. Without breaking stride, the board turned it
down—in unmistakable terms.

Undaunted, La Guardia caught a night train to Washington. Garrison recalled that "he came in after breakfast to see me. A bit rumpled
—from the trip—but full of vim and vigor." And it soon became clear
to Garrison that La Guardia was anxious for the War Labor Board—
and President Roosevelt—to take over the strike, because "he didn't
want Dewey monkeying around in New York City."

In the course of their conversation, La Guardia picked up a phone and told Garrison that he wanted to call his office to get the latest dope. Presumaby, he then spoke to his own mediator, who was trying to settle the strike, and was told that Dewey had gotten the employers to agree to arbitrate, which up to that point neither they nor the union would do. In addition to hearing La Guardia's part of the exchange, Garrison witnessed La Guardia's agitation. Now La Guardia was saying, "Oh, well, the union will never agree to that. They'll never agree to that."

Intrigued, Garrison watched as La Guardia busily had himself switched to where the actual negotiations were taking place, and he could hear a roar of voices at the other end of the wire. La Guardia said, "I hear the employers have agreed to arbitrate." A voice answered, "Yes, that's so." And La Guardia said, "But I'm sure the union won't agree." To which the voice answered, "They've just agreed—to arbitrate. And Dewey's going to appoint the arbitrator."

That sent La Guardia into a tailspin of despair; he hung up the receiver, held his head in his hands and groaned: "*Awwwwwww, ohhhhhhhh, ohhhhhh . . .*"

Garrison could not help but be amused. La Guardia had come to Washington to do what he could to settle the strike, and there he was groaning because it had been settled. Of course, he had wanted the strike settled, but not by Dewey, for he knew that Dewey had wanted to show him up, had wanted to get political kudos for settling a strike that was embarrassing and troublesome to New York City.

(Later, Garrison learned from La Guardia that Dewey had been successful in terminating the strike because he'd had an ace counsel up his sleeve. This counsel, the union's counsel, had not only been on Dewey's special prosecutor staff, but he liked Dewey and was loyal to him. Dewey, as a consequence, merely had to go to him, and the man, forthwith, persuaded the union to arbitrate. It had been as simple as that.)

When Dewey had not been a factor—which was at all other times—settling a strike was of prime, rather than secondary, importance. Though decidedly sympathetic to labor, La Guardia believed: "During strikes it must always be remembered that the public interest is paramount." In this, as in all cases, what he believed and what he did usually jibed.

Once a stalemated building trades strike had him in a tizzy, because the public interest was in jeopardy and because he abhorred inaction—stalemates. Pauline Newman, whom he'd appointed to labor committees, remembered La Guardia asking, "How's it going?" clearly wanting action and wanting it at once. "We're making progress," she'd say. And he'd come back with an impatient "Well, keep on making it."

It was therefore not at all surprising that he would want the building trades leaders to stop dragging their feet and come to terms, that—while he was at it—he would want to give them a graphic lesson, one they wouldn't forget, on the ethical necessity of being public-minded. He therefore gathered these leaders of the striking employees in a room in City Hall, went out and locked the door on them and then turned off the heat. La Guardia knew that as soon as the room became frigid, these "big shots" would have firsthand knowledge of what thousands would experience if a strike were to take place. It wasn't long after that, that they settled.

Pomposity—in labor leaders or anyone—annoyed La Guardia; but deflating pomposity gave him mischievous pleasure.

When Anna Rosenberg—thirty-two, petite and a dynamo of energy —became a hardworking part of the NRA, brass from Washington asked her to arrange a conference with Mayor La Guardia.

When they arrived, they proved to be very stuffy, very dignified, and obviously took themselves very seriously. Together with Anna Rosenberg, they went to the Mayor's office. Seated, La Guardia looked up at them, characteristically, over his glasses.

As someone started to make the introductions, La Guardia broke in with "I know her," indicating Mrs. Rosenberg with a movement of his head. "Last time I saw her, and at other times, too, she was in her nightgown."

A tangible silence and a general embarrassment. Finally, one of the men managed, "I beg your pardon, Mr. Mayor . . ."

At this point, Mrs. Rosenberg started to explain, but La Guardia broke in. "Never mind, never mind." His brown eyes were lit up, sparkling. "Let's get down to business."

After the business had been taken care of, Mrs. Rosenberg still felt obliged to explain. And as she explained, she could see that her audience was decidedly dubious about the story she was telling them. She had an older sister who had gone to an art school, that had had a poster-drawing contest. A congressman then and between marriages, La Guardia had served as one of the judges of the contest. Her sister had won, and La Guardia became quite fond of her and had taken her out. When he appeared at their home, Mrs. Rosenberg, then a child, would be in her nightgown, ready for bed. And it was to this that La Guardia had referred ambiguously.

The moment the NRA men left, Mrs. Rosenberg turned on La Guardia. "You really are the limit. To tell them that—"

"Did you see their faces?" La Guardia chortled. "Wasn't it—wasn't it funny? That brass really needed to be put down a little."

Mrs. Rosenberg went on, after that incident, to work on many labor disputes with the Mayor. And since he lived on upper Fifth Avenue and she at 96th and Fifth, he would often call her in the morning and say, "I'll be there in five minutes. I'll take you downtown," never bothering to ask if she were ready. And on the way—though he may have paid her the courtesy of not dictating letters to the recording machine in the rear of his limousine, as was his custom—he might say, "I'm going to stop at a fire." When she'd say pleadingly that she had to get to work, he'd answer, "Oh, take a little time." He'd then put on a fireman's hat and coat and leave her waiting to receive the remainder of her ride downtown. (Once La Guardia rushed into a burning restaurant on 51st Street. As one fireman came out of the building, he muttered, "Will somebody get the Mayor out of there." Even after the last fireman had emerged, La Guardia remained inside. When he finally appeared, he was so covered with soot that he was recognizable only because he appeared to be a silhouette of La Guardia. "I gave the refrigerator system a personal going over," he said, in explaining his delay. "I wanted to find out if the building code had been violated.")

Quite frequently, after the police had made a raid where there were slot machines, he'd stop on their way to work and take a hatchet, à la Carry Nation, to the slot machines. His fury erupted on these occasions; he wasn't posing, as he'd done with the sledge poised over a heap of slot machines, for public relations pictures.

The first time Mrs. Rosenberg saw him attack with the hatchet, she made the mistake of saying, "Oh, Fiorello, I love slot machines. I play them whenever I go someplace where they have them."

"Why, they're the most immoral thing." His scolding rose to a squeal. "I'm ashamed of you."

From then on, he made it a point to have her witness his slaying of slot machines with a hatchet, to impress upon her how evil they were.

This close, casual relationship carried over into their work on labor disputes. If she came to him and said, "Fiorello, I think there may be trouble. Do you want to come in?" he'd usually say, "No. You fix it. I'm not coming in until you tell me it's settled."

But before things were settled, conflicts would arise over procedures. Then one could say to La Guardia, "I can't do it that way. All right, if you want it that way do it yourself or get someone else to do it." That would make him furious, sullen. After a while, he'd bluster and listen. He then might say, "Oh, all right," or convince you that he was right.

Settling labor problems was less difficult with La Guardia as mayor, Mrs. Rosenberg felt. She explained that "although he got rough at times with management, it, like everyone, had confidence in his honesty. People didn't think because Consolidated Edison, or some other big company, was involved that that made any difference with Fiorello."

Even a satirical cocktail recipe, concocted with hostility, as well as some psychological accuracy, had La Guardia's "scrupulous personal honesty" as an ingredient: "Take five-feet-four [sic] of tireless energy as misdirected as that of a jack-in-the-box gone haywire, add a belligerency born of an inferiority complex, toss in a persecution mania and a fillip of Napoleonic grandeur, mix in a scrupulous personal honesty, flavor with a high-test brand of sophistry, stir in the bitters of class-consciousness, a jigger of demagogue, a pony of opportunism, fill the shaker to the brim with personal ambition, and presto!—you have the La Guardia Stinger."

La Guardia could be as rough with labor as with management; but when he warred with labor, his heart wasn't really in it.

No sooner had La Guardia come into office than he inherited a taxicab strike from his predecessor. In the course of indulging in some tax experiments, Mayor O'Brien had a city ordinance levy a five-cent tax on each ride. Meters were therefore calibrated to a twenty-cent, instead of a fifteen-cent, minimum. Then the courts ambled up and declared it all unconstitutional. In the meantime, $500,000 in tax nickels had been harvested.

La Guardia felt that the cab drivers were underpaid, and so he might very well have stated, as his opponents claimed he had, that the $500,000, collected unconstitutionally, should be turned over to the drivers. Some operators said the attitude of the drivers could be traced to that remark, and so they blamed La Guardia for the strike which started at 6:30 A.M. on a freezing cold February 2.

La Guardia learned of the strike on his way to City Hall, when he encountered a group of pickets on Lafayette Avenue. He had his chauffeur stop the limousine. Through the open window, ignoring the painfully low temperature, he discussed the strike with the pickets. Finally he said, "Come on down to City Hall, and tell me all about it." (This availability and display of warm and total sympathy irritated those to whom pro-labor amounted to pro-Satan.)

When La Guardia met the delegation of strikers at City Hall that morning, he told them, "I want to warn you against trying any rough stuff. If you do, I will get rough, too, and I can be rough if I try it. I warn you against hiring any strong men or gangsters, and I want you to inform me if you hear of any companies doing that." He went on to advise them, since they had no union, to seek the leadership of the American Federation of Labor; he, in the meantime, would get in touch with A. F. of L. President William Green and see what he could do to help them.

This talk took place on a Friday. On the following Monday, the strikers met in the suite of offices, at 285 Madison Avenue, of Attorney Morris L. Ernst—a defender of unions, a battler for civil liberties, an opponent of censorship—whom La Guardia had appointed as a mediator. Ernst went back and forth between meetings, held by strikers and operators in different rooms, carrying proposals, attempting to effect a compromise—but without success. At ten P.M., he interrupted his shuttling to have a talk with La Guardia, who was attending a baseball writers dinner at the Hotel Commodore. Then Ernst returned to his offices, and whatever ideas La Guardia may have given him failed to work.

At eleven o'clock, La Guardia suddenly appeared; and he dashed between the two sets of meetings as Ernst had done. (La Guardia, at this point, felt that the tax money should be split between the two parties, fifty-fifty. The drivers, however, wanted it all, claiming that the tax had curtailed tipping. On the other hand, the operators wanted 60 percent, arguing that though the tax may have caused the drivers to be deprived of tips, it had made them lose money simply because people had been forced by the tax to use cheaper forms of transportation.)

Finally, at 11:45, La Guardia emerged from the room in which the strikers were meeting, his face wreathed in smiles. After indicating that an agreement had been arrived at, he rushed off to catch a train for Washington and, as it turned out, to receive promises that he would be given $68,000,000 in loans for PWA projects.

It was while La Guardia was still in Washington that he heard, with amazement, that his joy over the settlement of the strike had been premature. This annoyed him, for the strikers had turned down what he regarded as a fair agreement. By way of threat, he said, "They must know there are 10,000 others waiting to be licensed to take their places."

During the following weeks, more "settlements" were announced. Once the strikers' leaders accepted, but not the rank and file. And throughout these negotiations violence occurred, the "rough stuff" La Guardia had forbidden. Strikers literally pulled apart cabs that were in operation, strewing the street with headlights, seats, wheels. They also manhandled drivers and passengers, telling the passengers, "Take the subway—Mayor La Guardia's car is one flight down." And before peace and a settlement were finally arrived at, sinister forces were seen in the taxi strike: communists, racketeers from Chicago . . .

The brand-new Mayor, as a result of this strike, found himself attacked right and left. The *American Mercury*, turned conservative after Commander-in-Chief Mencken withdrew from flailing the "booboisie" in its pages, charged that "La Guardia seemed to have no regard for the average citizen's welfare as long as he could make political capital out of championing the masses." And I. F. Stone in the liberal *New Republic* said of La Guardia: "He is a friend of labor, but he took New York's taxi drivers for a ride."

Without question, La Guardia was labor's friend, and a friend of long standing, and getting the labor vote was not the catalyst of his friendship. In 1912, in a garment strike, he picketed and also bailed out those pickets who had been arrested. When he was president of the Board of Aldermen, he mediated a strike and achieved a two-dollars-a-week raise for those who made children's shoes. As a congressman, he fought child labor and injunctions against strikes; he fought for unemployment insurance, old age pensions, a minimum wage, the right to bargain collectively. When he came back from visiting the striking coal mines of Pennsylvania in 1928, he gallantly had the House cleared of women because he knew his language in describing what he had seen was going to be too strong for their tender ears.

And after he became mayor, he continued to be on labor's side, concerning which Assemblyman Edward S. Moran, Jr., said, "The Mayor by intemperate speech and conduct has fomented and inspired disputes between capital and labor."

But if he "inspired disputes," he also settled them. (The Labor Party praised the way he mediated labor disputes. Part of his technique was to make use of a fact-finding board; he was the first public official to do this.) By trickery of the sort to be found in the denouement of Tom Swift or Rover Boys books, he settled a strike that started in the kitchen of the new and elegant Waldorf-Astoria and ended in a hurry when health inspectors, sent by the Mayor, came looking for violations. He settled a laundry strike by having his water commissioner turn off the water in laundries, thus siding with the workers, who were receiving extremely low wages.

Still another strike, involving truck drivers, came to a gimmicky end with comparable dispatch. On a day marked by negotiations that brought little in the way of progress, and much irritation to La Guardia, he had ancient Department of Sanitation trucks assembled in City Park. Late that afternoon, the negotiations still going on interminably, La Guardia turned to Newbold Morris and said, "When I give the signal, tell them to get those trucks started." (By this time a uniformed Sanitation Department driver stood beside each truck.)

Morris said in a whisper, "Where do you want those junk boxes to be moved? Some of those engines haven't been tuned up since the nineteen twenties!"

"Move them anywhere," La Guardia commanded. "Just get them going!"

Soon the old trucks, some of which had to be cranked, started with much backfiring and sputtering—a great deal of noise, noticeable noise —just outside the City Hall windows. La Guardia appeared not in the least disturbed by their racket; with exaggerated calm, he blew rings from his cigar. But the contending parties, with scarcely any more talk, came to an understanding and signed a contract. (This surprised Morris, for he felt that these hardheaded businessmen should have realized that no shipper would have entrusted a valuable cargo to those ancient sanitation hulks.)

There were times when La Guardia appeared to be going counter to labor's welfare; in any event, he never had shelter from squalls of criticism. When he stood unmovably against a bonus for New York City schoolteachers. When only World War II could interrupt his stand that opposed closed-shop agreements with New York subway workers . . .

The subway labor problem arose in connection with the unification of the two privately owned subway companies—the IRT and BMT—

and the city-owned IND. John L. Lewis, grand panjandrum of the CIO, whose declarations had the ring of divine law, declared that all employees of the subway system must be members of the Transport Workers Union; La Guardia—now, as he put it, an executive, not a legislator—declared with equal authority that the subway employees were civil servants and therefore bound by the civil service law and the constitution of the state of New York, which forbade them to belong to any organization outside of their own immediate associates or to strike. If they wished to negotiate about any matter, they were obliged to go to their immediate superior or to the state legislature.

William Chanler, the corporation counsel, and La Guardia believed they had a "pretty strong argument"; obviously, Lewis thought they had, too. After the attack on Pearl Harbor, Lewis called up La Guardia, whom he knew quite well. "Now that we're at war," he said, "let's drop the case. Let's forget the whole thing until the war is over." La Guardia and Chanler, out of patriotism, agreed to do this, and the subway employees did not become members of the Transport Workers Union.

(John L. Lewis waited patiently for the war to be over and for La Guardia to be out of office; then he started up the union's claim again. Chanler recalled: "When I heard that O'Dwyer and his corporation counsel were going to recognize them, I ran up to the Municipal Building to the corporation counsel and I told him what the law was and that we would have won the case if the war hadn't come along and Lewis hadn't persuaded La Guardia to drop it, because Lewis knew he'd lose. 'You don't understand,' the corporation counsel told me. 'Bill O'Dwyer wants labor's support. He's going to recognize them for political reasons.' So he recognized them and ever since then we've had trouble with strikes by the union that runs the subway.")

Criticism—in regard to labor and all other matters—never ceased, and even La Guardia found the going strenuous. Understandably, he would come down with colds. On one such occasion, he was offered well-meaning advice by Dominick Sorrenti of the Bronx, who wrote, "What you have to do now is to exercise in order to prevent catching cold again. And eat raw foods: salads. Join the YMCA. . . ." La Guardia answered, ". . . I will try very hard to take your advice about exercise, but exercise takes time and when a man is Mayor he has very little time for himself."

A month later, March 16, 1937, La Guardia's evaluation of being Mayor hadn't changed. This time, in answering a letter from Carlos M.

DeCastro, who had been elected a mayor in Puerto Rico and wanted information on Fire, Sanitation, Water Supply, Gas and Electricity, La Guardia, in addition to sending DeCastro the data that had been requested, wrote, "I am at a loss whether to congratulate or commiserate with you on your elevation to the post of *Alcalde de la Ciudad*. These are very hard times to be a Mayor."

CHAPTER TWENTY-ONE

T
HE ADVENT OF MAYOR FIORELLO H. LA GUARDIA, viewed through the scrim of nostalgia, could have an eerie, surrealistic quality. Reminiscing, Chief Magistrate Abraham Bloch said, "It seemed as though the town had been invaded by an army of small, plump men in big hats; he was everywhere." A busybody. La Guardia, in fact, was many busybodies. He would have commissioners meet with him at breakfast at seven o'clock and still be working at eleven that night.

En route with the Mayor to a meeting, William Chanler found the trip to be a series of verbal explosions. At a tie-up in traffic, La Guardia got on his limousine's phone and called Commissioner Valentine. "Hello, Lou. There's a terrible traffic jam and there's no cop around. Get busy!" No sooner had he hung up, than they hit a pothole. "Hello, Lou, there's a pothole at"—such and such a place—"nearly broke the spring. Get it fixed!" And so it went.

Obviously, Mayor La Guardia was not the archetypal administrator behind a cleared desk: a creator merely of policy, the details of which were attended to by a multitude of invisible subordinates and added up to a frictionless operation. When he came into office, he had had very little executive experience. He had merely directed a small personal staff. Now—suddenly—the electorate had dropped him into a cosmic whirlpool, turbulent with 140,000 employees and an annual expenditure of $600,000,000. To handle it all, one simple rule guided him: Give taxpayers the most for their tax dollar. Give them an efficient, therefore scientific, form of government, a government that gets things done.

What better way to get things done, in accordance with copybook dictum, than to do it yourself?

One day he showed up at La Guardia Airport shouting, "What's this I hear about the food being too high out here? Show me the menus, show me the refrigerators, show me the whole works!" The victim of this onslaught nervously gave La Guardia the first thing on which he could put his hands: a champagne list. This caused the Mayor to shout, "They can charge what they damn please for that stuff! What I want is a complete meal in this place for thirty-five cents, including coffee!"

And to save the taxpayer eighteen thousand tax dollars, he once set out, in person, to prove that the engineer who prescribed ventilators in an eight-block tunnel under Park Avenue was indeed what he called him, "an old faker." To show that the ventilating system wasn't needed, he followed a string of garbage trucks, twenty-four of them, and other smell-producing vehicles through the tunnel. Upon emerging, he said, "I've smelled worse smells than that."

To combat city noise, he saw to it that milk-wagon horses were shod with rubber shoes. Lifeguards, he decreed, should be required to take examinations to determine if they could really and truly swim—hardly too much to ask of a lifeguard. As for new shirts for policemen, he wanted to see the material to be used in these shirts, examined samples and also ordered the type of buttons they should have. Because of the number of such things that had to be done and their endless variety, his memos were in different colors—brown, pink, green, with the color indicating "the degree of priority."

Sorting out priorities by color didn't diminish the work load perceptibly. Robert Moses—one of the few who had been able to survive all of La Guardia's twelve years in office—stated flatly, decades after it was all over, with clearings of the throat that doubled as growls, that the idea of La Guardia not being able to delegate authority was "nonsense," was "rubbish." But why he didn't delegate authority made sense: "After all, there aren't a hell of a lot of people you can delegate authority to. And when you find out that they're no good, you have to get rid of them. And La Guardia was willing to do that. He was able to do that." Still, Moses felt that Al Smith was superior to La Guardia. "Let's not kid ourselves about it. . . . As an administrator in government, Smith was the best we ever had—in my time." More ferocious throat clearings. "La Guardia resented the fact that some people felt that way. He used to talk to me about it. He said, 'You think Smith is a greater executive than I am?' 'Well,' I said, 'yes, I do. I do.' Then he said, 'What's the matter with me?' . . . That doesn't mean that La Guardia wasn't a very superior fellow."

In assessing La Guardia, Moses would agree that a magnificent complex of contradictory traits can't be ignored: autocratic, humble; obscene, prudish; petty, generous; vindictive, charming; deadly serious, fun-loving. These and other warring personality elements entered into his behavior as an administrator. Still, Berle believed that "La Guardia wasn't a divided self that was looking for identity. He did what came naturally to him and he did it very rapidly and did it very well."

"Government by tantrum" was how one observer, and victim, summed up La Guardia's rule. (La Guardia did grab a notebook from the hands of a reporter who had offended him, and he did jump up and down on it.) But in numerous instances, it wasn't tantrum; it was a glorious lack of tact. "My dear Mr. Hessebein," he wrote. "Thank you very much for your letter of 8/3/37; also for the copy of your book, "Destiny," which I hope someday to find time to read." Far more cutting was La Guardia's response to an article, "Portrait of a Mayor: Fiorello La Guardia" by Karl Schriftgiesser, which appeared in the January 1938 issue of the *Atlantic Monthly*. La Guardia wrote to the magazine's circulation manager, who had sent him a copy and, obviously, expected words of praise. Instead, La Guardia told him that he had read the article and

it does not come up to the *Atlantic* standards in any way, shape or form. It is the most sloppy, inaccurate, indifferent piece of work I have ever read. The author seemingly knows nothing about my philosophy of government or economics or anything else I have been doing for the past 30 years. It's a conglomeration of excerpts from articles heretofore written and how it ever got by the *Atlantic* I am at a loss to understand. Better luck next time. With kind personal regards. . . .

Even in generously giving a quote concerning *George White's Scandals* to be used for advertising purposes, he said precisely what he thought: "a pleasing show—with tuneful music—quick moving continuity—and entertaining without the necessity of thinking."

If good public relations required little white lies, his attitude blared: "To hell with it!" Those who worked for him had to be able to take the truth, as he saw the truth. When Commissioner Blanshard had a report to make to La Guardia, though Blanshard was far from being a Milquetoast, he would call Betty Cohen, the Mayor's secretary, and ask, "How are things for a report today?" She would answer "fine" or "the weather tomorrow might be better." In spite of this precautionary dialogue, Blanshard might arrive on a stormy day—La Guardia in a black mood. When this happened, work that Blanshard had been on for months might be eroded in a hurry and washed away by a verbal deluge. (La Guardia believed, or rationalized, "I'd rather have an ungovernable temper than a governable mind.")

Stormy letters from City Hall bore the joy of creativity. Word choice, imagery, lilt, neat riposte—all indicate that the Mayor had a fine time writing them. He told Paul Windels:

Another one of your lousy decisions has popped up.

This is just to give you warning that you are disqualified from taking any retainers for Ex-lax, Pluto Water, Castoria or Cascarets, and that as an expert on recreational law, you take the Blue Ribbon. Of all the things I ever heard, Bob Moses getting jurisdiction of Comfort Stations under the new Charter on an Opinion of the Corporation Counsel, on the ground that "it is a recreational activity."

I am trying to get a WPA Project to collect all opinions for the last four years to be included in a bound volume, "Why Mayors grow gray."

But he handled differently (gently?) a communication from Edward C. Delafield of the Park District Protective League, who asked for information concerning a rumor in the Riverdale section that the Eighth Avenue subway was to be extended into Riverdale. La Guardia told Mr. Delafield, "I do not believe that you have anything to worry about for the next few days anyhow."

Countering with obliqueness—but a body blow, nonetheless—described his reaction to someone who dared criticize his administration and give unasked-for advice. A wire from Roderick Stephans, on March 31, 1939, to Fiorello H. La Guardia:

I submit that the deplorable accident on the city owned Independent Subway System coming so soon after disclosure of thefts and sale of jobs emphasizes need to fill vacancy existing since last June on New York City Board of Transportation. . . . I suggest consideration of Matthew J. Diserio. . . .

Three days later—clearly not sufficient time for La Guardia's pique to cool off—La Guardia answered.

Referring to your telegram. The other day I saw one of your coal trucks pass a red light and bump into another truck. Considering what might have happened, the damage was very slight. I also heard of drivers chiseling on weight although their employers had provided the full weight when the truck left the yards. All of this leads me to believe that you should have another vice president in your company and that you should appoint him at once. I therefore recommend Mr. Michael Murphy who has all the qualifications. His employment by you would be helpful in many directions.

Invariably, he used his abusive style on those close to him—the closer, the more abusive the style. He wrote John L. Rice, his commissioner of health, that he didn't understand one of his letters. He then went into detail.

Please talk just plain English that us honest folk can understand, rather than resorting to the language of the legal phraseologists and the verbiage technicians of the League of Nations.

Such outpourings were lukewarm compared to the heat one felt in the Mayor's presence. Budget Director Patterson—erstwhile bookkeeper, thin, nervous—helped mayors figure out what they ought to spend. La Guardia, he felt, was especially difficult; in the middle of March, La Guardia would move right into Patterson's office for a two-week, every-day-in-the-week study of the budget. Poor, poor Mr. Patterson. "I had to move out," he said poignantly, "and sit with Miss Pray—that's my secretary. Fiorello never went out to lunch. Sent out for hot dogs, which he ate with mustard, provided by us. We never got an appropriation for it either. . . ."

When the Mayor didn't get his way, a blast of hostility followed. This was also true in areas other than the budget. Pearl Bernstein Max felt that hostility. "He wanted me to fire a member of my staff on the Board of Estimate," she said, "because he didn't like the testimony that this man gave in a lawsuit about bus franchising that the city was contesting. He wanted the testimony his way." Because she felt that La Guardia's charge that the man was lying was a rationalization, she refused to fire the man; La Guardia retaliated by refusing to talk to her. (Refusing to see or talk to a person was a punitive pattern that he frequently followed.)

La Guardia fired employees himself, most ineffectively. He might just as well have shouted "Oh, go jump in the lake!" as "You're fired!" for both exclamations expressed nothing more than pure anger. Commissioners would joke among themselves about how many times they'd been fired and then taken back as though nothing had happened—no apology, no mention of the firing. This was all the more surprising when one considered La Guardia's emphasis in telling a commissioner he was fired: "absolutely and permanently, God damn you!"

Many left his administration, really left it, of their own accord. Commissioner of Housing Langdon Post departed "in disgust." Commissioner Ryan didn't complete a full year in office; Paul Windels stuck it out for a full term. Because of this sort of thing, the *World Telegram* observed, at the start of La Guardia's second term, "When the Mayor makes public service unbearable for some of his ablest associates and puts on a personal vaudeville act in the midst of important business, he is doing neither himself nor the city any good."

Even a La Guardia administrative technique could be horrendous. Berle experienced and described one—that the Mayor used in handling a problem—of which Berle "was scared to death."

He would pile up one's agony and worries to a point of crisis. Then he'd come through with a suggestion that we'd do thus and so. In mere relief everybody would seize it, and then he'd sit down and work out the details or have them worked out. The crisis would simply be defused. The mere fact that everyone was scared to death that he'd blow up Governor's Island or something or other was all right with him. He was quite content they should feel that way about it. But practically all the time he knew about where he wanted to come out.

And if he had to compromise, in order to come out where he wanted to, he was capable of compromising. But he more readily made concessions to the members of the Board of Estimate who were Democrats, part of the hated Tammany, than to his own colleagues. After all, he expected Republicans to go along with him. He'd blow up when they didn't. But he knew he couldn't blow up with the Democratic members, if he really wanted to get his programs through. So—he compromised.

Always, there was method in his apparent madness; it was as though La Guardia possessed a fairly uncanny daemon. Always he determined if something was right; if it was, he would go ahead. Therefore if a member of his staff wanted to move in a certain direction, he would cross-examine him to find out if such a move made good sense. He might then say, "I don't completely agree with you, but go ahead." Chanler said, "That's why I could get such a good staff. People who later became district judges wouldn't have run around saying 'yes, sir' to things they didn't agree with."

There were still others—besides those Chanler had in mind—who would not shy away from an argument with La Guardia.

Once, during the serious business of the finances involved in erecting new buildings and stalls at the Bronx Terminal Market, La Guardia strayed to his pet peeve. "Lawyers," he said, "have done more to retard civilization than cancer and smallpox."

Alderman President Bernard S. Deutsch could have let that pass like a balmy breeze. Instead, he spoke loudly and clearly into the silence that followed La Guardia's heated observation. "You wouldn't be here if you weren't an attorney, and I doubt if I would be either. But if anything goes wrong a lawyer is blamed for it."

"Well, it was a lawyer who ruled that it was legal to employ child labor"—La Guardia's body squirmed with anger—"and a lawyer who ordered runaway slaves returned to their original owner like chattels."

"It was a lawyer who freed the slaves."

La Guardia bellowed, "Not in his capacity as a lawyer!"

What took place at City Council meetings was as interesting—and as dramatic and amusing. Eddie Cantor offered $200 for records and transcriptions of the meetings to be used on his comedy show. "However," he stipulated, "I reserve the right to take out what I think is too funny." La Guardia turned Cantor's offer down, saying, "I am too good a friend of yours to stick you," though he went on to admit that the meetings were funny.

But in the serious business of decision making, it was La Guardia who decided what was right for the City of New York. And in the course of making those decisions, he didn't want any of his lawyers—Deutsch's brief in defense of all lawyers notwithstanding—to give advice or make suggestions, unless he asked them to. What they had to say must come later in the decision-making process. Being a lawyer himself—though a reluctant one—La Guardia knew with what gusto lawyers could mix up a policy decision by immediately pointing out that such and such a section prevented you from doing this, and another section prevented you from doing that. A man of action, La Guardia abhorred the mere mention of legalistic impediments.

A situation of unlimited dramatic potential began to develop when Chanler made Jeremiah Maxwell Evarts, an old college friend of his, a member of his staff and failed to make him aware of La Guardia's Commandment: "Thou shalt not butt in!" Chanler hadn't told Evarts that what an assistant corporation counsel did at a mayor's meeting was to take notes and listen and study and *then* tell the Mayor what one had to say.

From Vermont, Evarts not only had a New Englander's voice and sarcastic twang, but before coming to New York to practice law, he had been in the Vermont legislature (until he took up with a married woman) and had been accustomed to running things. Thus at a meeting in which La Guardia and Moses were in disagreement—a situation explosive in itself—Evarts, who knew a park commissioner's rights, told the Mayor what he couldn't do. Furious, La Guardia shouted, "What do you mean? Who are you?" Evarts went right on talking, telling the Mayor the section of the Charter that forbade him from doing what he wanted to do. La Guardia shouted again; this time, he shouted, "Shut up!"

Then La Guardia fired Evarts, "kicked him out" was the way La Guardia put it when he broke the news to Corporation Counsel Paul Windels. Windels then phoned Chanler to tell him what had happened to his friend Evarts. "What'll we do now?" he asked.

Chanler immediately went to Windels's office. He hadn't been there more than ten minutes when Moses phoned Windels. "I've just attended a meeting at the Mayor's office that your Assistant Corporation Counsel Evarts was at. He's the man I want to take charge of all my affairs. He's got guts enough to talk back to the Mayor."

Windels then worked it out with La Guardia that Evarts would be involved exclusively in Moses's affairs. (All went well for a year or two, until Evarts in his grating patois "told Moses where to get off and then Evarts went back to private practice.")

In addition to deciding what was right for his city—"his city," expressing the paternal proprietorship La Guardia always felt—he also, in guarding it, had to protect his own personal flank.

When Louisville had been devastated by a flood and mayors were sending police to keep vandals from raiding stores, Walter Binger, deputy and acting commissioner in charge of sewage treatment, told La Guardia, "Major, they're going to lose their water supply in Louisville. I could take the right crowd there of sanitary engineers, and it would be much better than just sending down some cops."

After a moment of thinking that over, La Guardia wailed, "Je-sus Christ, Binger, are you trying to get your ass in a sling?"

Binger in reliving the incident said, "I'd had experience with him before. And I knew he wanted to see whether he could scare me. He didn't care how I carried *my* behind. He meant, 'are you trying to get *my* ass in a sling.' That's what he was thinking of."

Binger also knew that when you spoke to La Guardia, you had to speak with the speed that you could get out of clipped words, clipped sentences. This was absolutely necessary, because La Guardia knew what you were going to say when you were halfway through a sentence, and it bored him to listen to the second half. So Binger spoke like a string of popping firecrackers in advancing his argument that he go to Louisville with a group of engineers. Finally he ran out of anything more to say.

For a moment, which Binger felt went on and on endlessly, La Guardia didn't look at him, looked off in the distance instead, as though mesmerized by the horizon. Meanwhile, Binger guessed what the Mayor was thinking: "Is this the guy to do it, if I do do it? Will he accomplish anything? How will I look if he doesn't? And how will I look if he does?"

Finally La Guardia turned back to Binger and said, "Come back to me in a half hour, with a telegram in my name to President Roosevelt."

Binger returned with the telegram, stating what he, La Guardia, could do by sending down this group of highly trained engineers, and offering to send them if the federal government thought it was desirable.

Two hours later, the surgeon general called La Guardia to find out—by that time it was three or four o'clock in the afternoon—if Binger and his engineers could leave the next morning on an early plane because of the seriousness of the situation. At once, La Guardia made arrangements with an airline to supply a plane. Binger and his expert crew arrived in Louisville like cavalry to the rescue, saved its water supply in a week's time and departed, guidons and spirits flying. Of course, La Guardia was as pleased as they. The thinking he had done during that long pause had clearly produced optimum results.

La Guardia was as careful, too, in not overstepping the boundaries of his jurisdiction, even in small, insignificant matters. One July day in 1937, Mrs. Charles A. Beston of New York City wrote her mayor—as a good, alert, concerned individual in a democracy should. She wanted him to do something about the heavy uniforms that those poor doormen had to wear in terribly hot weather. He told her that "their uniforms are quite beyond my jurisdiction. I have a little influence with the policemen's and firemen's uniforms and my office staff is open to suggestion, but beyond that the citizens are free to do their worst."

Earlier that year, a Dr. Henry Wallace let La Guardia know that the new West Side elevated highway should be named the Lindbergh Highway or Drive to carry on the name of Charles A. Lindbergh in a memorial. Yes, La Guardia agreed, "Lindbergh's name should be perpetuated." But he didn't have the authority to name a highway or a street, for that was in the jurisdiction of the Board of Aldermen.

And when William Borden of the New Jersey State First Aid Council wrote to La Guardia concerning the need for ambulances to be able to use the Henry Hudson Parkway, the Mayor had a not-to-be-missed opportunity to say a few words about the ineffable Robert Moses. "Your request seems a simple one, but let me assure you it is anything but that. I wouldn't any more ask Commissioner Moses to violate the chastity of his parkways for ambulances or anything else than I would make that request if I were in an ambulance and had to be rushed for a blood transfusion to save my life."

Jurisdiction was still sacred to La Guardia in 1943 when Gelett Burgess, famed for his "I never saw a purple cow" poem, wrote to the Mayor in verse that street signs should be made in such a way as to avoid confusion. He went on to explain that it was "hard to differentiate between a six, nine, three and eight."

"Dear Mr. Burgess," La Guardia answered,

> "We feel like lunatics," you say!
>   When through my mail my way I fight
> I share your feeling, day by day
>   And night!
>
> But sometimes, through the eyes hard glaze
>   A pleasure comes, a real delight.
> When query comes, like yours, in phrase
>   Polite.
>
> Every point's well taken and quite clear,
>   Each item covered and well said.
> But jurisdiction here will rear
>   Its head.
>
> Five borough presidents aligned.
>   In solemn, stately council meet
> And speak, in wisdom thus combined,
>   *re* street.
>
> Best not, piecemeal, change signs of tin,
>   The artist climbed high, alas,
> And barking every single shin
>   He has.
>
> A whole new set is what we want.
>   And meantime, praying on our knees
> Our general government to grant
>   Priorities.
>
> "A post-war project!" we will cry
>   And when a fleet of signs appears
> The City younger will look by
>   Eleven years.

Obviously, Gelett Burgess could not have received a more personal letter; form letters are just not composed in verse. La Guardia's unusual reply did not stem from public relations, to insidiously insure that Gelett Burgess would vote for the man who had taken the time to write to him in verse instead of prose. Clearly, La Guardia found the time—though how remains a mystery—to take meticulous care of nonearthshaking matters, because as an administrator his concern was for individuals as well as the abstractions of which they might be a part: the unemployed, an oppressed minority, those with a particular sensitivity, and on and on.

La Guardia's most important administrative skill was in letting nothing stop him from getting the best man for the job. In the thirties—far from the latter-day emancipation of the sixties—he even went so far as to appoint a black judge, Hubert Delaney, the first black man in New York City to receive such an appointment.

On coming into office, La Guardia told Burlingham to get a good legal staff for the Corporation Council's office and to pay no attention to politics whatsoever; all he wanted was people who had ability. Burlingham could therefore approach William Chanler, a first-rate litigation lawyer, even though Chanler had opposed La Guardia and had wanted McKee in City Hall.

Chanler felt a certain hesitancy about accepting. At the very least, he wanted to get clearance from the Mayor on a nasty letter he'd written about him during the campaign, which had been published in the *Times* as an editorial, over his signature, and had asked "How Can La Guardia Restore the City's Credit?" Chanler sent La Guardia the letter, and La Guardia returned it, after scribbling on its side, "Damn good political letter. Come along and write them for me." So Chanler went along, as chief of litigation, skillfully and effectively protecting the Mayor from "the Tammany boys who were being thrown out of office," for "they sued every move that La Guardia made," claiming that he was violating the Charter.

La Guardia never boasted about a success of this kind in the making of appointments. When Samuel Markewich, a lawyer, complimented him on two appointments which he had made to the Magistrates' Court, he told him, "All I can say about the appointments you referred to is what I always say about my appointments. If the two men I named turn out to be good, the credit is theirs. If they do not, the blame is mine."

He knew the truth of this from bitter experience. Just after he had appointed Herbert A. O'Brien as judge of Children's Court, he asked Judge Polier, "What do you think of my new appointment?"

"You couldn't have done worse," she said.

"That's like you, making a snap judgment."

"Look," she persisted, "I've followed him in the Queens Court. He's punitive, he's harsh, he's authoritarian. He's bigoted. . . ."

This savage evaluation of his appointee made La Guardia so furious that Judge Polier dropped the subject. But she had been right. Judge O'Brien sounded off like a disciple of Hitler, led the fascist Silver Shirts—an organization into which anti-Semites flocked. Finally, when La Guardia realized he had made a mistake, he admitted it with the classic "When I make a mistake, it's a beaut."

When Judge Polier saw the Mayor, sometime after he had made this admission of fallibility—of the highest order—she said, "I've got a good story to tell you. Your famous appointee, Judge O'Brien, wanted a low license number—and got it. It's the talk of the town, only he doesn't know it. His license number is IQ 16."

Aside from an occasional beautiful error, La Guardia did have an uncanny ability in the selection of really capable individuals. He simply judged a person on previous accomplishments and on the reputation based on those accomplishments. This would explain how La Guardia—something of a philistine—would pick Lewis Mumford, then known as a biographer of Herman Melville and an art critic, for a place on the Board of Education. He also would not even permit friendship to cause him to stray from the acquisition of the very best men and women for his administration.

He wrote to Frank H. Sommer, the dean of the New York University School of Law, who had recommended a member of his staff, Herman A. Gray, for "a judicial career":

My dear Frank:

I have your note. Coming from my own Dean, you may rest assured it will receive my very serious consideration.

The serious consideration mentioned is the typical, stereotype official term which, between you and me, does not mean very much. I have a long list of applicants for judicial appointment. You can check the list any time. Just take the "Red Book" under the heading "Attorneys." Omit the letter X and you will get a pretty good idea. It may be a long time before we get to the letter G.

How about getting together at the Brevoort for cocktails soon?

CHAPTER TWENTY-TWO

A FATHER MIGHT ALSO BE VIEWED AS AN ADMINIS-trator—directing and superintending what goes on in the home to achieve harmony (and love when possible), a reasonably balanced budget, the "finer things of life" . . . This analogy, of course, can be carried tiresomely on—all the way to boredom and beyond.

Upon becoming Mayor of New York City—actually, it wasn't until November 1934—La Guardia became a father again. He was almost fifty-two when he and his wife adopted Jean, six, and Eric, three. Jean, dark-haired, was the daughter of La Guardia's first wife's sister, who, stories claimed, gave up her child and then chronically regretted it. But Thea's sister did have to work; and so, at first, Jean stayed with the La Guardias a great deal, and then her mother agreed to the adoption. Eric, blonde, blue-eyed, had been in an orphanage.

In the role of administrator-father, La Guardia acquired a bedroom for the children. (When the apartment adjacent to his became vacant, he arranged with the apartment building's owner to have the wall between the two apartments broken through to create an additional room.) But because this bedroom was behind his, there had to be a door between the two bedrooms. This inept architecture upset La Guardia's personal physician, George Baehr. The doctor realized that the children, in order to go to the bathroom during the night and in the morning, had to go marching through their new parents' bedroom.

Finally Dr. Baehr went to La Guardia and said, "Look here, Fiorello. This is terrible. You have to move."

The Mayor asked why.

"Because the children go through your bedroom to get to the toilet. You come home late at night, and you want to sleep, and you're disturbed during the night."

La Guardia shook his head. "No. I like it. I want them to come through my bedroom. When am I going to see them, if they don't come through my bedroom?"

This was in the beginning of his parenthood. At that time, when he arrived home from a day's work at City Hall, after stopping at the Players or the Advertising Club for a scotch and soda, the first thing he'd do would be to get down on all fours and give his daughter a pony ride all around the living room. But as time passed, he began to expect more and more of his children—as he did of his commissioners. Just as he made it a strict policy to pick the best man for the job, it was as though he should have picked the best children for the role of his children.

One conjectures reflexively that he resented their trying to take the place of his real daughter, who never had a chance at life. Therefore, Jean and Eric could never—no matter what they did, or didn't do—be good enough. One senses this because La Guardia rarely mentioned his first wife or his child even to those closest to him, and because he appeared to have completely cut them from thought or memory. But far below the surface, an emotional residue caused him to respond to certain stimuli in a predictable way. Whenever WPA or PWA money was available, he took plans for district health centers to Washington and came back with a grant for the erection of a building. And when a center was established, he would walk through it, inspecting and asking questions. Among the many questions, he asked how they did case findings for tuberculosis. It had been during Thea's pregnancy that she developed a fulminating tuberculosis, for which there was no cure, no antibiotics at that time, and her child died of tuberculous meningitis. He passionately wanted poor women to know how to take care of themselves during the prenatal period. (Thea had been poor, had worked her way up from awful sweatshops.) He wanted poor women to give birth to healthy children.

And the safety of all children concerned him. Fire trucks, he ordered, must exercise caution in going around street corners in order not to strike a child at play. (It was as though he identified all children with his little Fioretta.) And they dare not go down play streets.

No matter how much La Guardia loved children, he was aware that one child, Eric, misbehaved. What did the fifty-two-year-old Mayor, who was the father of a three-year-old boy, consider misbehavior? A woman in a letter to La Guardia complained that park workers had been unnecessarily rough with a two-year-old boy who had been digging in a ball field with a toy shovel; they had dragged the boy and his mother off to the police station. La Guardia answered, with a carbon going to Moses:

As a parent I agree with you. As an official, I am compelled to uphold the action of city employees who do their duty and carry out instructions. . . . We had a similar experience in our own family. That was a tough situation for me, too. This is how we worked it out. Little Eric was a little over three years of age when he and another little boy took it upon themselves to go fishing in Central Park for goldfish that were in a fountain. One of the attendants chased the little fellows and my wife took Eric home. . . . We then impressed upon Eric that in so doing he was depriving other children of the pleasure of seeing the goldfish and that all people had to help in maintaining and protecting parks and all park property. We also told him that it was the duty of all police officers to watch public property and to prevent people from injuring it. . . . Although Eric was not quite four at the time, he kept ducking Commissioner Moses every time Moses would come up to the house. . . .

On the surface, it appeared paradoxical that quiet, bashful Eric should become increasingly difficult. La Guardia implied it was Marie's fault, that she didn't know how to bring up children, for he kept telling her, "Ask Katherine how to bring up children. Ask Katherine." Katherine was a neighbor with whom they were friends.

La Guardia—a progressive in politics—had no use whatsoever for newfangled ideas in the rearing of children; so he believed that the virtues of the past in this area should be held on to, believed this as a thoroughgoing conservative would. He therefore had no use for the Bureau of Child Guidance, because they championed modern claptrap. On at least one occasion, he said as much. It happened when a delegation of women—among them, Rosalie Lowe Whitney, one of La Guardia's close advisors, who had been appointed by him as a judge— met with La Guardia at City Hall to persuade him to approve an appropriation for the Bureau of Child Guidance.

"Why should we spend all these millions of dollars on the Bureau of Child Guidance?" he demanded of the delegation. "When I went to school, we didn't have psychologists, psychiatrists, tests, sociologists, social workers. We managed to get along without them."

Rosalie Whitney stood up. Even though she was short, she managed, in rising, to convey majesty, dignity, a strength to be reckoned with. "Yes, you got along without them," she said, with a rhythmic enunciation that contributed a thin layer of sarcasm. Then a long pause, serving as a contrasting backdrop for the scornful exclamation to come. "Ladies, *look at the sad thing!*"

La Guardia howled with laughter, slapped his heavy thighs. This merely meant that Rosalie Whitney had touched his funny bone, not necessarily his views. He lived in a milieu that was not psychiatrist-conscious; Freud had yet to supplant folk medicine. If Eric misbehaved, La Guardia felt that all he needed was to have someone "talk" to him—just the reverse of the verbal outpourings required of a patient in psychoanalysis. So a woman, an Italian spinster schoolteacher, received the assignment of "talking" to Eric, of straightening him out with the hammering of emphatic common sense.

Another neighborhood, a better one, might be good for the children; upper Fifth Avenue had begun to deteriorate faster and faster. To move, however, would be a bad move politically. It would appear that the Mayor had begun putting on airs, that he might no longer be interested "in helping the little fella."

Circumstances resolved this problem. First of all, Charles M. Schwab had a castle, though he was a president, U.S. Steel's first. Perhaps it made Schwab feel like a king to offer his castle, on Riverside Drive between 73rd and 74th Street, as a gift to the City of New York. The Board of Estimate wanted to accept, wanted to make an official residence out of the castle for the mayors of New York City.

When Borough President Levy pointed out to La Guardia that the castle would be nice for him to live in, La Guardia grumbled: "Why doesn't Charlie make a museum out of it? I don't want to live in a museum. I live in the same tenement house I did before I was mayor, and like it."

He therefore wanted the idea postponed, but when an outcry against postponement arose, he agreed with a begrudging "All right, all right."

When La Guardia had a look at the castle, saw the immensity of its seventy-five rooms and its regal elegance, he exclaimed shrilly, "What! *Me* in *that!*"

The city was already the possessor of, not a castle, but a mansion, Gracie Mansion, a beautiful—"lovely" was sometimes used in describing it—two-story frame structure, federal in design. It had been used as the Museum of the City of New York until the museum established new quarters uptown, on Fifth Avenue. Robert Moses regarded the mansion as historical, for on its property there had once stood a fort dating back to the American Revolution, and worthy of preservation.

He therefore spent considerable time trying to persuade La Guardia to move into it. If the structure's eighteenth-century look bothered La Guardia, there was a symbolic compensation in its location, at the north end of Carl Schurz Park, which runs along the East River from 84th to 89th, for the man after whom the park was named had been a liberal Republican, one whose "uncompromising manner made enemies."

La Guardia finally gave in to Moses' insistence. (He'd save Gracie Mansion for posterity. Perhaps having almost two acres to run around in would do Eric and Jean some good. He could move to this official residence and not be accused—since it was official—of deserting his old neighborhood. And he'd let Moses get to work on the place, which perhaps was Moses' prime motivation, and thus keep him quiet—on that subject, at least.)

Without delay, Moses let loose a horde of workmen, instructed to refurbish and restore the house as closely as possible to its original state. (It was in bad shape, because it had been occupied by only a caretaker, a careless sort who took little care of the place.) Then, like a ribbon around a gift package, Moses ran a protective four-hundred-foot-long, six-foot-high iron picket fence around the Mayor's House—the name the Park Department gave Archibald Gracie's mansion.

"Don't you know there's a war on?"—the standard rebuke for those who impeded the war effort in any way—was asked of Moses concerning the newly erected fence. As always, he fought back: the material in the fence had "no value" as scrap iron in the salvage campaign for war materials. Moreover, "That fence was made from junk, all junk, that we repaired with the WPA and park employees. Most of it had been there along the waterfront for years. It was all just junk until we fixed it up."

On Tuesday, May 26, 1942, the mansion was ready for occupancy. However, the day before, Fiorello left for Canada, ostensibly because he had business with the International Commission—and not because, even though a good family man, he wanted to escape the unique headache of moving. (Because the United Press thought of him as a good family man, their Mary Harrington contacted him; she was doing a feature story on how various famous men remembered their wedding anniversaries. She was sure he had a good plan, "like marking an X on every new calendar." This unwarranted praise failed to blunt La Guardia's cutting edge. "I have no formula, patent or copyright," he wrote. "I just *know* the date, that's all. It seems to me that any artificial reminder would indicate an indifferent relationship." But he did flee the country, leaving the moving to Marie.)

On Tuesday, five men and a van from the Columbia Warehouse Storage Company transported the first of four loads.

The next day at noon, Marie arrived at Gracie Mansion to supervise the unpacking. (Her husband, according to his shrewd schedule, would arrive that evening, when the books had been unpacked, the china and glassware removed from barrels, the furniture distributed to appropriate places in the mansion's nine rooms.) She went through the mansion's heavy, imposing iron gates, past the impressive, though small, sentry box which could contain one policeman and did and which had green, precinct-house lighting fixtures. En masse, the grounds' pansy beds, evergreens, rhododendrons and small shrubs concealed the circular drive on which she passed from the main entrance. The Mayor's House was white; porches with an intricate patterned railing bordered three of its sides. Neighborhood mothers were on hand, holding up their children so they might see the sights beyond the iron picket fence.

On entering the house, Marie found herself in a broad reception hall, with a large reception room on the right and, on the left, a roomy, high-ceiling study stocked with many historical volumes concerned with early New York and lent by the New York Public Library. And as she stood there, the movers and the painters—hurriedly applying a few last touches—got in one another's way, somewhat like children attempting their first ballet.

A *Times* editorial liked everything about the Mayor's new residence. It had spacious lobbies, well-proportioned and dignified rooms, marble mantelpieces, a beautiful winding staircase, a view of the East River and its Hell Gate, a treacherous, turbulent, narrow channel. And, in conclusion, it summed up its ecstasy: "The Mayor's House is no unworthy companion of City Hall."

Marie may have seen all this, but the bare floors, "that were awful," captured her attention and stirred up an overpowering distaste. (She later recalled that "they got Grover Whalen to give us a rug for the downstairs entrance hall." But the place had not the slightest suggestion of Gracie Mansion's eventual wall-to-wall carpeted elegance, of added, much-needed mayoral work space. She felt as though they were pioneers in an arid land, breaking ground for the mayors who were to follow. "We started it off, I guess you could say.") Unlike the *Times,* that thought Robert Moses had done a good job on the mansion, Marie told herself, as she looked around, that all Moses had done was "clean the place up a bit." Then she saw that directly behind the study was a dining room which led into a large combination pantry and kitchen—just a few feet from John Adams's desk—with white enamel sinks and a huge electric refrigerator. This struck her as lovely, like sunlight breaking through curdled black clouds.

Since all the city's museums had contributed furniture to the Mayor's House, Marie had the problem of deciding what was to be done with the pieces that made up their four loads of furniture. Fortunately, a large room in the basement could take care of all the excess.

La Guardia arrived that evening from his three-day trip to Canada. If he had any criticism, it may have been that the Duncan Phyfe chairs that came with the mansion should have had a bit less delicacy, curves that were not quite so graceful. Could this delicacy and grace bear up under his concentrated weight, the roughhousing of children? Would he not be more likely to see less of his children in this mansion with its spacious floor areas than he had in the comparatively minuscule Fifth Avenue apartment?

La Guardia's daily routine—as it related to his home—had been moved to Gracie Mansion along with the furniture. After rising early, he would have a big breakfast—meat, never cereal, or bacon and eggs. When he had been in Congress, Marie prepared his breakfast, but in the mansion, they had a maid, Juanita, who did—and she slept in. After the big breakfast, he would come hurrying down the porch's steps at 8:30 and head for the police prowl car waiting for him in the drive. Eleven hours later, he would be back from City Hall. "The minute he'd come in," Marie recalled, "the radio would go on. And always a station that had good music." He liked music; liked it with the volume turned up. And he also listened to the news. Sometimes he read the paper or spoke to the children. Dinner. No talk of his day at the office. "If there were worries or suspense," Marie said, "he never carried them home." All the lights were off at 9:30, except for those in his bedroom, for he worked until 11:00. He always did some reading for pleasure in bed—pulp Western magazines. Marie said, "He slept very well. Which was a saving grace, too."

Special activities broke the routine. Two weeks after the La Guardias moved into Gracie Mansion, La Guardia entertained colleagues on the Board of Estimate and their wives at a housewarming cocktail party. Because the party took place at five, after a Board of Estimate meeting in City Hall, it seemed an extension of work—which, in a very real sense, it was. In any event, Archibald Gracie's mansion, which had replaced an American Revolution fort, had seen entertainment on a grander scale. The guests alone indicate how grand: Louis Philippe, who would one day be king of France, John Quincy Adams, De Witt Clinton, Alexander Hamilton, Washington Irving, the Marquis de Lafayette . . . And the mansion would see little in the way of parties, for the La Guardias were not party goers or givers; and Fiorello viewed them with distrust, accusing cocktails of loosening one's tongue, which would, once loosened, say the wrong thing or reveal that which shouldn't be revealed. Besides, there *was* a war on.

But on a Saturday or a Sunday night, if La Guardia wasn't tied down, friends would arrive and La Guardia would cook for them—and put on a show in the process. This sometimes involved wearing his World War I medals, along with a towering chef's hat. La Guardia didn't bake. He prepared steaks, chickens, sauces—that Marie described as "terrific." A maverick, he wouldn't follow recipes. A progressive, his dishes were usually improvisations, made up as he went along. He had a standard, heavy, thick peasant soup loaded with a variety of chunks which, though it might have shocked the elegant Marquis de Lafayette or the sensitive cabinet maker Duncan Phyfe, satisfied the hungry. Marie claimed proudly—and with some amazement—that if she had something in a restaurant that she liked, Fiorello could tell her what ingredients it contained and reproduce it. ("It was just as good, if not exactly the same.") And as proudly, she observed that he was very messy—like a man who cooks. "A chef never cleans up," he said by way of excuse. He had a lot of fun with his cooking.

Sometimes La Guardia had an audience even when he ate. By coming to the south end of the mansion, where Moses' high iron fence came closest to it, people could look directly into the dining room and watch the Mayor—who didn't seem to mind—and his family as they ate. Eric and Jean may have minded, for they were both introverted and shy.

Some watchers, one Sunday, might also have seen La Guardia and his son out on the lawn throwing a baseball back and forth—a scene right out of Norman Rockwell. When two people are playing catch, the ball in passing from person to person does, in a sense, join them. Do fathers therefore want sons, according to the cliché, so that they can play ball with them or do they want them because they yearn to be close to them?

Sunday was also the day of La Guardia's broadcasts—which began with his routine appeal for patience and fortitude and then went on to cover a variety of topics. Eric went into action at the station. Because Eric was the Mayor's son, Seymour Siegel, the station's director, had to handle him gingerly. Siegel therefore attempted to steer Eric away from the microphones, loudspeakers and other equipment by offering him a typewriter, but Eric caught on, saw the offer as a ruse by an adult. Eric may have preferred a microphone to a typewriter, but he had also stuck doggedly to the practice of causing trouble on the assumption, the hope, that it would get him some attention. (He built a tree house and fell out of it; almost amputated a finger in shop at Horace Mann.) But he had very little chance in competing with his father for attention, when his father, for example, spoke over the air to the inhabitants of New York City as though *they* were his children, on the subject of eggs, potatoes and ballet.

Commencing tomorrow, April 24th, Grade A large eggs will be sold in retail stores in New York City from 45¢ to 47¢ a dozen, without cartons. I cannot tell you any more than to advise you that your children cannot eat the cartons and that they are not worth 2¢. So arrange to buy your eggs without the cartons. . . . Take your old carton and take the eggs out of the carton in the store, and put them in your old carton. It will cost you 2 cents less. . . . I cannot recommend Grade B eggs too strongly. They are fine eggs, so take advantage of the 39-cent price. You ought to hear the involved technical explanation of a Grade B egg. It is so involved and technical that it does not make sense. . . . Another thing about brown eggs and white eggs. I need not tell you we do not eat the shells. The inside of each is exactly the same. It is just a little trick of the trade to play up white eggs. Now in Boston, somebody is telling the consumer that white eggs are as good as brown eggs, because in Boston they played up brown eggs and there they cost more. The same is true in Cleveland, Ohio. So buy brown eggs, because you can get them for a penny a dozen less.

A dozen Grade A large eggs at 45 cents a dozen, without the carton, should weigh a pound and a half. So watch that, please.

Then he issued another warning, this one about potatoes.

Do not pay more than 15 cents for 5 pounds.

Then on to bacon.

Bacon is just too high and I am not going to plug it. If you do buy bacon, the sliced bacon is 42 cents a pound now, and slab bacon is 33 cents. If you have large families, I recommend buying the slab bacon because you cannot cut it as thin as the sliced bacon in stores and, therefore, you get more of the nourishment to the children in the thicker slices. . . .

Incidentally, I am watching the price of retail milk in New York City. *I hope that politics will not interfere with baby's milk.*

Man does not live by bread alone—which includes grade B eggs, slab bacon, potatoes and milk. There's also ballet. After plugging the Ballet Russe de Monte Carlo, because it was at the City Center, he went on to say:

I want you to know that our friend Hurok has a ballet going at the Metropolitan Opera House. You see, we are not competitors. His ballet is good, too. It is very good. Try and see Mr. Hurok's ballet dancers.

And he didn't restrict himself to being a dance critic.

Last night Marie and I went to a movie. We saw Abbott and Costello, and it is an awfully funny picture. You have nothing to worry about while you are looking at it; you don't have to try to follow a plot—it's just funny.

And all Eric could do was fiddle with the forbidden apparatus of the radio station. On the other hand, his sister surrendered to the reality of her personality, and—because she had no way of getting attention—she melted into the background or sought the pitiful, figurative concealment to be found in the corners of rooms. (Perhaps her adjustment was, in part, a copying of Marie's, for if La Guardia was substance—and he was that, overwhelmingly—Marie was shadow, "the quiet little lady beaming proudly on the sidelines.") And Jean, thin as a young child, began gorging her way to obesity. And because she was diabetic, she had the opportunity of eating what was as forbidden to her as WNYC equipment was to her brother.

A childhood friend of Jean's recalled an excursion with Jean to the boardwalk in Asbury Park, New Jersey. Before leaving, her mother said, "Don't let Jeanie eat any sweets, because it's not good for her."

So we had the most awful walk on the boardwalk, because every step she was buying something. We couldn't say no. I mean, she'd hate us. She was grown up—maybe eighteen, sixteen, I don't remember. . . . And just every step on the boardwalk, there was food. And this girl was eating and we knew it would kill her. Instead of dieting—as a diabetic, you're supposed to diet to have a minimum amount of insulin—she did the reverse. She took larger and larger quantities of insulin to cover her indulgences. Very tragic. . . .

And this same friend—to whom La Guardia was like a second father—recalled her association with the La Guardia family "as the biggest prize," as a most wonderful experience.

Because we did such exciting things and, as a kid, to sit in the chauffeured limousine of the Mayor and have everybody staring at me was just the biggest pleasure you can imagine. . . .

She also found going up to the McMillan Theatre with Marie, to see the Tony Sarg puppets "okay." But Marie, who was always "warm and loving," didn't generate the excitement that Fiorello did.

Every year at Jeanie's birthday party, Fiorello would go. And it would be an outstanding party. Jimmy Durante would be at the house. Or one year we went to see *Claudia* and the birthday cake and the party were backstage with the actors. They were serving *us* [Jean and Eric's friends]. And every year—we have pictures—of us at the circus, us at the rodeo, us at the bicycle races. All of these events that occurred, *he* took us to—all the kids. He went with the kids. He was the most wonderful host. And he stayed the whole time, enjoying every minute of it. And we'd sit right down there in the box belonging to the Mayor. Every clown, at a circus, would come up and talk to us in the box. And we got anything we wanted to eat.

However, there was a price tag on all these good times.

He was warm to *us*. And very loving to *us*. But you always felt that he demanded that you perform. He really expected a good deal of us. And his kids were pushed very much in the background. He didn't pay any attention to them. Maybe he did, but he was just so domineering that they—Jeanie, particularly—just stayed away.

As a consequence, when there would be company at the mansion, Jean would sit alone upstairs. But her friends enjoyed being with the company, especially since La Guardia was there.

It was fun watching him. He was like an actor—an actor. We enjoyed being there because if I opened my mouth, he would listen to me. We knew who was center stage and we knew who was the hero, but we felt that we were sharing the spotlight with him. We felt very important. He made us feel very, very important.

In spite of all this adulation—and fun—she knew Jean and Eric didn't have a chance "in that household," because their father was more than strict with them. He was dictatorial. She therefore said, "I wouldn't have wanted to have been his child for a million dollars."

She recalled how he could squelch you with an annihilating "Shut up!" Since she had seen the way he ate scallions, she could never eat them again. He liked scallions.

And he would grab one, and we were sitting down at a table with linen and flowers. And he'd grab and he was short so he had to put his whole belly on the table and he'd grab three or four scallions and then he'd go crunch in a very, very loud voice. You know, you'd just hear that crunching. And then he'd burp. A *loud* burp. And as a kid it just repelled me so. I thought the man was just so vulgar.

But he was also tender; part of his complexity stemmed from such contradictions. So he could be both indulgent to his children and as strict as a staff sergeant.

Mrs. Anna Rosenberg Hoffman remembered an incident of La Guardia performing as a parent.

I was out at Hyde Park once, and he came out with the family. And we were at the swimming pool. And he had a whistle. He would whistle and the children could jump in the pool. He would blow the whistle, so that you thought there was a fire, and they would have to get out of the pool. He thought that was discipline. He indulged them terrifically, but he thought he was a great disciplinarian.

Another father at Hyde Park had trouble with his children. The demands of his high office had something to do with it—as was undoubtedly the case with La Guardia. "One of the worst things in the world," Roosevelt observed with intense feeling, "is being the child of a President."

His wife blamed him, to a certain extent, for this; she felt he should have worked more at the solution of his children's problems. Marie, on the other hand, spoke not of Fiorello's role, but of her own: "No matter how independent women want to be, they're still the nucleus of the family."

As for Mayor La Guardia, from all appearances he simply felt that, like the City of New York, children should be handled in the efficient, scientific, hard-hitting ways of enlightened Fusion government—but with considerable good-time fun thrown in.

LA GUARDIA'S LINGUISTIC TALENTS CONTRIBUTED
to his creativity in being abusive, and Tammany—without question—
served as a compelling target. For example, when Tammany spent millions for a park at Jamaica Bay, which turned out to be four feet
underwater, and La Guardia strolled through it, in a manner of speaking, in a motorboat, he christened Tammany's handiwork "Larceny
Park." He could be devastatingly subtle, too. Upon the permanent
passing of Brooklyn Boss John McCooey, he said with appropriate
solemnity, "He was a good husband and father." This appeared to
have all the weight and sincerity of a punch line in a eulogy, unless
one knew that McCooey's son, a so-so lawyer, had been made a Supreme Court justice by his father, and that McCooey had also been
generous with city jobs to a host of relatives.

For politicians—in general and individually—La Guardia dipped
into his special lexicon of virulence: "pinochle player," "clubhouse
loafer," "pay-roll leech," "*gonif*," "treasury looter," "correspondence-
school incompetent." Luminous with poetry, his appellations dripped
poison. In his eyes, every time one of these "lousy bums" approached
an official, it was for something improper—as was also the case when a
voter approached them. President Roosevelt told William Allen White
a story about such a voter who "took $4.00 from the Republicans and
$2.00 from the Democrats and almost voted the Democratic ticket on
the ground that it was the more honest, but ended by staying away
from the polls altogether after he was given a pint of liquor by a
Prohibitionist leader."

Naturally, La Guardia wouldn't, for a moment, think that he fit
under the politician heading. "My kind of politics," he said, with nice

understatement, "has been unorthodox." That this was the case didn't endear him to most of his fellow Republicans or to any machine Democrats. Al Smith, for one, didn't tire of putting on a particular skit for his Tammany friends, because their inevitably pleased reaction gave him pleasure. The skit consisted of Smith's approaching the fiercest tiger in the Central Park Zoo, putting his face fairly close to the bars and growling, "La Guardia!" Then the symbol of Tammany invariably obliged with ferocious snarls and lunges at the bars as if he did, indeed, detest La Guardia.

During his childhood in Arizona, in a heroic fantasy which children, in their insecurity, require, La Guardia may have stalked one of the Tammany-labeled tigers which he had seen in *World* cartoons, their habitat, and shot it dead. An element of fantasy—or naivete—also entered his defeat of Tammany in 1933, for he felt that since he had put Tammany out of the running for all time, his being in office for another term would be unnecessary.

In the back of his mind, there was also an inescapable fact: no reform mayor had ever been reelected. But obviously, La Guardia was La Guardia, and La Guardia was *sui generis*. This included knowing the practical and the dirty aspects of politics, that reformers Mitchel and Low didn't know. Mitchel, perhaps because he was only thirty-four, even lacked some of the nuances of his trade. For instance, in the course of his "improving" the school system, classes were shifted around and as a result there were several lunch hours instead of one. In those days, women hadn't as yet acquired the right to vote, but it had already been ordained by custom that they slave in the kitchen. Naturally, making a number of lunches per day lacked appeal, and they pestered the master of the house not to vote for Mitchel and his "improvements."

Though the job of a politician is to get reelected, La Guardia had more important things to do. He maintained, "The man in office who has his eye on another office is like the automobile driver with a pretty girl at his side. He can't keep his mind on his work. I've never worried about the next election."

Evidence supported this claim. Before his first month in office had ended, La Guardia sent President Roosevelt a wire on the occasion of the President's fifty-second birthday: ". . . You can count on New York City doing its part by following your splendid leadership in the great battle now being waged against Depression, poverty and unhappiness." Thus the Mayor made it clear—if he hadn't already done so, by working for Roosevelt's social legislation during his last days in the House—that he had aligned himself with the New Deal. Of course, this and his progressively closer relationship with Roosevelt widened the gulf between him and conservative Republicans and intensified the loathing of organization Democrats. (Liberal Democrats, without pangs of conscience, could vote for La Guardia, because he equalled the New Deal on a municipal level.)

The very next month, La Guardia tried, unsuccessfully, to have a talk with the President at Hyde Park. Stephen Early, assistant secretary to the President, suggested another possibility in a wire: "Be here Saturday morning and ride with the President from Washington to New York en route Cambridge. The train will leave Washington nine A.M. reaching New York at twelve-fifty-five P.M. and affords opportunity for conference without taking you away from your affairs for more than the forenoon. . . ." (This exotic request didn't faze La Guardia. He and Berle once had a conference while he reviewed a Legion parade and another while marching at the head of the 1934 Memorial Day Parade; they found both settings "as private as any other," "quiet," "satisfactory.")

And during that month, a letter La Guardia wrote to President Roosevelt was indicative of a growing intimacy.

> I submit the enclosed proposed draft in the course of a pourparler looking to an exchange of diplomatic communiques. After reading the enclosed draft, I admit it is sort of a cross between Gertrude Stein's poems, the Einstein theory and a Mrs. Sanger's essay on birth control. That ought to qualify it as a diplomatic document.
>
> Hoping you will get a few hours of much needed rest and quiet.

This familiarity—Republicans who disliked La Guardia might call it rudeness—extended even to the First Lady. Once, after having had lunch with her in her apartment on 11th Street in New York City, he told her, "My wife never asks me where I have been nor whom I have seen, but she always asks me what I have had to eat. Today, I can truthfully say I did not have too much!"

Nonetheless, La Guardia had numerous appointments with Eleanor Roosevelt's husband—and sometimes for lunch. Because constant, pressing problems occupied the Mayor and the President, finding intervals when they were both free required intricate reshuffling of appointments; this involved many wires and phone calls. Sometimes La Guardia would wire merely to say that he would be at the Mayflower at such and such a time, and if the President should want to see him, he was available. And what was truly remarkable was how solicitous La Guardia would be in not wishing to intrude on the President: "Any time convenient to the Chief, without rushing or crowding, please. . . ."

That they were becoming increasingly closer could also be seen by the salutations of La Guardia's letters. At first, it had been "Dear Mr. President," then "Dear Chief" and "Dear Skipper." Anna Rosenberg Hoffman, who knew both of them very well, said that they were sincerely fond of each other. "La Guardia liked FDR, because he was a doer. And he liked his personality. Sometimes they were both Peck's Bad Boys. They would laugh about it. . . ."

Politically, they also had need of one another. La Guardia's need intensified when, five months after he entered office, Arthur Cunningham, the city's comptroller, died of a heart attack while horseback riding in a Queens park. Ironically, this gave new life to a moribund Tammany.

Government organization under the old city charter made this possible. Like the national government, New York's was bicameral. The Board of Estimate and the Board of Aldermen were comparable to the Senate and the House of Representatives, respectively. The Mayor, like the President, was the chief executive. He was also on the Board of Estimate and had three votes. The comptroller and the aldermanic president had three votes. The borough presidents of Manhattan and Brooklyn had two votes; those of Queens, the Bronx and Richmond one each. All New York City legislation and appropriations had to be passed by both houses and then was subject to the Mayor's approval or veto.

Thus with Comptroller Cunningham's death, La Guardia had not only lost a valuable associate, but three votes had suddenly been placed in jeopardy. To snare those crucial three votes, La Guardia and Tammany scrambled to get their choice for comptroller in office. The night before the election, La Guardia said, "If I lose my comptroller, Tammany will stage a comeback. In that case, you're going to see one hell of a fight." Tammany won.

The following year, Tammany struck another telling blow at the Fusion administration in much the same way. President of the Board of Aldermen Bernard S. Deutsch, possessor of three votes, died, and Tammany maneuvered their man, Timothy J. Sullivan, into Deutsch's office. Thus Tammany, seemingly with divine help, gained control of both Houses, and the victory over Tammany which Fusion had won in 1933 dwindled into something less than victory. The power La Guardia had taken from Tammany was slipping from him. Now he had to run for reelection in 1937 to wrest the power back from Tammany.

To be sure of defeating Tammany, La Guardia needed President Roosevelt's backing and the advantage that would come his way by having the popular Tom Dewey run for district attorney on his ticket. Finally, he needed the Republican Party's nomination, for without it all was lost.

La Guardia must have known that he jeopardized that all-essential Republican support by campaigning in 1936 for FDR and for Lehman for governor of New York. Little wonder, that only Berle—of all La Guardia's supporters—thought he had a chance of being reelected.

Tammany had reason to be confident. In '36, they had lined up the new American Labor Party's 250,000 votes for Roosevelt and against Alfred M. Landon of Kansas. This party consisted of an alliance of labor unions, among them the garment workers union; and it had been blessed by CIO leader John L. Lewis. Since the Labor Party had behaved as Tammany had wanted it to once, Tammany deduced—without taking into account all the factors required by logic—that the Labor Party would be on their side and against La Guardia.

Naturally, the President wanted the Mayor to be a guest at his second inauguration. A newspaper story, however, revealed that La Guardia wasn't aware of this.

When the Board of Estimate was discussing a date for a meeting of the Committee of the Whole today, someone suggested January 20.

"Aren't you going to the inauguration of Pres. Roosevelt?" inquired Bronx Borough President James Lyons, turning to Mayor La Guardia. "That is set for the 20th."

"I haven't been invited," replied the Mayor.

Roosevelt's memo of 1/16/37 to "Mac," Marvin McIntyre, his secretary: "Make sure he really did get invited." On the memo, McIntyre scrawled, "Went out special delivery 1/15/37."

Invited, La Guardia still did not go. He wrote a note in longhand, the day after the inauguration:

at home sick

> My dear President:
> Speech—magnifico! Sincere best wishes for next four years.
> Faithfully,
Fiorello

Such devotion—in part, at least—made Roosevelt want to find a berth for La Guardia in his cabinet. Berle wrote to Roosevelt concerning this on February 4, 1937:

In Buenos Aires you asked me whether Mayor La Guardia intended to run again for Mayor of New York; otherwise he might be brought into the government. He expects to run, feeling that if he takes a job with your government and declines to run, he will be accused of making a deal by which in return for a safe berth in Washington he clears the decks for a combination between Tammany and Farley. I think he is right. As things stand now, he has a better than even chance of being elected. Anyhow we would rather be defeated trying to do something we believe in than throwing up the sponge.

I hope you can keep clear of this. As in 1933, there is nothing in this for you.

Politically, FDR could be cautious, daring, opportunistic, compromising. He knew the need for caution where Tammany was concerned. Edgar Pitske, a lawyer, wanted the President to become a member of the Society of Tammany; he wrote to Farley, pointing out that Andrew Jackson was the only President who had been a member and that because there were many parallels between Jackson and Roosevelt, Roosevelt, too, should become a member. Farley queried the President, and the President replied, "Politically unwise and furthermore couldn't break the rule of not joining anything."

But Roosevelt attempted to keep Tammany's goodwill. On the anniversaries of the society's founding, he would send such star-spangled greetings as "with best wishes that this Society so venerable in years, will always uphold the highest traditions of true Americanism."

And as late as August 11 of the election year 1937, he issued a statement that he would remain neutral in the New York City mayoralty election, offering Tammany this half loaf of negative support.

Dewey proved more of a trial; and because he was a Republican, he had less excuse for being difficult. Dewey's work as a DA, as a "crime buster," had also been an effective public relations job, making him well known—and even admired, in some quarters. For him to run for district attorney on La Guardia's ticket would, the reasoning went, be a vote getter.

But as Berle put it, "Dewey's vanity, always disagreeable, was working overtime." As a consequence, Dewey made outlandish demands: (1) he wanted both the governor of New York and the President of the United States to ask him to run; (2) a guarantee of a $300,000 campaign fund; (3) a public clamor, three days in duration, that he run; (4) assurance that his running for office was essential to La Guardia's victory. This last stipulation outraged Berle. Ever La Guardia's loyal and deeply devoted guardian, Berle declined to agree to this demand. "In the first place," he maintained, "it is not true; in the second, it would merely mean trouble later. No head of any government should admit that an outsider was essential to his government even if it were true which it is not."

At breakfasts, La Guardia and Berle—who found himself functioning as campaign manager—worked on the Dewey problem. They variously decided "to let him come in or stay out," "to give him the absent treatment," "to let him stew in his own juices." Finally, magnanimously, Dewey announced his candidacy.

The Labor Party, whose support Tammany had taken for granted, came out for La Guardia, primarily because of La Guardia's labor record. He had been labor's champion for decades, picketing for the garment workers, giving his legal services to the Brotherhood of Sleeping Car Porters, backing labor before it could repay its supporters with a substantial bloc of votes . . . Labor also felt that La Guardia was the first mayor who had given labor a fair deal.

Since the Communists were also pro-labor, they backed La Guardia instead of Tammany. One didn't have to be an astute politician to realize that this was not a blessing. And La Guardia forthwith declared, "They will get no aid or comfort from me." After all, his administration—according to innumerable impassioned utterances—was nonpolitical.

Naturally, the Tammany opposition could not have been more pleased by this development. Thrusting logic to one side, they reasoned that if the Communists were for La Guardia, this clearly meant that La Guardia was a Communist, a Red. Their candidate, former Supreme Court Justice Jeremiah T. Mahoney—huge, red-headed—cried "Red!" in his campaign speeches, and this came to convey desperation, a last-ditch attempt to somehow discredit the Mayor's impressive four years in office.

This tactic didn't capture the Italian vote. What kind of an Italian, after all, would vote for someone named Mahoney when they could vote for a La Guardia? And La Guardia had the vote of the Jews, who were not only liberal politically, but fearfully alarmed by the German Bund whose people thought of Dewey as "Jewey of New York," called Roosevelt "Rosenfeld" and his New Deal the "Jew Deal," and denounced La Guardia as "the Jew La Guardia." (All that Mahoney could offer was that he had opposed America's participation in the 1936 Olympics, held in Berlin.)

A letter which La Guardia received in 1937 from a Mr. A. W. Brown of the Bombay Oil Company in Rochester, New York, indicated that anti-Semitism wasn't restricted to Nazis.

Did you know the Jews plus the bankers through Governor Lehman and Morgenthau, who is United States Treasurer and nephew of Governor Lehman by marriage, have had this Country by the throat for the last four years and won't let go?

What are you going to do about that, Mayor?

Brown also asked that La Guardia back the Wagner Housing Bill and keep it from being administered by Jews.

La Guardia acknowledged receipt of the letter most cordially, and then wrote:

Should you come to New York City I would suggest that you contact Dr. Earl Bowman. I think he might understand your case. He is in charge of the psychopathic department at Bellevue Hospital, 29th Street and First Avenue.

Eventually, the Republicans—warring among themselves—had to declare for La Guardia, though they would have liked to be eternally rid of this person who stood for the progressivism of the La Follettes and the New Deal of Roosevelt and the Democrats. FDR, too—by his alleged neutrality—was on La Guardia's side. If he had been against La Guardia, he undoubtedly would have proclaimed it publicly—well, might have. Lehman had—and so had Jim Farley. So the President's silence, as clearly as speech, revealed where he stood in the New York mayoralty race.

Just a few weeks before the election, he called Farley to find out what Farley could tell him about the campaign.

Farley didn't tell Roosevelt to end his neutrality. Instead, jokingly, he said, "If La Guardia really gets tough, I'll pin his ears back."

"Watch out," Roosevelt advised him. "He might bite you."

"He's too short to reach above my ankles."

Much might be read into this banter; possibly, some of it would be right. There was no question about the meaning of the song the Fusionists were singing—to the tune of "The Daring Young Man on the Flying Trapeze"—and that a joyous certainty of victory inspired it:

Oh!

> We'll get all the votes with the greatest of ease,
> Mahoney Baloney is nothing but wheeze,
> The heelers are howling—there's no graft to seize—
> Good Government's now here to stay!

"Now here to stay" taken literally, meant forever and ever; only poetic license justified such hyperbole—poetic license and the ebullience of a winning side. The ebullience had certainly been justified, for La Guardia did more than merely break the jinx of a reform mayor's inability to be reelected; he won overwhelmingly: 1,344,630 votes to Mahoney's 890,756. (At ten o'clock election night, FDR was already on the wire congratulating La Guardia.) Though half of the 480,000 votes that La Guardia received from the Republicans were unenthusiastic, they had the same value when counted as the enthusiastic ones. Together with the American Labor Party's 482,790 votes, they spelled victory. (La Guardia's victory swept Dewey into office. And because it appeared that La Guardia had finally destroyed Tammany, the deputy police commissioner, to symbolize this event, sent La Guardia the skin of a tiger he'd shot in India.)

Victory failed to change La Guardia's unorthodoxy as a politician. Instead of smothering with verbose appreciation those who had worked diligently for him, he said, "I hope our relations continue pleasant, but I wouldn't be surprised if by the Fourth of July you were damning me as the Republicans did. I am going to continue to administer the city as I did the past four years. There will be no change at all. My attitude toward political parties will be just as in the past."

CHAPTER TWENTY-FOUR

N O SOONER HAD LA GUARDIA BEEN REELECTED
than he felt the irresistible pull of another office, the Presidency of the
United States. It had tugged at him before; and this explained, in some
measure, his ever-closer ties with the New Deal. Was it merely the
gossamer of a lulling daydream: the son of an Italian immigrant who
becomes a successor to ineffable giants, Washington, Jefferson, Lincoln
—and Franklin Delano Roosevelt? Well, there was the substantial actuality of his having beaten Tammany decisively twice in a row. There
were the urgings of his friends, among them Berle, whose shrewdness
matched his lean, sensitive face, whose deep devotion did not distort
the clarity of his evaluations.

And when you want something desperately, even encouraging letters from strangers take on a not completely justified significance.
Nathan L. M. Ferber, a lawyer in Detroit, congratulated La Guardia
on the beginning of his second administration. He concluded, "And I
don't think I am amiss in stating that in the minds of all those many
thousands, your succession to the Presidency of the United States
should follow."

Another letter touched caustically upon a topic—Roosevelt's seeking
a third term in 1940—which was of deep concern to presidental aspirants. It arrived right after La Guardia's reelection from Miss B.
Mordant Wilson of Woodhaven, Long Island.

I am sure the President of the United States is no friend of yours. He means
to see that you shall not hold that position. He means to have a third term,
maybe a fourth—for he loves power. . . . Mayor La Guardia, it is your duty
to run if the people want you. . . .

La Guardia could, when necessary, be modest. He informed Miss Wilson, "I fear that in this instance there are not many who will agree with you." And he had work to do; to be diverted could be disastrous.

This disclaimer notwithstanding, his latest full-bodied victory over Tammany had thrown the national spotlight on him. He thereupon went traveling all over the West to meet the Voter.

When he appeared before the Illinois Agricultural Association in the winter of 1937–1938, he spoke of coordinating industry, labor and agriculture.

First of all I want you to know I'm not a city slicker. . . . I don't know anything about farming, but I do eat.

He then employed a gimmick he had used in Congress; he took a ham sandwich from his pocket—in order to illustrate price parity for farmers.

I bought this sandwich for a dime. The amount of corn represented by this slice of meat could be weighed on a jeweler's scale. We wonder where the actual cost is. Perhaps in the bread? But no, it's mostly air. You can't blame the farmer.

Before concluding, he spoke of the reports being circulated by politicians.

I am not running for any office. I have all I can do to keep the enemy at bay in my own city.

It was at this time that William Allen White elevated La Guardia to the rank of presidential possibility. (Previously, his *Gazette* had declared La Guardia "the Republican Party's Modern Day Lincoln." The needling of reactionary Republicans was something White did to relieve the oppressive heat of a Kansas summer.)

"White is a good friend of mine," La Guardia countered, "and when he said that he spoke as a mother speaks of her favorite blue-eyed baby boy. . . . It's bad to be thinking of another office when you have one. It's vain and impairs the office holder's usefulness."

White persisted, maintaining that La Guardia was the "type" of presidential candidate to be selected in the future. Country boys could no longer aspire to the presidency.

Even the rural sections would not accept the "clodhopper type" now. . . . The country has gone from the rural to the urban state, and the country boy has to give place to the city boy.

The *New York Times* pointed out, to set White straight, that though La Guardia was born in New York, he grew up "in wider-open spaces than any farmer-boy President since Abraham Lincoln."

In any event, the Mayor didn't behave like a city boy, for with the coming of spring, his thoughts turned, presumably, to agriculture—to its problems. These problems, he said by way of justifying his traveling so far from City Hall, affected the people of New York City.

But way out west, the voters were intrigued by the idea that they might be getting a look at the next president of the United States. In Wichita Falls, Texas, Dr. O. B. Kiel, in whose home La Guardia was a guest, proclaimed that La Guardia could do for all the country what he had done in New York. And Governor James V. Allred, in introducing La Guardia to an audience, coyly referred to the possibility of La Guardia's being called to a bigger job in national affairs. In reacting to the governor's implication, La Guardia stated flatly, "I have a contract with the people of New York City which still has almost four years to run."

Guthrie, Oklahoma, performed more exotically than Wichita Falls. The visitor from the East was not only christened Chief Rising Cloud, but Wolf Tooth, an ancient Cheyenne, speaking in his ancient tongue, nominated him President of the United States. These carryings-on struck one member of the press as strangely familiar; then his déjà vu meshed with Calvin Coolidge of the long Indian warbonnet and the even longer silences.

A realist, La Guardia would not be taken in completely by the various receptions. The welcoming crowds might signify mild approval plus curiosity; the backing of politicians was an altogether different sort of affection. The Republicans tolerated him; the Democrats regarded him as a maverick in New Deal clothing. When La Guardia asked Ickes if he could get the nomination, the curmudgeon's answer could scarcely have been briefer, more incisive; he said no.

La Guardia didn't have to ask Ickes to go into more detail. He himself had said that no one with an Italian name could be elected president; besides, he would be fifty-eight in 1940, which was even a year older than Wilson when he became president; and the anti-Semites would make much of his Jewish mother, his switching from backing Dewey for governor, in 1938, to Lehman, a Jew. However, many thought La Guardia was a Catholic. And Al Smith had been defeated for the presidency because he *was* a Catholic.

Roosevelt went into much more detail than Ickes, in a talk with

Berle. Personally, he thought La Guardia "was easily the ablest of the lot," would make "a first-rate liberal President"; practically, he expressed doubts about the acceptance, in the farm belt, of the man's New York language and accent. Roosevelt had also said that "for President, [La Guardia] was just a little flamboyant."

Of course, all probing and conjecture concerning 1940 could have been put off, for it was all academic until one overriding question was answered: would Roosevelt run for a third term? Tugwell, in a debate with fellow brains truster Moley, before the *Herald Tribune* Forum, argued that Roosevelt should run, simply because of the unfinished business that he alone could finish. This infuriated La Guardia; he raged for a week before quieting down. Tugwell understood what had caused La Guardia to boil over; La Guardia "had set his heart on something so unlikely that he ought not have entertained it even as a vague idea."

La Guardia took stock. The Democrats had no one better than him to succeed the President; and without him as their candidate, the Republicans couldn't win. Self-confidence—and a degree of dispassion—took this inventory. He found some hope in a 1939 *Fortune* poll to determine the most likely presidential candidate. Though he tied for second place with Senator Vandenberg of Michigan, and Dewey came in first, he still had time to displace Dewey. He then resorted to an old trick. If the two parties, he vowed threateningly, put up "political palookas," a third party would arise—in wrath and righteous indignation—and the implication was plain that he would be its leader.

The Mayor had three advantages which the other presidential aspirants wouldn't have. The following year, the World's Fair, associated with his name, would draw the entire country to New York City, and the Fair's wonders were going "to be translated, properly and legitimately, into a sales talk for the Mayor." That year the entire country would also come to know of "the world's greatest airport," the eastern terminus of four major airlines, that he had brought to New York City after battling Newark, New Jersey, for that right. Called the New York City Municipal Airport—and generally known as North Beach Airport—it would eventually be named La Guardia Airport in the Mayor's honor. (At its dedication on a beautiful October Sunday, skywriters wrote across a cloudless sky, in mile-high letters, "Name it La Guardia Airport." And the letters lingered in readable form for at least ten minutes.) Finally, La Guardia had the advantage of having been president of the United States Conference of Mayors. It had became the strongest lobby in Washington, and the help he managed to get for cities made them his friend.

La Guardia received special World's Fair publicity when he announced that he would not permit Germany to have an exhibit at the Fair. Having forbidden that country—categorically—he added that if it somehow were to exhibit, he would put a wax facsimile of Hitler, whom he called "a brown-shirted" fanatic, in the Museum of Horrors. As for Goering, La Guardia described him as "a perverted maniac."

Secretary of State Cordell Hull made an official, formal apology to Germany. La Guardia, forthwith, blasted the Nazis again with colorful verbal dynamite. Again Hull apologized. (FDR remained silent about the matter. However, when La Guardia came to the White House to keep an appointment, the President smiled, extended his right arm and said, "Heil, Fiorello!" La Guardia snapped to attention, extended his right arm, and said, "Heil, Franklin!")

At one point, Goering vowed to bomb New York City from Governor's Island to Rockefeller Center merely to "stop somewhat the mouths of the arrogant people over there."

When the German consulate asked for police protection, in case angered Jews struck back, La Guardia provided some of New York's finest—Jewish cops.

It wasn't surprising that the Mayor should receive a threatening note, its signature a crayoned swastika. "You will get this [a live .22 caliber long cartridge, enclosed in a small box] if you continue to attack the German Nazi party."

The war between La Guardia and the Nazis made good newspaper copy, made him better known nationally. Still, in the fall of 1938, La Guardia continued his travels, which could not help but erode those xenophobic feelings of the hinterland mentioned by Roosevelt; the three-week itinerary would take him to El Paso, Phoenix, Prescott, Fort Worth, San Francisco and Los Angeles, where he would spend a week at the American Legion Convention.

As his train pulled out of Knoxville, a dignified white-haired man shouted from the platform, "The Mayor of New York and the next President of the United States, and you can tell him that comes from an Alabama Democrat."

The train stopped in Chattanooga, and the reporters clambered aboard to find out La Guardia's plans for 1940.

La Guardia laughed. "I don't know anything about politics. Besides I'm too busy running New York City. . . ." (He ran New York City by means of constant telephonic and telegraphic communication. In his breast pocket, he carried two watches; one told him New York time and the other railroad time. They also served as a symbol of his nationwide influence.)

In Phoenix, he said to reporters who asked him about 1940, "I couldn't get a ticket together to get into the gallery of a good theatre."

He varied this for Los Angeles reporters. "I couldn't get a gallery ticket to either party's conventions."

In addition to traveling, he gave himself pep talks. What had been the pattern of his political life? Rejection—followed, inevitably, by acceptance. It might very well happen again, and this time Fusion might put him in the top office in Washington.

And if the presidency eluded his reach, the vice-presidency might not. Garner, of course, was not the only one who regarded the second-highest office in the land as "not worth a quart of warm spit." But La Guardia told Berle of his interest in that office. Berle saw Cordell Hull-La Guardia as a possible ticket—a pragmatic balance of moderate and progressive, but he would have preferred to have had the ticket reversed, with Hull in the second spot.

La Guardia shuttled between hope and despair. In despair, he explained why he couldn't be vice-president: "Because the son of a wop who lives in a tenement doesn't get nominated for vice-president." And yet he could still hope that he would be his country's first Progressive president.

Everything hinged on the answer to a question. Would Franklin Delano Roosevelt run for a third term? As early as 1937, the President told a reporter who asked him the question to go stand in a corner and put on a dunce cap. Events would reveal that Roosevelt's frustrating silence did not stem from indecision, but was, rather, one stratagem of a sagacious political battle plan.

President Roosevelt and Mayor La Guardia were not at war; they were the best of friends. La Guardia did not covet the presidency, but he did want it. Not much political sagacity was needed, however, to realize that an aspirant had a chance only if FDR did not run for a third term.

At the end of August 1938, the La Guardias went to Hyde Park to call on the Roosevelts. Eric, to some extent, was responsible for the visit. Once when his father had returned from Hyde Park, he asked him why he didn't bring the President home with him sometime.

"The President is a very busy man," La Guardia told his seven-year-old son, "and is much too busy to see little boys."

Unimpressed, Eric said, "Aw, I don't think he's so hot."

La Guardia thereupon arranged a trip to Hyde Park that would include Eric, Jean and a few of his children's friends.

FDR showed off his new cottage, in process of construction, a retreat made of native stone which once marked the fields, built on a hilltop behind his wife's retreat. It would be a place devoid of political talk. And the items of civilization that it would not have revealed what Roosevelt intended for the rest of his life. The cottage would be without telephone, radio, secret service men—who would be displaced by a fantasy science-fiction gun that would mow down any intruder who passed through an electric beam. To feel even more removed from the present, he even considered that the cottage's lights should be powered by kerosene rather than by electricity.

Clearly, Roosevelt did not appear to be a man greedily intent on getting his hands on that third term. When Fiorello spoke in praise of Franklin, those assembled at the little outing smiled their approval. Then FDR—tilting his chin, jerking his head characteristically as he spoke—asked anyone who had influence with either Mr. or Mrs. La-Guardia to exert it in persuading them to purchase land in Duchess County and to become neighbors.

It rang true that he wanted the quiet, bucolic life for himself and the La Guardias. And when this Duchess County squire said that he did not want a third term, he spoke the truth, even though he also, at the very same time, lied. Ambivalence explains the paradox.

Two terms had whittled him down physically. His wife also could not countenance four more years in the White House. She jokingly, yet seriously, gave a rundown on what she had to do during those eight years of her life.

Always be on time. Never try to make any personal engagements. Do as little talking as humanly possible. Never be disturbed by anything. Always do what you're told to do as quickly as possible. Remember to lean back in a parade, so that people can see your husband. Don't get too fat to ride three on a seat. Get out of the way as quickly as you're not needed.

Understandably, Eleanor Roosevelt urged her husband to ready a successor. This led to Harry Hopkins being brought into the Cabinet, as secretary of commerce.

What must have given her some hope was the hold tradition had on her husband; and the tradition of no-third-term—rooted in the democratic ideology that no man was indispensable—had become an inviolable tradition. The Republican press gave the electorate the impression that a third term would be in defiance of the Constitution. Actually, the Constitution makes no mention of a third term—for or against. It merely says, "The executive power shall be vested in a president of the United States of America. He shall hold his office during the term of four years. . . ."

That "that man in the White House" might possibly run for a third term had the conservatives shaking with fear—which amused Roosevelt. The third-term game also intrigued him with its endless possibilities, and the politician in him could not resist being a participant. First of all, he must run and appear not to be running. Otherwise, voters would damn him with the charge of being a dictator, a dictator hungry for uninterrupted, unending power. There was only one way to win this game. He must be drafted.

A virtuoso at political maneuverings, Roosevelt offered incontestable proof that he did not want to run for the third time, by his encouragement of others to enter the race. He did not encourage just one or two, but a half dozen or more, so the public could not help but notice. In addition, by placing so many contestants in the field, the power of any single one would be diluted, the division among them would be great, and defeating this distracted lot would be a sure thing.

After receiving La Guardia's consent, Berle, in a talk before the Affiliated Young Democrats, told them "that unless the Democratic Party were progressive enough to take in a La Guardia, it could not possibly win the 1940 election." The Republicans knew they did not have a chance unless they picked La Guardia. Still, Wendell Willkie proved to be their candidate. A big, bulky man, a Hoosier, a lawyer-businessman with an outspoken antipathy for the New Deal. He had once been in Tammany, but denied this. He wanted to have La Guardia as his running mate, but his advisors feared "that La Guardia would take occasion to decline publicly and announce forthwith for the President."

International crisis changed everything that election year. According to the polls: (1) vast majority against a third term; (2) majority against FDR's having a third term; (3) some regarded a third term necessary in case of crisis. The crisis began in April, with Nazi armies on the march, continued through the summer and the Republican and Democratic conventions. The third term issue, as a consequence,

faltered and died. Even the New Deal dried up as a source of antago-
nism, and it took second place as FDR's reason for being a candidate. Now survival came first. And a cliché fit the people's thought:
one did not change horses in the middle of a turbulent stream.

La Guardia stumped for Roosevelt. Seabury even claimed, angrily,
that La Guardia had appointed Jimmy Walker as impartial chairman
of the women's garment industry, at a $20,000-a-year salary, in order to
get votes for Roosevelt, for many were still enthralled by the ex-
Mayor's charm. The October 21 issue of *Life* ran "Roosevelt Preferred"
by Fiorello La Guardia. The editors pointed out that La Guardia, in
addition to writing the article, had volunteered to choose pictures and
write captions for it. They said they had "accepted this unusual offer
and trust readers will forgive any minor eccentricity in caption style."

La Guardia wrote about the President's accomplishments, and also
hammered away at Willkie's inexperience. He then concluded:

Remember this is not an election for a municipal alderman—this is not an
election for a mayor. Bear in mind that we are electing this year a President
of the United States—to the most difficult job in the world. The people's
candidate is Franklin D. Roosevelt.

Roosevelt did indeed prove to be the people's candidate, preferred
not only by La Guardia but by the electorate.

With pride, Mrs. La Guardia said, "Public office, to serve the public.
Why, Fiorello regarded that as an honor and privilege. Not like some
of your politicians who just think what they can get out of it, what's in
it for them."

After two terms as mayor, his hair beginning to show gray, the office
consumed his energy, but could not satisfy his appetite for accomplishment. He liked FDR, a doer. He believed women should be doers,
should be more than "breeders." "Don't be just a breeder," he told a
young girl who was studying music, by way of prodding her into
working hard on her lessons.

Driven to achieve, La Guardia appeared to play at being president,
in Walter Mitty fantasy. Even before he attempted to actually become
president, he participated in the office—by mail.

Your daring foreign policy which you frankly discussed, has given me many
sleepless nights and nightmares. I hear bugles calling and drums beating
and cannon shots all night. Please do be careful and be sure of our friend
Johnny Bull. . . .

The President reassured him.

Don't stay awake nights thinking of drums and bombs. The Navy program is having an excellent effect in Berlin, Rome and Toyko [sic]. Enough said!

On another occasion, La Guardia pointed out the strategic locations of the Cape Verde Islands and the Azores and the possibility of acquiring them.

He made use of cables, too. One, in May 1940, went to His Majesty King Victor Emmanuel III.

Recalling our days together in 1918 and even remembering your desire for peace and love for humanity I am taking the liberty to tell you that the American people are united in support of our President in his efforts for peace. . . . Realizing the wild ambitions of the Nazi government the American people sincerely hope that Italy will not sacrifice her sons for Hitler. . . . Let us stand together for peace and freedom as we did in nineteen eighteen.

(When La Guardia was billed $51.13 for the cable, he objected mildly in a note to Berle, then assistant secretary of state. Berle answered: ". . . The Congress of the United States in its corporate awfulness and wisdom ruled that whenever the Department sent a cable in a private interest, it should get the private interest to pay the bill. . . . Once I asked why Congress made such silly rules about this Department, and they told me you put through the Act in question!")

An innocent enough wire went to FDR on the occasion of his fifty-ninth birthday:

The City of New York wishes the President many happy returns of the day and it's [sic] Mayor sends his personal greetings and best wishes for continued good health, plenty of pep and the maintenance of the good old wallop.

"And continued attempts," he might have added, "to reward me adequately for my work in your behalf during the presidential campaign of 1940." Of course, La Guardia had slightly more subtlety than that. Besides, the President didn't have to be reminded; he was working assiduously trying to find something that would suit La Guardia. Ambassador to Britain? When La Guardia heard that appointment was under consideration, he let it be known that kneepants would hardly flatter his figure. Ickes recorded in his diary that FDR spoke of selecting La Guardia as an executive assistant, a liaison between himself and the new defense setup. FDR also asked him what he thought of La Guardia for secretary of war. Ickes answered that "it would be a good appointment." A week later, however, when the President sounded him out on La Guardia's remaining in New York, Ickes thought that a good idea, because of the subversive activities there. "La Guardia, with his liberal record, could go further than anyone else to check those activities without too much criticism." (Ickes on the subject of La Guardia in New York must be weighed against Ickes' desire to be secretary of war.)

In his diversity of problems, Roosevelt curiously had a local one: the policing of the National Capitol, traffic accidents and general traffic conditions. So while La Guardia strove to reach distant horizons, the President took on the hue of a mayor. He contacted La Guardia and told him he thought the solution might reside in having more policemen. "What would you think of lending me Valentine and his principal traffic officer for three or four days to give me personally and unofficially their slant on the trouble . . . ?"

The traffic situation couldn't mar Washington's appeal in the spring. La Guardia and his family flew there from La Guardia Airport. (This had a newsworthy element. Since 1934, La Guardia had made it a point not to fly with Marie—in order to protect Jean and Eric from the possibility of losing both parents in a crash.) The weather proved perfect for flying; the children had become increasingly air-minded; and La Guardia was eager to show the children points of interest in the Capitol, including the House chamber where he had sat as a member of Congress. On boarding the plane, La Guardia said, "I was happier then."

The accuracy of nostalgia's assessment of the past can't be trusted, but that such an assessment is made may indicate malaise. The White House knew of this unhappiness too. A memo to the President from James Rowe, Jr., concerned the reappointment of John Morin, a friend of La Guardia's, a capable person, but refused a reappointment by FDR because of his age.

La Guardia really wants this. La Guardia has been making a lot of unhappy noise since the election. A lot of people will tell Morin they got the President to make the reappointment. For many obvious reasons I suggest you let La Guardia know he is responsible and I attach a memorandum from you to him to that effect. NOTE: La Guardia's Italian quotation, in his memorandum to you, reads: "Accursed old age is despised by all." Your reply in Italian reads: "The old are happy when protected by the good."

The memos which Rowe referred to are:

April 11, 1941

Memo from
La Guardia to FDR

> La vecchiaia maledetta
> e da tutti disprezzate

Please do not turn John Morin down. He has been on the job for twelve years. He has been a real and loyal friend.

Fiorello

April 22, 1941

Memorandum for: Mayor Fiorello La Guardia
John Morin
I vecchi sono felici cuando
sono difesi dai buoni
All right, Fiorello, you win!

FDR

In addition to doing a favor for "a real and loyal friend," and taking care of his city threatened by a subway strike, La Guardia quite obviously had cast himself, at the very least, in the role of presidential assistant. A memorandum for the President dated 4/21/41 clearly indicated this.

Mayor La Guardia 'phoned. He wants to talk to President about Newfoundland. He is going to Canada tomorrow and would like to fly back to Washington Thursday morning and see the President. I have given him twelve o'clock tentatively.

He asked that the President not sign the Home Defense Plan until he, La Guardia, has presented a few suggested ideas to be included.

The Mayor also stated he was addressing England from Ottawa, Canada, Wednesday. He wanted to know if the President had any message or any thought that he would like included in this address by the Mayor.

A month later the President, finally, decided how to channel all this inexhaustible, extracurricular energy. (This still needed doing, even though La Guardia, in addition to being Mayor, was chairman of the American section of the Joint Permanent Defense Board, an agency set up to coordinate defense between this country and Canada, and president of the United States Conference of Mayors, an agency that coordinated the work of municipalities throughout the country.) Roosevelt made La Guardia director of the Office of Civilian Defense, charged with the task of providing "adequate protection of life and property in the event of emergency," and this involved mobilizing vast numbers to engage in volunteer defense work. (Roosevelt had heard that in January of that year, La Guardia had sent firemen to England to learn how the English took care of fires started by incendiary bombs; thus the Mayor had jumped the gun on his appointment and, conceivably, had suggested it.)

Of course, the appointment was considered a political one, the President paying off La Guardia for helping him become President for the third consecutive time. Ickes viewed the appointment as ridiculous. Granted, La Guardia couldn't be surpassed at handling the defense assignment, but he simply had too much to do. "After all, Fiorello is not God and he has to eat and sleep like other human beings." Eugene Meyer, of the *Washington Post*, agreed with Ickes, telling him "that Fiorello La Guardia as head of Civilian Defense is a joke. . . . He already had his hands full as Mayor of New York."

Apparently La Guardia didn't have to eat and sleep, for on the night of his appointment he told New York City in a radio talk that his OCD duties would in no way interfere with his duties as Mayor. The next day he called a press conference, mentioning that "black and white ties will not be necessary." To still possible alarm, he pointed out that there was a 95 percent chance that the defense volunteers would never be needed. Then he said, "We can't take a chance on the remaining 5 percent." He also let the press know that "we will not require elaborate and luxurious offices." (He was to receive no compensation—besides satisfaction and honor—for being head of the OCD.) Finally, he declared, "This department is going to be different."

After getting his organization settled in an old brick mansion in residential Washington, La Guardia began an arduous, superhuman schedule. From Tuesday morning, when he caught a plane at La Guardia Airport, to Thursday night, he was in Washington running the OCD. If there was a Cabinet meeting on Friday, he stayed over, for his attendance at Cabinet meetings had been a concession to induce him to take the directorship of OCD, to make him feel that he did more than keep the streets of a little town on the Hudson clean—his denigrating hyperbole for the job he did as Mayor of New York. The *Times* reported that on a single day in June La Guardia had fourteen appointments on his schedule, and that he might possibly squeeze in a few more. His last appointment of the day—being present at the opening concert of the Lewisohn Stadium—was made with the proviso that he would be on hand if he was in town. There would be much-needed escape for him in that amphitheatre, "listening to a world which offers symmetry in an age of chaos, design in a time of destruction, beauty in a world at war."

War had been the crisis that made FDR's third term imperative. La Guardia, too, had FDR's ambivalence about continuing in office. Besides, Marie didn't want him to run again, and he had promised her he wouldn't. He told biographer Henry F. Pringle, "I haven't the enthusiasm I had before. I figure that this world is going to be in turmoil for fifty or a hundred years. There's work for me to do. If I'm not cleaning the streets of New York I'll be doing something else." But there was over two months before election day. And New York, in La Guardia's own words, was "the logical and most attractive and tempting target for a foreign enemy." It could be argued that just as FDR had to run, not simply for the sake of saving the New Deal, but for survival itself, La Guardia had to remain in office not merely to keep Tammany out, but to keep New York from being destroyed.

The precarious international situation favored La Guardia's chances. This stiffened the resistance of conservative Republicans. Their animosity flamed ever higher, and their John R. Davis—who wished "to rebuild the Republican Party on a conservative and old-fashioned basis" —gave La Guardia a hard time in the primary.

O'Dwyer, the Mayor's Democratic opponent, faced a number of hurdles. Though tall, handsome, an immigrant Irish boy who had moved from hod carrier to district attorney of Brooklyn—in which capacity he eliminated Murder, Inc.—he still had to overcome La Guardia's eight years of good government. He wasn't Tammany-picked, but he had been chosen by the Brooklyn machine. He claimed to be a New Dealer, but that meant nothing in the way of votes, for La Guardia was a veteran New Dealer. He had fought crime, with something of Tom Dewey's dash, but there was talk that he had strong ties with the underworld. (Luciano complained to Costello: "We gave O'Dwyer a pisspot full of money, now what the hell are we getting back for it?")

The Democrats fell back on the old communist cry, but it rang even less true now, sounded even weaker than it had in '37. With some justification, they also called La Guardia a part-time Mayor. Then a political error, as though heaven-sent, helped them. In the course of the campaign, La Guardia's temper flared and he accused Governor Lehman of being "a thief and a double crosser and a fixer," because the governor had never backed La Guardia and he was now supporting La Guardia's opponent. Lehman supporters thereupon turned on La Guardia, and La Guardia's advisors urged La Guardia to apologize. La Guardia refused, though he knew this would mean the loss of thousands and thousands of votes.

Finally, his political common sense almost triumphed over a costly, emotional indulgence. He half apologized. He told those whose votes he was losing, "I didn't call the Governor the names he's said I called him. I was referring to the political bosses."

None of all this touched the general voter apathy. The whirlpool of war, that would in a matter of only a month suck their country into its vortex, held their attention, and the personal-political tiff between Lehman and La Guardia could not divert it. Besides, the widespread view that La Guardia was sure to win hardened voter apathy. Even good government had lost its tang—and good government was still La Guardia's battle cry: "There is just one issue. Do the people want to retain this administration, with its record, or do they want to return this city to Kelly, Flynn and Sullivan. . . . If you want us to continue we will, with one promise only, to give you clean, honest, decent government."

The losses to La Guardia as a result of the Lehman matter were somewhat offset by a memo which Roosevelt read—with his telling nuances and expert timing—to a press conference, held little more than a week before election day.

Although my voting residence has always been up-State, I have lived and worked in the City of New York off and on since 1904. I have known and observed New York's Mayors since that time. I am not taking part in the New York City election, *but*—[Laughter]—what are you all laughing at?—[More laughter]—*but* because the City of New York contains about half the population of my State, I do not hesitate to express the opinion that Mayor La Guardia and his Administration have given the City the most honest and, I believe, the most efficient municipal government of any within my recollection. . . . That's all.

La Guardia acknowledged the President's support by wire immediately.

THE PRESIDENT

Merci

FIORELLO

La Guardia won a photo-finish race, the closest election since 1909. (An enfeebled Fusion only gained control of the Board of Estimate.) So FDR snared the presidency for the third time, which kept La

Guardia from ever having it, and thrust a third term as mayor upon him. Thoreau saw no purpose in going on making pencils, after succeeding in making a good one; La Guardia had achieved good government for New York City. . . . That a Gallup poll put him in fifth place to succeed FDR in 1944 offered La Guardia little in the way of hope or consolation.

CHAPTER TWENTY-FIVE

I

N A MATTER OF WEEKS, A DAY THAT WOULD LIVE IN
infamy catapulted La Guardia out of the doldrums. On that day, December 7, 1941, the Mayor of New York happened to be primarily the
director of the OCD and was therefore in Washington. The news sent
him riding about in a police car, siren in full cry; La Guardia, meanwhile, shouted, "Calm! Calm! Calm!"

The Mayor hadn't contributed to calm in his running of the OCD.
His first error in judgment had been to acquire the President's wife as
his associate, reasoning that she could do much for the entire operation
in the way of prestige and publicity, ignoring the disparity between
them, which ran far deeper than her tallness and his shortness.

Roosevelt had wanted his wife involved in defense, so that she
wouldn't bother him about a slackening, due to the war, in New Deal
efforts. Still, he anticipated trouble, for what individuals had said to
him concerning making La Guardia secretary of war was fresh in his
thoughts. La Guardia wouldn't work with others. The analogy of his
running all over the field with the ball was a euphemism on the side of
kindness. He failed to work with the country's governors; instead, set
up his own organizations in the states, and this, of course, made "the
governors hot under the collar."

To pin down the mercurial La Guardia, FDR called in Anna Rosenberg, known for her consummate skill in directing warring individuals
or groups down peaceful paths. "I don't want to take sides between
Eleanor and Fiorello," he told her. "You go in there and keep peace. I
don't have time for that."

The urgent, unprecedented international situation created some of
the conflict, and some sprang from two strong-minded individuals at-

tempting to work together. She had certain ideas of how things ought to be done, and who should be brought in to do them. He, on the other hand, had his own ideas. And their interests differed radically. His ran to the dramatic: air raid–warning systems, practice blackouts, fire-fighting methods. Mrs. Roosevelt concerned herself with gaining the understanding of people.

Mrs. Anna Rosenberg Hoffman recalled how she detonated highly charged encounters.

Their ideas were seldom irreconcilable. If you talked to both of them and said, "Look, it can be done this way." Or "he feels very strongly about it," I'd say to Mrs. Roosevelt. "He means well, please do it his way." Next time I would show them where it could be reconciled, or I would say to him, "Look, you think she's the most marvelous woman in the world"—and he did—"and I agree with you. Now if she has an idiosyncrasy or wants to do something this way. It isn't going to do any harm. Why not let her do it this way?"

Her way lacked the pyrotechnics which his idiosyncrasies required. He would lure women volunteers with irresistibly stylish, sex-snappy uniforms, but she felt obliged to first of all determine what they were going to do as volunteers and, after that, she actually favored something in the way of a uniform that was practical and cheap, around three dollars, and which had a dreadful, blue-gray denim institutional look. On the other hand, a half dozen beautiful girls modeled La Guardia's selection and he posed for the newsreels with them.

Besides this difference, essentially one of personality, La Guardia's part-time status made him hurry up meetings, for he had planes to catch, vital duties not related to defense to perform. As a consequence, decisions were arrived at which really should have had more careful consideration. Sometimes, too, department heads and Mrs. Roosevelt herself couldn't stop the ever-moving director of OCD long enough for an important discussion. (And Mrs. Roosevelt found "every activity which Mayor La Guardia did not want in his part of the program was thrust into my division.")

The evening of the Pearl Harbor attack, La Guardia, after pleading in the streets for calm, told James M. Landis, head of the New England OCD, to get his wardens and auxiliary policemen to march, to get "a big parade going in Boston tomorrow."

"Mayor, my men don't march. They don't know how to march."

La Guardia persisted, as though war automatically required marching, and since this was a war . . . "You ought to get them to march," he said.

The next morning, La Guardia and Mrs. Roosevelt flew to the West Coast, where Japanese subs lurked offshore like man-killing sharks waiting for a propitious moment to strike, to still any hysterical alarm and to build morale.

The trip began with a bit of slapstick comedy. As La Guardia was being served his dinner, the plane hit an air pocket and a glass of milk drenched him. The next feature of the double bill turned out to be melodrama with a suggestion of grim personal tragedy. After the spilt milk incident, La Guardia went to his compartment for the night. Therefore, it was to Mrs. Roosevelt that the pilot came with the news —flashed by the Associated Press—that San Francisco had been attacked.

Shaken, she went to La Guardia's compartment. When he stuck his head between its curtains, he looked "for all the world like a Kewpie." As soon as she told him the news, he said that she should get off at the next landing and contact Washington for verification. "If it is true," he added, "we will go directly to San Francisco." La Guardia's unhesitating response impressed her. "One could be exasperated with him at times," she wrote, "but one had to admire his integrity and courage." (The army had failed to inform the mayor of San Francisco of a practice blackout and this led to the false report of a bombing raid.)

However, the state of civil defense in the cities all along the West Coast appalled Mrs. Roosevelt, and it was then she definitely felt that La Guardia hadn't done an effective job and couldn't on a part-time basis. Her facts and those of her associates convinced the President. La Guardia didn't make his being fired an easy task, pointing out to the President that the press had conspired against him, arguing for a differentiation between protection and participation in civil defense— but he finally capitulated.

Just being Mayor of New York still didn't offer him enough challenge; that he had failed in the OCD assignment scarcely squashed his self-assuredness. One week when chicken was cheap, he told all women within range of WNYC's sound to use chicken. They, of course, didn't know how to prepare chicken in different ways; so he'd give them a good recipe. No sooner had he finished telling them the recipe, than he said, "Now listen, Winston Churchill. . . ." He thereupon told Winston Churchill, the "blood, toil, tears and sweat" leader of England, that Churchill had done something he didn't like, and he spoke as though Winston Churchill were eternally tuned in to WNYC.

When someone pointed out how funny the incongruity was between a recipe making use of cheap chicken and a scolding delivered to Prime Minister Winston Churchill, he growled, "What do you mean funny? Churchill was wrong!"

And he continued to act as though he held the position of First Assistant to President Roosevelt.

> Dear Skipper:
>
> I sent word to you a few days ago that I felt a definite statement should be made by you very soon concerning Italy's future. The subject is being kicked around in political circles, and inasmuch as you have definite views on the subject, the statement should not be delayed, and in addition will do a great deal of good where it is needed in Italy.
>
> Another matter that I think should be decided real soon is a joint statement that Rome should be an Open City and not bombed. . . .

The diplomatic mail pouch—through his friendship with Berle—served to convey personal letters abroad, though Berle said he wasn't "sure how many rules and regulations we are violating."

Some bore traces of diplomacy. A La Guardia-type account went to John G. Winant, U.S. Ambassador to Great Britain, The American Embassy, London, England:

The story is I started blabbing about fashions one day on the radio and got wheedled into talking about how English women wore their stockings. Now I am in trouble. (A Miss Mumford had pointed out that stockings in England required two clothing coupons. And she also wrote, "Give the British woman really decent 5th Ave. stockings and she will soon show you how to wear them, and wear them right, too.") I want to make your life easier and avoid a diplomatic incident. I am sending a pair of the best nylon stockings to the young lady and will greatly appreciate it if you will mail them.

One letter, at least, had the stamp of compassion. Berle pointed this out to Fiorello.

The enclosure to your letter of February 20th is going forward by pouch to London. I think it was extremely gracious of you to take so much time and trouble in answering the inquiry of a mother who wanted to know where and how her boy died; and I am sure that both she and the London Embassy will greatly appreciate your unfailing kindness.

That boys were dying while he merely occupied a swivel chair, which he claimed had "ruined more men than chorus girls and liquor," must have bothered him. His wife explained his seemingly small-boy penchant for going to fires: he felt he should be where his men were in danger, give them the morale they needed. But, unquestionably, in addition to duty, he savored what Theodore Roosevelt called war's "crowded hours of glorious life" and, as was true of Roosevelt, there was something in the nature of uniforms which gave him special pleasure. He had worn a uniform in World War I, purchased a uniform for this new World War and continuously made a nuisance of himself in order to be able to wear that uniform—in action. Between being addressed as Mr. Mayor or Major, he preferred Major. This time he reached for the far grander Brigadier General.

In a wild, fat scrawl—so wild and fat that only eight or so lines fit on a page—he told FDR of his deep-down need.

> I still believe General Eisenhower—can *not* get along without me and am awaiting your order (but as a soldier)—
>
> Food, man-power, prices and wages are still our big trouble and headaches.
>
> Let me know how and when I can help.
>
> I hope to see you soon—in the meantime
>
> Con amore
> Fiorello

The President responded six weeks later, affirmatively, as though to rectify for all time his having attempted to force a man of La Guardia's spiritual dimensions into the narrow mold of civilian defense, a defense, moreover, which might very well never materialize.

Next time, in a manic, this-is-it letter to Harry Hopkins, the flow of La Guardia's longhand flattened into an undulating, lyrical line.

> I saw the Chief yesterday and I am so happy that I can be of service to my country—besides cleaning the streets of N.Y.C.—I expect to get my medical exam next week— The Chief indicated I could be commissioned right after I finish the Executive Budget, in early April. I am to be assigned to General Eisenhower's staff and am confident that I will be able to do a good job and be really useful. . . .
>
> Writing this by hand as I do not want office to know until last minute.
>
> F

Early April came. The press reported the Mayor's age as sixty, his weight as 175, his probable imminent destination as North Africa, his function as administrator of conquered territory or, eventually, of a liberated Italy.

June brought its customary perfect days, but none for La Guardia, for he was still waiting. But he could muster a touch of whimsy.

> Dear Chief:—
>
> Soldier La Guardia reports to the C in C that he awaits orders.
>
> He believes General Eisenhower needs him now more than ever.
>
> > F. La Guardia
> > Major U.S. Air Service
> > 1st WW

La Guardia received a memorandum from the President, but not on *the* subject. Two sentences, a rebuking tone in each: "I, too, would have censored your address. Soon you will see why and you will wholly agree!" (La Guardia was doing a weekly broadcast for the Office of War Information, and his broadcasts required censoring, because the OWI was not permitted to broadcast anything that was intended "to stir up revolution against the Italian Government." After vowing that he would make no more broadcasts, he would show up punctually, make a broadcast that required censorship, vow he would make no more . . .)

Obviously, the Mayor would not behave until he could wear a uniform. FDR, apparently, refused to face up to this fact, possibly because he feared La Guardia was even capable of disrupting a war. And so the President took to *Survey* editor Paul Kellog's idea, sent to Mrs. Roosevelt, that La Guardia go to Italy, in mufti, to assist in the reawakening of Italian democratic sentiment. ("If in World War I," Kellog mused, "why not in World War II?") FDR suggested that Eleanor send the idea to Hull, and she did. Hull simply said that it was up to the President, adding, "I should cheerfully concur in any move he might make along those lines."

By this time it was mid-August, and FDR asked Hopkins in a memo, "Will you speak to me about this?" Hopkins appeared to know the real La Guardia, for he pointed out: (1) La Guardia will not accept unless he is in army; (2) he does not want to be commissioned until about the middle of November; (3) he does not think it politically wise for him to go to Italy prior to the election.

Secretary of the Navy James V. Forrestal stepped into the tangled skein at the end of August.

Italy would "hold no substantial interest for anyone of such energy and diverse qualities as the Mayor."

This thought occurs to me: As we take islands in the Pacific there will be need for administration, particularly in the Philippines, where I should think Fiorello's talents would be useful, and I should think it would be an interesting challenge to him. . . .

This plan by the secretary of the navy struck Secretary of War Henry L. Stimson as unsatisfactory, for—he told the President—it overlooked the War Department's plan for the Philippines.

The light reign and the early withdrawal of the Army from civil affairs, which this plan proposes, does not seem to me to be the sort of position that suits the temperament of the Mayor. I am afraid that the insertion of this vigorous personality into this picture might jeopardize the smooth execution of the plan.

He suggested that La Guardia

be used as advisor in the civil administration of the Pacific Islands already occupied. . . . Take it up with Navy, if you wish. Recommend La Guardia be commissioned initially as a *captain in the Navy* or a colonel in the Army.

Added in longhand:

If Jim Forrestal wants him to have a higher rank I should have no objection to his being made an admiral!

A mere three weeks later, Stimson's mood and thought changed drastically, judging by a letter that he wrote to Harry Hopkins.

I have determined that I need La Guardia in the army with the rank of Brigadier General.

I have some important assignments that I want him to do during the next year and their accomplishment will require his being in uniform. He should be commissioned around the middle of November.

I do not plan to use him for the time being in Italy, although it may develop later that I will want him to go there for a time.

Apparently the secretary of war meant this, because a few days later at a presidential press conference the matter of a proposed trip by La Guardia came up, and the President offered nothing new concerning it. Someone observed that La Guardia had his uniforms all ready "from the last time, when he thought he was going over a year ago." The President said, "Oh, I know—I know. I hope they still fit."

Two weeks after this press conference, on October 18, 1944, La Guardia had not made the talked-about trip. Instead, he wrote a letter that began "Dear Chief," and expressed the idea that "a good soldier never questions a command," but he then went on to question one, saying, "I do want to make it clear that I would not care to go anywhere where we do not have combat troops." He then told the Commander-in-Chief not to send him to Italy "unless I would be in charge with full authority and your complete backing and support and equal say with the British. . . ."

The runaround—Hopkins viewed it as a raw deal for La Guardia—ended with the selection of former Lieutenant Governor of New York Charles Poletti and Brooklyn D.A. William O'Dwyer for the trip to Sicily, the job to be done there.

President Roosevelt could look down at La Guardia from the heights of sardonic good humor—and he did just that. At a press conference, he drew laughter in the course of saying, "I see my friend the little Mayor—is—has stirred up a hornet's nest in respect to how to prepare coffee." (La Guardia had proposed to housewives that they get more mileage out of their coffee by using the coffee grounds.) "We will have a lot of grave issues like that during the coming year."

The hornet's nest that the Mayor stirred up with the OCD stemmed from his failure to operate that organization successfully and his subsequent disappointment. (Both "civilian" and "defense," as concepts, could not possibly ignite La Guardia's enthusiasm.) Prior to a citywide blackout in New York, he announced that it was perfectly all right for baseball fans at the Polo Grounds to smoke. Disdain underscored the way he put it: "Hitler could not see lighted cigars or cigarettes from the air." The army and the OCD disagreed, maintaining "the flare of a match in lighting up could be seen from thousands of feet in the air."

La Guardia's irritability—"he could be morning one minute," Anna Rosenberg Hoffman recalled, "dark evening the next minute"—also caused him to take a poke at the administration for failing to put him in uniform. The poke consisted of refusing to recognize the midnight curfew on places of entertainment, for the purpose of conserving electricity and showing the armed forces that the home front would make sacrifices in supporting them.

In a call to War Mobilizer James F. Byrnes, "Fiorello talked as if New York City would secede from the Union if its night clubs were forced to shut down so early; he expressed doubt that I had any power to 'invite' the closing and told me that such activities would continue in New York City until one o'clock in the morning." (Byrnes didn't argue. Instead, he phoned General George C. Marshall, who "always put duty and country above self," who issued an order to military personnel that any club that failed to comply with the closing regulation would be placed off limits. Admiral Ernest King issued the same order in behalf of the navy.)

La Guardia still had to leave City Hall with head held high as he walked toward the setting sun. He let it be known that if he ran for a fourth term, he would definitely win, but he had decided against running, for he believed the office should not be held too long by one individual and, besides, people might conceivably be getting a little tired of him. FDR's death was also a factor in his decision. It had occurred at 4:35 P.M. on April 12, 1945, and was made public at a quarter of six; a half hour later, La Guardia—shaken by Roosevelt's sudden death—told "all New Yorkers," over WNYC, "to carry on." But he knew that he could not carry on as mayor. After all, Harry Truman, now in power, had not only opposed his becoming a brigadier general, but there would be no federal help from him for New York City. La Guardia was also well aware that his years in office had eroded his health and that the Republicans had refused to give him the nomination.

Forty-five Republicans who backed La Guardia decided that if they could get state officials to support him, the Mayor could then swing the nomination. A letter asking for this support went out; it roused little interest. The forty-five especially hoped Dewey, because of his importance, would get behind the Mayor, but he "gave the letter the silent treatment."

As proof that he didn't want another four years in office, La Guardia acted indifferent, aloof, utterly carefree. He revealed that in the corner of his 1944 Christmas card he had the number 814. Esoteric? Not at all; 814—as everyone surely knew—was the number of the Furniture Handlers Union; so this, obviously, meant that at least as far back as that Holy Day he had decided on leaving City Hall and Gracie Mansion—bag and baggage and furniture.

Dr. Vincent A. Caso, a Brooklyn newspaper publisher, expressed his sorrow that La Guardia was not going to run again. Then he made a request which evoked sad memories.

My daughter Thea will be 21 years of age on May 19, it would please her very much if you will send her a letter of congratulations, the reason for this request is, she knows that she was named after a charming, intelligent and lovable lady, upon your request.

The enclosed letter [from La Guardia to Caso, dated 5/22/24, which congratulated Caso on the birth of a daughter. "To little Thea I send all my love and may she grow to be as charming, intelligent and lovable as was her beautiful namesake."] is a copy of the original, of course. My daughter is charming, intelligent, lovable, but not beautiful, but she surely is "simpatica," red hair, five feet six. . . .

When Thea lived, he had wanted passionately to be mayor and he had wanted it for her. Now he was through, and the future—by comparison to the past—appeared downhill.

If one needed more evidence that he was through voluntarily, there was his offer to back O'Dwyer—and O'Dwyer *had* been made a brigadier general, *had* been sent to Sicily. But La Guardia turned briskly from O'Dwyer, because O'Dwyer not only refused to run independent of the bosses as La Guardia insisted, but had picked up a distinct underworld odor.

The Democrats, however, decided on running O'Dwyer once more, this time against Jonah Goldstein, a Tammany man turned Republican. Old Fusion warriors pointed out shrilly that the voters had no choice; O'Dwyer and Goldstein were an Irish Tweedle Dum and a Jewish Tweedle Dee. Newbold Morris bolted his party because of the Goldstein selection. He toyed with the idea of joining up with O'Dwyer, and La Guardia advised him to, saying, "You can thumb your nose at the Republicans, and you'll surely be elected." After a moment's thought, however, La Guardia said glumly, "No, Newbold, *you* can't do it. *You couldn't live* with those people!"

La Guardia, who still had great influence, underwrote Morris's running on an independent ticket. Some felt, perhaps with justification, that La Guardia set out to split the Republican vote and thus insure O'Dwyer's victory. With O'Dwyer in office, their reasoning went on, La Guardia's administrations would, by contrast, take on unmistakable luster.

In any event, O'Dwyer won so handily that he did not need the votes he gained by the party's having been split. He thus became the first Democratic administrator of the city after twelve years of Fusion.

Precisely as the code in La Guardia's Christmas card had predicted, furniture handlers arrived at Gracie Mansion, now a dirty grayish white. Other workmen, readying the place for O'Dwyer, said that Mrs. La Guardia was "a mighty fine housekeeper," and that they found little evidence of occupancy by a family with two young children.

On the last day of 1945, at three o'clock in the afternoon, La Guardia left his office, empty now except for a blue poster on the mantelpiece which bore one word in large white letters, *Hope*. But there were other words, in small letters; they, as though with prescience, asked for contributions to the cancer fund. The message of the poster—in the large and small letters—was a foreshadowing; not knowing, La Guardia simply turned his back on it. (As soon as he left, workmen brought in poinsettias and other flowering plants to brighten up the room for the arrival of his successor.)

The next morning, La Guardia and his wife rode to City Hall in her Ford sedan. O'Dwyer arrived a half hour after them, and La Guardia met him on the steps of City Hall, escorted him to the office and, turning over the city government to him, wished him "the best of luck." The ritual then required that O'Dwyer say that he hoped he would do as well as La Guardia had done.

Before stepping into his wife's car, La Guardia turned, took off the big black hat that had become his trademark and, smiling broadly, held the hat high as he waved to City Hall and said good-bye. The photographers had him repeat that wave twice. Even these contrived waves and smiles conveyed his happiness, partially uncontrived. (Right after O'Dwyer had been elected, he called on La Guardia at City Hall. La Guardia immediately popped out of his seat, and seizing O'Dwyer by the arm, shoved him into the chair he had just vacated. "Now," he cried, "*you'll* have a perpetual headache!")

La Guardia's last Sunday "Talk to the People" just before turning over the city to O'Dwyer differed from his past performances in quite a few respects. For one thing, many outgoing officials, appropriately solemn, were present to see the outgoing Mayor depart from the municipal airwaves, just one of the steps in his complete leave-taking. For another, there was a general air of departure—desks, chairs, typewriters, files, turned and heaped in ways not consonant with their functions.

Today La Guardia exclaimed, "Happy New Year!" Then he confided, in a most benign manner, "There are a great many things I want to say today, but I'm not going to say them. Oh, no! This is the holiday season and good cheer abounds." Thereupon, he said a great many things on a great many subjects. He then embraced the microphone and told his audience, "You know, I do want to keep busy. I *love* my city. I hope I'll be able to help others who want to do the right thing." (La Guardia had already let it be known that he intended to keep an eye on Mayor-elect O'Dwyer and give him helpful suggestions.)

"I do want to keep busy" was blatant understatement. For the time being, conducting two radio shows and writing a couple of weekly pieces comprised his schedule. When asked where he would find the time to do so much writing, he answered, "It does not take long to write the truth."

As always, truth—written or spoken—made him vulnerable to trouble. *Liberty Magazine*, which contracted to sponsor his Sunday night, fifteen-minute news commentary, had promised, obviously quite rashly, that he could say anything he pleased. La Guardia did. *Liberty* so disliked what pleased him that they dropped their sponsorship, claiming that La Guardia was too controversial, that he made "reckless and irresponsible" statements. La Guardia responded like an epic hero. "I have lost 'Liberty' but I retain my soul." (He also retained June Dairy Products Company as sponsor of his Sunday noon WJZ show.)

La Guardia's two million listeners made him attractive to commercial radio, for these two million not only listened to his truths but obeyed like obedient children. When he said, "If the kids get tired of potatoes or dumplings, try cornmeal," the mothers of the New York area tried cornmeal. And he had women wearing their rubbers, as "a little favor" to him. The weather, after all, was treacherous. "If you don't wear your rubbers you may slip and fall," he warned them. "You may slip and fall and hurt yourselves. Then we'll have to take care of you, and we don't like to ask our doctors and nurses to take care of any more patients. They are very busy already. So won't you please be sensible and wear your rubbers?"

The radio executives made a flying deductive leap: if all those listeners wore their rubbers on his say-so, they would buy brand X soap or whatever if he told them to. That fallacious reasoning received a fatal blow, for La Guardia said, as quoted in *Variety*, "If they announce that the sponsor is not responsible for their commentator's sentiments, I'll announce that the sponsor's product is not necessarily endorsed by the commentator."

The writing business also had its trials, among them the technical view of critics. La Guardia's writing, one authority said, tended to be thin, more paprika than meat. Another exposed La Guardia as one who dictated rather than wrote and who was "probably under the impression that you can make a sentence emphatic by saying it louder."

In April, a treacherous month, requiring rubbers, President Harry S. Truman called La Guardia to appoint him to what La Guardia was later to call "my unhappy job," a job in which he dealt "with the statistics of death," and which would keep him, usually a sound sleeper, awake and tossing. In this job, as director general of United Nations Rehabilitation and Relief Administration (UNRRA), he had "to feed, clothe, and give material hope to several hundred million human beings who were victims of the war." Governor Lehman had been UNRRA's first administrator, one with the patience of Job—Eleanor Roosevelt's assessment—but still his patience ran out.

Patience and fortitude, virtues that La Guardia plugged for years at the beginning and close of his radio program, gave way at first to a cry for "impatience and activity." (Mrs. La Guardia observed, "There were times when I was amazed at the patience he had with situations—just amazed at it. When it was important, he was very patient. Over trivial matters, he had no patience, wanted to get them out of the way, do something about them.")

A delegate to an UNRRA meeting couldn't resist an obvious pun: "UNRRA has no wheat, but it's got a little flour." The Little Flower went after the wheat.

Wheat has no political complexion, and I'll buy wheat any place in the world where I can find it. And I start right off now in extending my very best personal greetings to General Peron and to say to him that here is an opportunity for Argentina to show that it desires to cooperate with the democracies of the world.

To get food, he conferred with Stalin in Moscow, the Pope in Rome, Marshal Tito in Yugoslavia. There had been far too much talk, talk, talk.

The people are crying for bread, not advice. I want plows, not typewriters. The people need relief, not sympathy. I want fast-moving ships, not slow-reading resolutions. People can't eat resolutions and even the people in our country have learned through a period of depression that ticker tape ain't spaghetti.

He also knew of immoral waste.

In my own city we waste enough food to feed a city of 350,000 people every day. That is a correct statement I know. I picked up that garbage for twelve years.

And he refused "to be stopped by pettiness, the greed or selfishness of man." Weariness, however, slowed him down. In Washington, in a hotel suite, after an impossible day of labor, he would sometimes fall asleep before a radio concert with the volume turned up as loud as it would go.

CHAPTER TWENTY-SIX

LA GUARDIA HAD KNOWN WEARINESS LONG BEFORE UNRRA. Physical collapse—according to his mind set—was sudden, complete—and yet, paradoxically, always imminent. "That's what's going to kill me, of course," he lamented, "unless I do something about it. I don't get any real exercise." (This panacea, on one occasion, went off to Fire Commissioner Walsh in the form of an executive order, signed by the Mayor: "The Fire Commissioner is hereby ordered to take exercise on Saturdays by playing golf at nearby golf links. ORDER TO TAKE EFFECT IMMEDIATELY.)

Just three months after the start of his first term as mayor, he told Senator Robert Wagner, Sr. that sometimes he was so tired he could "hardly stand it." His belief in the doctrine of imminent collapse appeared in a phone conversation with Harry Hopkins, who was planning to be in New York over a weekend. He asked Hopkins to look him up. "Be sure to look me up," he reiterated. "I may be in a hospital, but look me up."

The first thing La Guardia did upon becoming mayor was to call Dr. George Baehr—with death on his mind. "George," he said, "I want to be examined."

After a thorough examination, he said, "Now, George, tell me. Can I live seven years?"

Baehr, bald, with a fringe of white hair and a gray mustache, must have appeared capable of answering such a question. "Fiorello, why just seven years?" he asked.

"I never earned much money as a lawyer, and I couldn't save anything on a congressman's salary. I want to know if I can live seven years, because if I can live more than seven years then it would pay me to put all the money I can save from my salary as Mayor into the pension fund, because that's all my family's going to have when I die. If I can't live seven years, it won't do any good. I just better put it in a savings bank. Because that's all they're going to have."

"Fiorello." The way Dr. Baehr set "Fiorello" off with pauses indicated that he was going to give it to him straight. "You have a bad build. You're overweight. You have bad habits. You eat too much, and you come from a short-lived family. The odds are against you. But I can't find anything wrong with you, physically, and I think you should take a gamble on living more than seven years."

Friends over a long period, Dr. Baehr and La Guardia had enough in common to make them kindred spirits. Dr. Baehr had engaged in an adventurous expedition to Serbia to determine the cause of typhus, and regarded himself a radical because he wanted to make medical help more available to the poor. Two days after the bombing of Pearl Harbor, he issued a statement to the press concerning American women "who up to last Sunday were trying to find defense work that wouldn't interfere with their bridge or their matinees." He suggested, as La Guardia might have, that they volunteer for nursing jobs, which he felt were on a par with action in the first-line trenches. And both men had a consuming interest in public health.

Friendship didn't prevent La Guardia from treating his personal physician as though he were a commissioner—watched, tested, put on guard. Once Dr. Baehr requested that since La Guardia's urine hadn't been tested in some time, he drop off a specimen on his way to City Hall. A few hours after La Guardia had complied with this request, he phoned. "George," he said, "did you examine the specimen?" Baehr said he had, and that it was negative. "You did a sink test," La Guardia snapped. (He was referring to the practice of lazy—or overworked —technicians who, instead of doing a test, poured a specimen in the sink.) Dr. Baehr objected. The examination had been done very carefully. "Did you examine it for sugar?" La Guardia asked. The doctor had. "Did it have any sugar?" La Guardia demanded. "No." "I say it has." "I say it didn't." "I say it had." The doctor finally asked, "How do you know?" A triumphant La Guardia shot back, "Because I put it in." "Fiorello, you took it out of the sugar bowl, didn't you?" "Yes." "That's saccharose. That's not glucose. It doesn't give the test that we do." "Oh," La Guardia said, "I learned something." "Sure. You got a lot to learn, Fiorello."

And just as he put commissioners in their place, he let Dr. Baehr know that he was above some of his frills—X ray, for example. Once when La Guardia thought it a waste of time to be x-rayed for a possible kidney stone, he stealthily placed a key behind his kidney, in the course of being x-rayed, so that the key would show up in the developed picture and frighten the doctor. (He later claimed he had swallowed the key "by accident in an absent-minded fit of irritation.")

One Sunday, he introduced Baehr to his radio audience: "He's my doctor, but he's a terrible doctor. And you want to know why? Because he won't let me eat spaghetti. *He* says I'm too fat."

Mrs. La Guardia introduced the preternatural into her husband's being "heavy for his build" by maintaining that all he had to do was look at food and he would gain weight. Actually, this phenomenon had a simple cause-effect explanation: La Guardia's looking at food was followed by his consuming what he saw and then by an inevitable increase in weight. "Well, he nibbled," Dr. Baehr said. "He nibbled and he nibbled." And he nibbled because of tensions, and he was always torn by tension. Even at mealtime, while waiting for food, he'd nibble bread or anything else on the table that was edible.

"My doctor says I oughtn't to eat lunch the way I do," La Guardia complained, while standing and eating a frankfurter off a paper plate, "but I think it's better than eating a heavier lunch at a table. Anyhow, I couldn't go out to lunch if I wanted to."

Because he didn't go out to lunch, but ate at his desk, his wife prepared a sandwich for him to take with him to City Hall. Mrs. Anna Rosenberg Hoffman recalled one particular lunch. "Come on," he said to her. "Sit there while I eat, so I can talk to you." As she sat down, he opened a desk drawer and drew forth the smelliest, the most highly seasoned Italian sausage imaginable. "You eat the sandwich," he told her. "I'm going to eat this." It was as though Dr. Baehr had never cautioned him not to eat highly seasoned foods. When Mrs. Hoffman brought up the matter, he said, "I know what's good for me." This annoyed her. "Who do you think you're fooling?" she said. "The doctor or Marie? You're fooling yourself." Masticating a mouthful of sausage—grumbling, too—he managed a semiaudible "Never mind."

La Guardia could not completely ignore Dr. Baehr, who "became worried about the Mayor's inability to lose weight." The doctor had a reluctant La Guardia admitted to Mount Sinai Hospital and put on a diet—considered generous by La Guardia, but low on calories. He set out to show La Guardia that by means of a proper diet one could lose a pound a day, that it could be done.

In the course of this strictly controlled regimen, La Guardia said,

"George, you know I'd love to have something tasty. Do you think I could have a piece of herring?" The doctor said he could. The next day, a furious La Guardia told Dr. Baehr, "You're a lousy doctor. Here I am, and it's costing me all this money to be in this private room and I gained a pound since yesterday."

After some cross-examination, Dr. Baehr uncovered two unalterable truths. La Guardia had not eaten just "a little piece of herring," but an entire herring, and a salty one at that.

"Why, you're full of salt," Dr. Baehr scolded, as one would a bad boy. "And therefore you retain water. You don't have to get mad at me. It's your fault. You ate too much herring."

Dr. Baehr put La Guardia back on his herringless diet, and thus, by taking away his salt, he removed more than a pound the following day. This satisfied La Guardia, and Baehr—pro tem—was not a lousy doctor.

The ten pounds that were removed in ten days eventually returned. But La Guardia's stay in Mount Sinai produced something of enduring value, something that began with Dr. Baehr's sudden realization that it would be a good idea to have a public health center at each of New York City's medical schools "so that they could teach the students the protection of the people's health in the community." Taking to the idea instantly, La Guardia ordered the deans of the five medical schools brought to his room in the hospital, and the deal with the schools was made then and there. (Washington provided the money for the construction of the five health centers, and each center had two stories devoted to teaching.)

Dr. Baehr regarded La Guardia a well person; colds, excessive weight are, after all, the lot of the normal man. But La Guardia took a great deal of punishment. He said concerning the Mayor's office, "Every year that a man puts into this job takes five years off his life." Sixty years, if one took that reckoning literally, had been taken, and UNRRA also took an inestimable toll in weariness of body and spirit. He resigned from its director generalship at the close of 1946, an acknowledgment of defeat, when the absolutely essential support of food and cash by the United States and Great Britain had been withdrawn.

In April of the following year, bowed by ill health, pain, bitterness, La Guardia was once again admitted to Mount Sinai Hospital. Dr. Baehr knew at once that his friend had cancer of the pancreas, inoperable, fatal.

I told his wife. But I didn't tell Fiorello, because I thought that as long as he lasted he could earn some money for the first time in his life, and this was all the money, except for the pension amount, that would be left to his family. It was my duty to him. I knew he would want me to do it—not to tell him, to let him keep on working until he dropped. And so he kept on as a broadcaster.

Dr. Baehr had to tell the press something; he told them that La Guardia was suffering from inflammation of the pancreas. Later, he reported that "further tests for a diabetic condition were being taken." On May 1, O'Dwyer visited La Guardia in the hospital. And on that day, to give credibility to his story, and to vary it a bit, Dr. Baehr told reporters that La Guardia "was doing very well."

The facts didn't jibe with that report. Weeks went by, and La Guardia had to have friends substitute for him on the radio. In addition to fooling the public, Baehr also had to deceive Fiorello, who now had another sort of weight problem, an apparent loss of weight. La Guardia could now have eaten a whole herring and not have gained a single ounce.

I had to tell him a cock and bull story, that the duct from the pancreas had narrowed down and closed. But it was open again and the inflammation subsided. And since the digestive juice of the pancreas was not getting into his intestinal tract to digest food, he was losing weight for that reason.

Dr. Baehr began to doubt that he was pulling the wool over the eyes of his dying friend, far too bright to be so easily fooled. It appeared that La Guardia—as in an O. Henry story—was also playing a game of deceit, that he knew he had cancer and was dying, but he never revealed that he knew or asked questions. Instead, he assumed a phony faith and naivete.

George, I have great faith in you. If you tell me I have an inflammation of the pancreas and you're going to cure me, I believe you. But before you cure me, I'm going to die of malnutrition because I'm wasting away.

And Mrs. La Guardia continued in the role of a wife who did not know that her husband was drawing close to death.

Dr. Baehr did not attempt to keep the truth from Berle, because he was one of La Guardia's closest friends. Berle wrote in his diary:

Yesterday, July 24, I went to Riverdale to see Fiorello. He was sitting in the sun, in the little garden in back of his house. We talked of the state of the Union, re getting some of the historic American progressive sentiment going and of concentrating progressive force in districts where it had a chance to win; and of the fact that anybody who was a member of the 80th Congress is guilty of something until he proves an alibi. . . . And so forth through the afternoon hours.

The doctor came in to give him an injection and took me downtown in his car. I asked the obvious question. "Off the record, probably three or four months," was his answer. He has not been told anything, and they are keeping the office and all political arrangements standing, even making speaking engagements for him in October. . . .

Late that summer, anyone who saw La Guardia knew. Robert Moses knew.

I was shocked at the change in him. He was in bed, so shrunken, so chapfallen and yet so spunky, and so obviously on the way out. To tell the truth, I felt like crying. It was a battle that not even the most courageous fighter could win.

Berle didn't want La Guardia to think that he couldn't win, didn't want to think it himself.

I went to see him once. He opened up his gown—and said, "This is awful." I said, "You've been meeting awful situations all your life." And then we kidded.

As summer turned to autumn, La Guardia fell into a deep sleep that lasted for days, from which he could not be roused. Newspaper headlines made use of the word coma—a dramatic, newsworthy word. People in the streets, in the subways spoke of La Guardia, told their individual stories or made observations concerning him, and it was as though he were already dead. And visitors came to the house in Riverdale, came, stayed briefly, left. And the steady flow of arrivals and departures, with something of the silence of shadows, created a hushed expectancy. The curious came, merely glanced at the house—once in passing it and then again after turning around on the dead-end street. An ice deliveryman parked his truck a distance away, so as not to disturb La Guardia.

Baehr finally surrendered. He used "critical," but could not bring himself to say "cancer"; instead, his official statement used "an inoperable condition of the pancreas." (During his first term as mayor, La Guardia had used the word in connection with Tammany—"Tammany is a cancer in the very heart of the city." And unlike Dr. Baehr, he had a cure: starvation, "withholding all patronage from it.")

When, finally, La Guardia's sleep turned to death, people found it hard to believe. They had known his incessant energy for so long, the fact that it could run down seemed impossible.

A *Times* editorial the next day remembered his accomplishments.

He did not find us brick and leave us marble, but he rescued our public credit, put non-partisan experts in charge of city departments, expanded parks and playgrounds, developed clinics, public markets, housing projects, airports. He did much of this in an uproar of controversy but he did it.

He lay in state in the Cathedral of St. John the Divine; for ten hours, at the rate of four thousand an hour, individuals moved past his bier. Some merely paused to look, some crossed themselves, some moved their lips in silent prayer, some wept openly, some attempted to conceal their tears. One woman tossed a rose into the coffin, saying, "Poor Mayor La Guardia. He's gone." A man said, "I feel he helped all of us." (He had indeed "spent more time balancing the budgets of the poor than he had trying to keep a lid on metropolitan spending.") Only one floral offering was on the bier, a bank of roses inscribed "To Daddy" from the La Guardia children, Jean, eighteen, and Eric, fifteen.

The funeral service also took place in St. John the Divine. One present in the vast nave, listening to old, beautiful biblical words vibrate from loudspeakers, sensed something not quite right about these proceedings for Fiorello.

It was merely that his whole history and temperament suggested different obsequies. He should, one thought, have been borne down crammed and populous streets, hardly wide enough to get through; and there ought to have been singing in a packed and none too beautiful church where the women crowded into the pews and sobbed. There should have been elbows all around, and Fiorello making his last journey on earth through them.

When the cavalcade left the cathedral, the streets were not narrow, "crammed and populous," and the streets it passed through were the streets of Harlem and those on the West Side to 110th Street. Thousands lined those streets; the elbows motionless, well behaved. And what impressed one was the silence, so complete that "you could hear the click of the traffic lights as the cavalcade went by." And this silence somehow said that these people in the streets felt that they knew La Guardia and were saddened by being witnesses to "his last journey on earth."

BIBLIOGRAPHY

Berle, Beatrice Bishop, and Jacobs, Travis Beal, eds. *Navigating the Rapids,* *1918–1971; from the Papers of Adolf A. Berle.* New York: Harcourt Brace Jovanovich, 1973.

Blanshard, Paul. *Personal and Controversial.* Boston: Beacon Press, 1973.

Brown, Charles H. *The Correspondent's War.* New York: Scribner's, 1967.

Burns, James MacGregor. *Roosevelt: The Lion and the Fox.* New York: Harcourt, Brace, 1956.

Byrnes, James F. *All in One Lifetime.* New York: Harper, 1958.

Caro, Robert A. *The Power Broker.* New York: Knopf, 1974.

Cuneo, Ernest. *Life with Fiorello.* New York: Macmillan, 1955.

Curran, Henry H. *Pillar to Post.* New York: Scribner's, 1941.

Ellis, Edward Robb. *Epic of New York City.* New York: Coward-McCann, 1966.

———. *A Nation in Torment.* New York: Coward-McCann, 1970.

Farley, James A. *Jim Farley's Story.* New York: Whittlesey House, 1948.

Flynn, Edward J. *You're the Boss.* New York: Viking Press, 1947.

Fowler, Gene. *Beau James: The Life and Times of Jimmy Walker.* New York: Viking Press, 1949.

Franklin, Jay. *La Guardia: A Biography.* New York: Modern Age Books, 1937.

Freidel, Frank. *Franklin D. Roosevelt: Launching the New Deal.* Boston: Little, Brown, 1973.

Garraty, John A. *The American Nation.* New York: Harper, 1966.

Garrett, Charles. *The La Guardia Years.* New Brunswick, N.J.: Rutgers University Press, 1961.

Goldman, Eric F. *Rendezvous with Destiny.* New York: Knopf, 1952.

Goldston, Harmon H., and Dalrymple, Martha. *History Preserved: A Guide to New York City Landmarks and Historic Districts.* New York: Simon and Schuster, 1974.

Gosch, Martin A., and Hammer, Richard. *The Last Testament of Lucky Luciano.* Boston: Little, Brown, 1974.

Hamburger, Philip. *Mayor Watching and Other Pleasures.* New York: Rinehart, 1958.

Hapgood, Norman, and Moskowitz, Henry. *Up from the City Streets.* New York: Harcourt, Brace, 1927.

BIBLIOGRAPHY

Hudson, James J. *Hostile Skies.* Syracuse, N.Y.: Syracuse University Press, 1968.

Ickes, Harold. *The Secret Diary of Harold Ickes: The First Thousand Days, 1933–1936.* New York: Simon and Schuster, 1954.

———. *The Secret Diary of Harold Ickes: The Inside Struggle, 1936–1939.* New York: Simon and Schuster, 1954.

La Guardia, Fiorello H. *The Making of an Insurgent: An Autobiography, 1882–1919.* Edited by M. R. Werner. Philadelphia: Lippincott, 1948.

Lash, Joseph P. *Eleanor and Franklin.* New York: W. W. Norton, 1971.

Limpus, Lowell M. *Honest Cop: Lewis J. Valentine.* New York: E. P. Dutton, 1939.

———, and Leyson, Burr. *This Man La Guardia.* New York: E. P. Dutton, 1938.

Manchester, William. *The Glory and the Dream.* Boston: Little, Brown, 1973.

Mann, Arthur. *La Guardia: a Fighter Against His Times, 1882–1933.* Philadelphia: Lippincott, 1959.

———. *La Guardia Comes to Power: 1933.* Philadelphia: Lippincott, 1965.

Millis, Walter. *The Martial Spirit.* Cambridge, Mass.: Literary Guild, 1931.

Mitgang, Herbert. *The Man Who Rode the Tiger.* Philadelphia: Lippincott, 1963.

Moley, Raymond. *After Seven Years.* New York: Harper, 1930.

———. *27 Masters of Politics.* New York: Funk & Wagnalls, 1949.

Morris, Newbold, and Thomas, Dana Lee. *Let the Chips Fall.* New York: Appleton-Century-Crofts, 1955.

Moscow, Warren. *Politics in the Empire State.* New York: Knopf, 1948.

———. *What Have You Done for Me Lately?* New York: Prentice-Hall, 1967.

Nearing, Scott. *The Making of a Radical.* New York: Harper, 1972.

Nevins, Allan. *Herbert H. Lehman and His Era.* New York: Scribner's, 1963.

Norris, George W. *Fighting Liberal.* New York: Macmillan, 1945.

Page, Thomas Nelson. *Italy and the World War.* New York: Scribner's, 1920.

Pearson, Drew, and Allen, Robert S. *Washington Merry-Go-Round.* New York: Liveright, 1931.

Pringle, Henry F. *Alfred E. Smith: A Critical Study.* New York: Macy-Masius, 1927.

Rankin, Rebecca B., ed. *New York Advancing: A Scientific Approach to Municipal Government, 1934–1935.* New York: Municipal Reference Library, 1936.

Roosevelt, Eleanor. *The Autobiography of Eleanor Roosevelt.* New York: Harper, 1961.

Russell, Francis. *The Shadow of Blooming Grove.* New York: McGraw-Hill, 1968.

Salter, J. T., ed. *The American Politician*. Chapel Hill: University of North Carolina Press, 1938.

Sayre, Wallace S., and Kaufman, Herbert. *Governing New York City Politics in the Metropolis*. New York: W. W. Norton, 1960.

Schlesinger, Arthur M., Jr. *The Coming of the New Deal*. Boston: Houghton Mifflin, 1959.

Soule, George. *Prosperity Decade*. New York: Rinehart, 1947.

Spalding, Albert. *Rise to Follow*. New York: Holt, 1943.

Summerhayes, Martha. *Vanished Arizona Recollections of My Army Life*. Salem: Salem Press, 1939.

Swanberg, W. A. *Citizen Hearst*. New York: Scribner's, 1961.

Terkel, Studs. *Hard Times*. New York: Pantheon, 1970.

Thomas, Norman, and Blanshard, Paul. *What's the Matter with New York?* New York: Macmillan, 1932.

Tugwell, Rexford G. *The Art of Politics*. Garden City, N.Y.: Doubleday, 1958.

———. *The Brains Trust*. New York: Viking Press, 1968.

Wecter, Dixon. *The Age of the Great Depression*. New York: Macmillan, 1948.

Whalen, Grover A. *Mr. New York*. New York: Putnam, 1955.

White, William Allen. *The Autobiography of William Allen White*. New York: Macmillan, 1946.

Zinn, Howard. *La Guardia in Congress*. Ithaca, N.Y.: Cornell University Press, 1959.

Congressional Record
Fiorello H. La Guardia papers in the Municipal Archives and Records Center
Oral History transcripts of Columbia University
At the Franklin D. Roosevelt Library in Hyde Park: material relating to La Guardia in the papers of Franklin D. Roosevelt, Harry Hopkins, Adolf Berle, and the papers and diaries of Henry Morgenthau

The New York Times
American Magazine
American Mercury
Atlantic Monthly
Collier's
Current History
Fortune
Harper's Monthly
Life

Literary Digest
The Nation
The New Republic
Newsweek
The New Yorker
The Outlook
The Saturday Evening Post
The Survey
Time

INDEX

INDEX

INDEX